# ONE WEEK LOAN

# Sport, Rhetoric, and Gender

# SPORT, RHETORIC, AND GENDER

## Historical Perspectives and Media Representations

*Edited by*

*Linda K. Fuller*

SPORT, RHETORIC, AND GENDER
© Linda K. Fuller, 2006.

First published in 2006 by
PALGRAVE MACMILLAN™
175 Fifth Avenue, New York, N.Y. 10010 and
Houndmills, Basingstoke, Hampshire, England RG21 6XS
Companies and representatives throughout the world.

PALGRAVE MACMILLAN is the global academic imprint of the Palgrave Macmillan division of St. Martin's Press, LLC and of Palgrave Macmillan Ltd. Macmillan® is a registered trademark in the United States, United Kingdom and other countries. Palgrave is a registered trademark in the European Union and other countries.

ISBN-13: 978–1–4039–7328–3
ISBN-10: 1–4039–7328–8

Library of Congress Cataloging-in-Publication Data

    Sport, rhetoric, and gender : historical perspectives and media representations / Linda K. Fuller, editor.
       p. cm.
    Includes bibliographical references and index.
    ISBN 1–4039–7328–8 (alk. paper)
     1. Sports—Social aspects. 2. Sports—Language. 3. Gender identity. 4. Mass media and sports. I. Fuller, Linda K.

GV706.5.S7364 2006
306.4'83—dc22
                                2005056635

A catalogue record for this book is available from the British Library.

Design by Newgen Imaging Systems (P) Ltd., Chennai, India.

First edition: September 2006

10 9 8 7 6 5 4 3 2 1

Printed in the United States of America.

*Madison, Delia, and Violet*
*aspiring athletes*
*(Thanks to Title 1X)*

# CONTENTS

## Part III  Print Media Representations

## Part IV  Broadcast Media Representations

## Part V  Visual Media Representations

# Part VI  Classic Case Studies

# Introduction

*Linda K. Fuller*

* *When a girl joins the ball team, what is she afraid the boys will do?*
   *Answer: Soccer*
* *In what country are the scores always even?*
   *Answer: Thailand*
* *Why did the baseball manager hire Aunt Jemima?*
   *Answer: Because she makes great batters*
* *Who can run faster than light?*
   *Answer: Mrs. Light, when she's angry.*
* *Why are there 9 men on a baseball team?*
   *Answer: Women aren't allowed*
* *A sultan with 20 wives won what event at the Olympics?*
   *Answer: The marrython.*

These silly *Sports Riddles* from a 1989 book of that name by Everett Hafner provide a bizarre encapsulation of this quite serious study of sport, language, and gender. Taken from the top, it concerns itself with boys/men and girls/women, bodies, business, power, barriers, and the wide world of sport.

*Sport, Rhetoric, and Gender: Historical Perspectives and Media Representation* makes an important contribution not only to the study of sport but also to gender, linguistics, marketing, fandom, media, human behavior, historical perspectives, studies of celebrity, literature, education, ethnic stereotyping, interpersonal and intercultural communication, and more. While sports represents a $60+ billion industry in the United States alone, its implications worldwide account for extensive historical, economic, political, psychological, religious, sociological, ideological, anecdotal evidence, and other areas that may surprise you.

Contributors to this volume represent a range of countries, colleges and universities, departments and disciplines, even professional and amateur athletes. The volume is, quite clearly, international and interdisciplinary, a unique compilation of approaches marking the first time gender and language have been applied to the field of sport. What follows is a brief literature review of the field, a discussion of sports in general, the underlying theory of hegemonic masculinity, overviews of gender and language vis-a-vis language, all leading to the subject of sports language. After that, *Sport, Rhetoric, and Gender* is described and delineated to engage you, the reader, to considering its incredible interconnections.

## LITERATURE REVIEW ON SPORT(S)

> Sport does not exist in a world of its own but reflects the world around it. If there are gender issues in our society, then these issues are likely to appear in sport; and if language is central to human behaviour, then the language of sport is likely to provide interesting *evidence for how we view men and women differently. Research projects and investigations on sporting topics are popular.*
>
> —Adrian Beard, *The Language of Sport*

When you peruse "sports" in mainstream bookstores, most of the offerings deal with "how-to" s or biographies or simple statistics. Fortunately, there is also growing interest in the field amongst academics and informed practitioners. For example, there has been work on audiences, the economics of sport, culture/social relations, ethics/values, gender, law/legalities, media, the Olympic Games, politics, psychology, sportscasting/sportscasters/sports journalism, sport marketing and management, and more, such as drugs and doping, homophobia, physicality, religion, even theories. Of the many citations here, many of course cross categories, but it is hoped that this bibliography will be helpful to future research on sport. What follows is a brief review:

- Audiences (Harris, 1994; Real, 1996; Wann, 2001)
- Culture/social relations (Andrews and Jackson, 2001; Martin and Miller, 1999; Miller, 2001; Rail, 1998; Rowe, 1999)
- Economics (Andrews, 2001; Aris, 1990; Fizel, Gustafson, and Hadley, 1999; Graham, 1994; Rosentraub, 1997; Sheehan, 1996; Staudohar and Mangan, 1991)
- Ethics/values (Arnold, 1997; DeSensi and Rosenberg, 1996; Loland, 2000; Lumpkin, Stoll, and Beller, 1994; McNamee and Parry, 1998; Whannel, 2002)

- Ethnicity and race (Bloom and Willard, 2002; Eisen and Wiggins, 1994; Jarvie, 1991; King and Springwood, 2001; Kirsch, Harris, and Nolte, 2000; Shropshire, 1996; Wiggins, 1997)
- Gender (Birrell and Cole, 1994; Burstyn, 1999; Cahn, 1994; Cohen, 1993; Costa and Guthrie, 1994; Creedon, 1994; Drinkwater, 2000; Festle, 1996; Hall, 1996; Hargreaves, 1994; Lenskyj, 1986, 1994; McKay, Messner, and Sabo, 2000; Messner, 1992, 2002; Messner and Sabo, 1990; Nelson, 1991, 1994; Salter, 1996; Sandoz, 1997; Sandoz and Winans, 1999; Scraton and Flintoff, 2002; Smith, 1998; Tomlinson, 2001)
- Law/legalities (Berry and Won, 1993; Champion, 1993; Cotton and Wilde, 1997; Cozzillio, 1997; Dougherty, 1994; Greenberg, 1993; Hladczuk, 1991; Jarvis and Coleman, 1999; Jones, 1999; Quirk, 1996; Weiler, 2000; Wong, 1994; Yasser, McCurdy, and Goplerud, 1990)
- Media (Baker and Boyd, 1997; Boyle and Haynes, 2000; Klatell and Marcus, 1988; Rowe, 1999; Wenner, 1998; Whannel, 1989, 1992, 2002)
- The Olympic Games (Barney, Wenn, and Martyn, 2002; Daddario, 1998; de Morgas Spa, Rivenburgh, and Larson, 1995; Findling and Pelle, 1996; Fuller, 1989, 1996; Guttmann, 1992; Hoberman, 1986; Larson and Park, 1993; Lenskyj, 2000; Mandell, 1971, 1987; Roche, 2000; Senn, 1999; Talbot, 2001; U.S. Olympic Committee, 1996)
- Politics (Allison, 1993; Arnaud and Riordan, 1998; Sage, 1990; Vinokur, 1988)
- Psychology (Anshel, 1994; Butler, 1996; Diamant, 1991; Horn, 1992; Murphy, 1995; Russell, 1993; Singer, Hausenblas, and Janelle, 2001; Stein and Hollwitz, 1994)
- Sociology (Bale, 1994; Birrell and McDonald, 2000; Cashmore, 2000; Coakley, 2001; Coakley and Dunning, 2000; Dunning, 1999; Eitzen, 1999; Gerdy, 2002; Gruneau, 1999; Ingham and Loy, 1993; Jarvie and Maguire, 1994; Kew, 1997; Lapchick, 1996; Leonard, 1993; Maguire et al., 2002; Rowe, 1995; Simon, 1991; Wise, 1994)
- Sportscasting/sportscasters/sports journalism (Anderson, 1994; Catsis, 1996; Fischer, 1995; Fuller, forthcoming; Gibson, 1991; Kuiper, 1996; O'Donnell, Hausman, and Benoit, 1992)
- Sport marketing/management (Brooks, 1994; Cuneen and Sidwell, 1994; Graham, Goldblatt, and Neirotti, 2001; Masteralexis, Barr, and Hums, 1998; McDonald and Milne, 1999; Miller, 1997; Mullin, Hardy, and Sutton, 1993; Parks, Zanger,

and Quarterman, 1998; Pitts and Stotlar, 1996; Schlossberg, 1996; Scully, 1995; Shank, 1999; Stotlar, 1993; VanderZwaag, 1998; Wascovich, 1993)

In addition, there are sport-specific books, such as on basketball, football, soccer, golf, bodybuilding, wrestling, and the like, as well as country-specific studies, such as Canadian hockey or British hooliganism. Other sports-related topics include drugs and doping (O'Leary, 2001), homophobia (Griffin, 1998; Rogers, 1994), nationalism (Houlihan, 1994; Ingham and Loy, 1993; Maguire, 1999; Wilson, 1994), physicality (Cole, Loy, and Messner, 1993; Guttman, 1996; Lenskyj, 1994; Weitz, 2003), religion (Higgs, 1995; Prebish, 1993; Price, 2001), theories (Graham, 1994; Maguire and Young, 2002; Morgan, 1994), ad infinitum.

## Sport(s)

*Sports have become a microcosm of national life. Once relatively isolated from national issues, sports in recent decades have lost whatever innocence they might have once enjoyed and moved into the mainstream of national life. At times they have mirrored national trends and issues, at other times they have forced national policymakers to act.*

—Richard O. Davies, *America's Obsession*

Dating from the days of Greek reverence for the body beautiful, athletes have been our gods, sports our supreme escape and entertainment. Today, more than ever, we continue to worship sports stars, spend inordinate amounts of money on sporting events, and sell and succumb to sports-related commercialism and sponsorships. In essence, we live in a sports culture, reducing race and class into a simple equation of winners and winning. It is a multibillion dollar global, all-pervasive societal industry, incorporating governments, educational systems, mass communication, businesses, players, and participants. Sport as a social, "gendered institution" (Messner, 1992, p.16) is spectacle, demanding our attention and our support, both as audiences and as spenders. An integral part of our political economy, sport also operates as a socializing agent, sometimes even working as an agent of social change. Stars can spur trendy hairstyles or happenings, and often it can be for positive outcomes. In many instances, it has become something of a national addiction (Gerdy, 2002).

It presents something of a paradox, as Eitzen (1999) has pointed out: "Sport, a seemingly trivial pursuit, is important. Sport is a fantasy—a diversion from the realities of work, relationships, and survival. Sport entertains. Why then do we take it so seriously? First and foremost, sport mirrors the human experience" (pp.2–3). Whether embedded in a society emphasizing physical skill and strength or ones that rely on strategizing, sport in the world arena may vary in terms of competitiveness or commitment but it usually well represents cultural values, regulated by local traditions and taboos. For minorities, women in particular, the stakes in the political economy of sport are considerably complicated.

## HEGEMONIC MASCULINITY

*If those of us who are committed to a more theoretically informed feminist politics of sport want to bring others who are less certain about the value of the project on board, then our theorizing must be relevant to sport and developed in clear, precise, accessible language.*

—M. Ann Hall, *Feminism and Sporting Bodies*

First introduced in the 1930s by Italian political theorist Antonio Gramsi, the idea of hegemony refers to privileged societal groups imposing their rule as validly legitimate. While this concept informs the bulk of essays in *Sport, Rhetoric, and Gender*, there are a number of theories developed around or beyond it. Whether couched in cultural studies, semiotics, semantics, media effects, or even systems theory, they provide invaluable bases beyond mere reportage. Fortunately, a majority also incorporate ethics and social issues, such that many studies reported here encourage replications.

Recently, popular cultural texts and traditions have emerged as significant sources for examination of gender studies. Research here has primarily centered around notions of a "masculine-powered society" (Fuller, 1999; see also Davis, 1997; Messner, 2005; Trujillo, 1991), Messner (2002) reminding us that, "Examining the ways that the televised sports manhood formula cuts across sports programming and the accompanying commercials provides important clues to the ways that ideologies of hegemonic masculinity are both promoted by, and in terms serve to support and stabilize, the collection of interrelated institutions that make up the sport-media-commercial complex" (p.126).

## GENDER AND MEDIA/SPORTS

*Men and masculinity have frequently been treated as the "norm"*
*and men's portrayal in the media have often been seen as unprob-*
*lematic or even exemplary.*

—S. Craig, *Men, Masculinity, and the Media*

The ideology of sport is such that it commands our attention in terms of public policy. Add to that an underpinning of sex and sexuality, and it is easy to see why gender has always played a critical role. Whether referring to the Baron Pierre de Coubertin's 1912 comment about the modern Olympic Games he founded as, "The solemn and periodic exaltation of male athleticism with internationalism as a base, loyalty as a means, art for its setting, and female applause as reward" (Fuller, 1989, p.4–10), or to golfer Annika Sorenstam's brave, if beaten, foray into the PGA Tour, not much really has changed. Men still mostly fear being "beaten by a girl."

Like its female counterpart, masculinity is a social construct, the body eroticized to become an object of desire. In nearly every culture, men are socialized to be aggressors, women to be victims. Historically, sport has come to be seen as a form of male entitlement, little boys continuing to play into adulthood. And while women have made enormous strides since the Victorian period, when they were thought to be too weak to partake in sport, formation of the Women's Sports Foundation in 1974 marked a high point for bringing awareness to fitness for females. Concurrent with the issues involved in Title 1X (Suggs, 2005), which the U.S. Congress passed in1972, feminist scholars around the world began to critique sport as yet one more sexist institution, "male-dominated and masculine in origin," as exemplified in Nancy Theberge's 1981 pioneering article in *Social Forces.*

Sexism in sports abounds. Whether the emphasis is on scantily clad cheerleaders, women performers gazed at as sex objects, and/or sports-caster comments emphasizing female frailties rather than performance, a number of challenges remain.

## LANGUAGE AND SPORTS

*Given that both language and sport can perpetuate male privilege,*
*it is not surprising that the language of sport also favors men.*
*Examples of sexist language in sport include gender marking*
*(e.g., using "Lady" or "ettes" as part of the women's team name),*

*referring to female athletes as "girls," focusing media coverage on
women's physical attractiveness or marital status rather than on
their athletic prowess, and assuming that the "real" event is the
men's event and the women's event is "other."*

—Janet B. Parks, *"Influence of age, gender, and content"*

Spiced with metaphors from everyday life, the language of sport
ranges from talk about playing hardball to sticky wickets to cheap
shots. Routinely, whether in our homes, offices, or in boardrooms, we
talk about offensive and defensive tactics, game plans, Monday morning
quarterbacking, being team players, playing tough and playing fair. If
we can't talk the talk, we are denied access to "level playing fields"
(Fuller, 1992). Consider this comment by Bob Andelman (1993,
p.89): "Football provides many (men) with conversational confidence,
especially young men. Conversational competence depends on knowing what's going on, and many conversations in an office or on a job site
or in social situations pivot around sports . . . . If you can't join in and
have something to say, you're left out." Murphy and Zorn (1996) state:

> Sports talk is the unofficial small talk of American business. Not only
> are scores, plays, and statistics daily topics of conversation, but business
> talk itself is peppered with sports-oriented phrases. It is not uncommon
> to hear meetings, proposals, strategies, and the like described in terms
> such as *slam dunk, out of bounds, below the belt, score one for our side,
> struck out, defensive play, end run, dropped the ball, your turn at bat, the
> whole nine yards, easy lay up,* and *pass the ball.* (p.218)

## SPORT, RHETORIC, AND GENDER

As a predominantly male discourse, sport-talk tends to be militaristic,
sexual, even violent. Considering that much of it is played on a *battle-
field*, much of sport argot involves martial metaphors like *bombs, bullets,
training camps, shoot-outs, shotguns, sudden death, veterans, ammuni-
tion, attacks, blitz, flanks, victories and defeats, gun-downs, blockades,
minefields, zones, trenches, snipers, detonations, casualties,* even *suicide
squads.* With our current obsession on *weapons of mass destruction,* it
is easy to see from whence the vocabulary originates.

Sex doesn't even have to have innuendoes. There are risks to
*"going all the way," grinding, getting sacked, using bump-and-run
stratagem, dinking, balling, clutching, heading, hitting the "sweet
spot," penetrations, naked reverses, exploitations, butt-blockers, squeezes,*

and of course there is always the possibility of a *hurry-up, firing a blank*, or *faking it*. *Protection* for "*scoring*," however, is tough to come by, and only tennis includes *love*, snooker a *kiss*. One wouldn't want to be categorized as *bush league*.

The really scary part, though, is the amount of violent sport language that is thought to perpetuate pornographic and stereotypical forms of intimidation. Tactics tend to be *offensive, oppressive, killing, tackling, fought, shot, dominant, destruction-oriented, pinch-hitting, biting the bullet, knock-outs, unstoppable*, and *conquest* is the goal. Aggression and violence prevail, whether or not one has to *pull punches* and/or *take his lumps*.

Although this book is universal by design, it is being published in English, so not all expressions or idioms might cross boundaries or cultures. Nevertheless, it is quite clear that examinations of sport in terms of gender and language are long overdue. The 21 chapters that make up *Sport, Rhetoric, and Gender: Historical Perspectives and Media Representations* fall neatly into these categories: sports language per se, historical perspectives, print media representations, broadcast media representations, visual media representations, and classic case studies. Information about the contributors appears at the end, followed by an index.

Part 1 begins with Marlene Mawson's suggestion of the term "Sportswomanship," followed by Segrave, McDowell, and King's invaluable review of sports-related linguistic conventions and Faye Linda Wachs' ethnographic study of the term "throw like a girl." Historical perspectives comprise Part 11, Nancy Rosoff's analysis of athletic women from 1880–1920 leading us to Mike Sowell's female sportswriter Winifred Black (aka Annie Laurie) and Jane Stangl's study of George Helgesen Fitch's "Siwash" stories about football antics. Print media representations are featured by Susan Burris relative to the Women's National Basketball Association (WNBA), by Cheryl Cooky relative to the now-defunct *Sports Illustrated for Women*, Marie Hardin and Julie Dodd relative to *Runner's World*, Jennifer Smith Maguire in various fitness texts, and Orchard, Stark, and Halas in the magazine *Maxim*. Televised workouts by Denise Austin inform Melissa Camacho's chapter, as does James Hallmark's examination of women's basketball by ESPN. Part V, on visual media representations, includes Kimberly Bissell's coverage of professional women's tennis players, Linda K. Fuller's stereotypes of women in baseball films, and Sabiston and Wilson's views of Britney Spears and music videos. Classic case studies include Scott A.G.M. Crawford's of NASCAR's Jeff Gordon, Kim Golombisky on Little League mothers, Sally Cole

Mooney on girls' soccer, Diana Tucker on football coaches' wives, and Susan Zieff 's "GirlSpeak" reports on pre-teen and teen girl athletes in their own words.

## IMPLICATIONS

*Athletic achievements are concrete, visible, measurable, and cultur-ally valued: obvious, tangible proof of what people can do. Boxer Jackie Louis, baseball players Jackie Robinson and Roberto Clemente, runner Jesse Owens; they seemed to succeed not only for themselves, but for all African-Americans, all Hispanics, all people who felt over-looked or discriminated against . . . Similarly, female, athletes have symbolically surmounted sexism.*

—Mariah Burton Nelson, *"Intro"*

As you might well imagine, it has been my supreme privilege to bring together these wide-ranging reports on the nexus between rhetoric, sexuality, and sport. Aiming to deconstruct the role of language in the multibillion dollar infotainment business—particularly, as it relates to sporting aspects of our popular culture, *Sport, Rhetoric, and Gender: Historical Perspectives and Media Representations* hopes to inspire much more research in this area. The idea is that once we better understand the vocabulary of sexploitation (see Brackenridge, 2001), the better prepared we will be to take action(s). Critical, relational studies, whether theoretical and/or empirical, of gender, language, and sport can move us to see the wider world through another prism.

## REFERENCES

Allison, L. (Ed.) (1993). *The changing politics of sport.* Manchester: Manchester University Press.

Andelman, B. (1993). *Why men watch football.* Lafayette, LA: Acadian House.

Anderson, D.A. (1994). *Contemporary sports reporting,* 2nd ed. Chicago, IL: Nelson-Hall.

Andrews, David L. (Ed.) (2001). *Michael Jordan, Inc: Corporate sport media culture, and haté modern America.* Albany, NY: State University of New York Press.

Andrews, David L. and Stephen J. Jackson (Eds.) (2001), *Sports stars: The cultural politics of sparking celebrity.* London: Routledge.

Anshel, M.H. (1994). *Sport psychology: From theory to practice.* Scottsdale, AZ: Gorsuch Scarisbrick.

Aris, S. (1990). *Sportsbiz: Inside the sports business.* London: Hutchinson.

Arnaud, P. and Riordan, J. (Eds.) (1998). *Sport and international politics.* London: E. and FN Spon.

Arnold, P.J. (1997). *Sports, ethics, and education.* London: Cassell.

Baker, A. and Boyd, T. (Eds.) (1997). *Out of bounds: Sports, media, and the politics of identity.* Bloomington, IN: Indiana University Press.

Bale, J. (1994). *Landscapes of modern sport.* Leicester, UK: Leicester University Press.

Barney, R.K., Wenn, S.R., and Martyn, S.G. (2002). *Selling the five rings: The International Olympic Committee and the rise of Olympic commercialism.* Salt Lake City: University of Utah Press.

Beard, A. (1998). *The language of sport.* London: Routledge.

Beray R.C. and Wong, G.M. (1993). *Law and Business of the sports industries: Common issues in amateur and professional sports.* Westport, CT: Praeger.

Birrell, S. and Cole, C. (Eds.) (1994). *Women, sport, and culture.* Champaign, IL: Human Kinetics.

Birrell, S. and McDonald, M.G. (Eds.) (2000). *Reading sport: Critical essays on power and representation.* Boston, MA: Northeastern University Press.

Bloom, J. and Willard, M.N. (Eds.) (2002). *Sports matters: Race, recreation, and culture.* New York: New York University Press.

Boyle, R. and Haynes, R. (2000). *Power play: Sport, media, and popular culture.* Harlow: Pearson Education Ltd.

Brackenridge, C.H. (2001). *Spoilsports: Understanding and preventing sexual exploitation in sport.* London: Routledge.

Brooks, C.M. (1994). *Sports marketing: Competitive business strategies for sports.* Englewood Cliffs, NJ: Prentice Hall.

Burstyn, V. (1999). *The rites of men: Manhood, politics, and the culture of sport.* Toronto: University of Toronto Press.

Butler, R.J. (1996). *Sport psychology in action.* Oxford: Butterworth-Heineman.

Cahn, S.K. (1994). *Coming on strong: Gender and sexuality in twentieth-century women's sport.* New York: Free Press.

Cashmore, E. (2000). *Making sense of sport,* 3rd ed. New York: Routledge.

Catsis, J.R. (1996). *Sports broadcasting.* Chicago, IL: Nelson-Hall.

Champion, W.T., Jr. (1993). *Sports law in a nutshell.* St. Paul, MN: West.

Coakley, J.J. (2001). *Sport and society: Issues and controversies,* 7th ed. New York: McGraw-Hill.

Coakley, J.J. and Dunning, E. (Eds.) (2000). *Handbook of sports studies.* London: Sage.

Cohen, G.L. (Ed.) (1993). *Women in sport: Issues and controversies.* London: Sage.

Cole, C., Loy, J., and Messner, M. (Eds.) (1993). *Exercising power: The making and remaking of the body.* Albany, NY: SUNY Press.

Costa, D.M. and Guthrie, S.R. (Eds.) (1994). *Women and sport: Interdisciplinary perspectives.* Champaign, IL: Human Kinetics.

Cotton, D.J. and Wilde, T.J. (1997), *Sport law for sport managers.* Dubuque: A. Kendaw/Hunt.

Cozzillio, M.J., and Levinstein, M.S. (1997), *Sports law: Cases and materials*, Durham, NC: Carolina Academic Press.

Craig, S. (1992). *Men, masculinity, and the media*. Newbury Park, CA: Sage.

Creedon, P.J. (Ed.) (1994). *Women, media and sport: Challenging gender values*. Thousand Oaks, CA: Sage.

Cuneen, J. and Sidwell, M.J. (1994). *Sport management field experiences*. Morgantown, WV: Fitness Information Technology.

Daddario, G. (1998). *Women's sport and spectacle: Gendered television coverage and the Olympic Games*. Westport, CT: Praeger.

Davies, R. (1994). *America's obsession: Sports and society since 1945*. Fort Worth, IN: Harcourt Brace.

Davis, L.R. (1997). *The swimsuit issue and sport: Hegemonic masculinity in Sports Illustrated*. Albany, NY: SUNY Press.

de Morgas Spa, M., Rivenburgh, N.K., and Larson, J.F. (1995). *Television in the Olympics*. London: John Libbey.

DeSensi, J.T. and Rosenberg, D. (1996). *Ethics in sports management*. Morgantown, WV: Fitness Information Technology.

Diamant, L. (Ed.) (1991). *Psychology of sport, exercise, and fitness: Social and personal issues*. New York: Hemisphere Pub.

Dougherty, N. J. (1994), *Sport, physical activity, and the law*. Champaign, IL: Human Kinetics.

Drinkwater, B.L. (Ed.) (2000). *Women in sport*. Oxford: Blackwell Science.

Dunning, E. (1999). *Sport matters: Sociological studies of sport, violence, and civilization*. London: Routledge.

Eisen, G. and Wiggins, D.K. (Eds.) (1994). *Ethnicity and sport in North American history and culture*. Westport, CT: Greenwood.

Eitzen, D.S. (1999). *Fair and foul: Beyond the myths and paradoxes of sport*. Oxford: Rowman and Littlefield.

Festle, M.J. (1996). *Playing nice: Politics and apologies in women's sports*. New York: Columbia University Press.

Findling, J.E. and Pelle, K.D. (Eds.) (1996). *Historical dictionary of the modern Olympic movement*. Westport, CT: Greenwood Press.

Fischer, H-D. (1995). *Sports journalism at its best*. Chicago, IL: Nelson-Hall.

Fizel, J., Gustafson, E., and Hadley, L. (Eds.) (1999). *Sports economics: Current research*. Westport, CT: Praeger.

Fuller, L.K. (1989). Olympics access for women: Athletes, organizers, and sports journalists. In *The Olympic movement and the mass media: Past, present, and future issues*. International Conference Proceedings, The University of Calgary. Canada: Hurford Enterprises Ltd. 4/9-4/l8.

———. (1992). Reporters rights in the locker room. *Feminist Issues* 12, 1 (Spring): 39–45.

———. (1996). Olympic documentary films. In *Historical dictionary of the modern Olympic movement*, ed. Findling, John E. and Pelle, Kimberly D., 404–414. Westport, CT: Greenwood Press.

———. (1999). Super Bowl speak: Subtexts of sex and sex talk in America's annual sports extravaganza. In *Sexual rhetoric: Media perspectives on sexuality, gender, and identity*, ed. Carstarphen, M.G. and Zavoina, S.C., 161–173. Westport, CT: Greenwood Press.

Fuller, L.K. (Forthcoming). *Sportscasting: Principles and practices.* Binghamton, NY: Haworth Press.

Gerdy, J.R. (2002). *Sports: The All-American addiction.* Jackson, MS: University Press Mississippi.

Gibson, R. (1991). *Radio and television reporting.* Boston: Allyn and Bacon.

Graham, P.J. (Ed.) (1994). *Sport business: Operational and theoretical aspects.* Madison, WI: WCB Brown and Benchmark.

Graham, S., Goldblatt, J.J., and Neirotti, L.D. (2001). *The ultimate guide to sports marketing.* New York: McGraw-Hill.

Greenberg, M. J. (1993), *Sports law practice,* Charlottesville, VA: Michie Co.

Griffin, P. (1998). *Strong women, deep closets: Lesbians and homophobia in sport.* Champaign, IL: Human Kinetics.

Gruneau, R. (1999). *Class, sports, and social development.* Champaign, IL: Human Kinetics.

Guttman, A. (1991). *Women's sports: A history.* New York: Columbia University Press.

———. (1992). *The Olympics: A history of the modern games.* Urbana, IL: University of Illinois.

———. (1996). *The erotic in sports.* New York: Columbia University Press.

Hafner, E. (1989). *Sports riddles.* New York: Viking Kestrel.

Hall, M.A. (1996). *Feminism and sporting bodies: Essays on theory and practice.* Champaign, IL: Human Kinetics.

Hargreaves, J. (1994). *Sporting females: Critical issues in the history and sociology of women's sports.* London: Routledge.

Harris, J.C. (1994). *Athletes and the American hero dilemma.* Champaign, IL: Human Kinetics.

Higgs, R.J. (1995). *God in the stadium: Sports and religion in America.* Lexington, KY: University Press of Kentucky.

Hladczuk, J. (Comp.) (1991). *Sports law and legislation: An annotated bibliography.* New York: Greenwood.

Hoberman, J. (1986). *The Olympic crisis: Sport, politics, and the moral order.* New Rochelle, NY: A.D. Caratzas.

Horn, T.S. (Ed.) (1992). *Advances in sport psychology.* Champaign, IL: Human Kinetics.

Houlihan, B. (1994). *Sport and international politics.* New York: Harvester Wheatsheaf.

Ingham, A.G. and Loy, J.W. (Eds.) (1993). *Sport in social development: Traditions transitions, and transformations.* Champaign, IL: Human Kinetics.

Jarvie, G. (1991). *Sport, racism, and ethnicity.* London: Falmer.

Jarvie, G. and Maguire, J. (1994). *Sport and leisure in social thought.* London: Routledge.

Jarvis, R.M. and Coleman, P. (1999). *Sports law: Cases and materials.* St. Paul: West.

Jones, M.E. (1999). *Sports law*. Upper Saddle River, NJ: Prentice-Hall.

Kew, F. (1997). *Sport: Social problems and issues*. Oxford: Butterworth-Heinemann.

King, C.R. and Springwood, C.F. (2001). *Beyond the cheers: Race as a spectacle in college sport*. Albany, NY: SUNY Press.

Kirsch, G.B., Harris, O., and Nolte, C.E (Eds.) (2000). *Encyclopedia of ethnicity and sports in the United States*. Westport, CT: Greenwood.

Klatell, D.A. and Marcus, N. (1988). *Sports for sale: Television, money, and the fans*. New York: Oxford.

Kremer, J. and Scully, D.M. (1994). *Psychology in sport*. London: Taylor & Francis.

Kuiper, K. (1996). *Smooth talkers: The linguistics performance of auctioneers and sportscasters*. Mahwah, NJ: Lawrence Erlbaum.

Lapchick, R.E. (Ed.) (1996). *Sport in society: Equal opportunity or business as usual?* Thousand Oaks, CA: Sage.

Larson, J.F. and Park, H.S. (1993). *Global television and the politics of the Seoul Olympics*. Boulder, CO: Westview Press.

LeFeber, W. (2002). *Michael Jordan and the new global capitalism*. New York: W.W. Norton & Co.

Lenskyj, H.J. (1986). *Out of bounds: Women, sport, and sexuality*. Toronto: Garamound.

———. (1994). *Women, sport and physical activity: Selected research themes*. Gloucester, Ontario: Sport Information Resource Centre.

———. (2000). *Inside the Olympic industry: Power, politics, and activism*. Albany, NY: State University of New York Press.

Leonard, W.M. (1993). *A sociological perspective of sport*, 4th ed. New York: Maxwell Macmillan.

Loland, S. (Ed.) (2000). *Fair play in sport: A moral norm system*. London: Routledge.

Lumpkin, A., Stoll, S.K., and Beller, J.M. (1994). *Sport ethics: Applications for fair play*. St. Louis: Mosby.

MacClancy, J. (Ed.) (1996). *Sport, identity, and ethnicity*. Oxford, UK: Berg.

Maguire, J. (1999). *Global sport: Identities, societies, civilisations*. Cambridge, UK: Polity Press.

Maguire, J. and Young, K. (Eds.) (2002). *Theory, sport, and society*. Amsterdam: JAI/Elsevier Science.

Maguire, J., Jarvie, G., Mansfield, L., and Bradley, J. (2002). *Sport worlds: A sociological perspective*. Champaign, IL: Human Kinetics.

Mandell, R.D. (1971, 1987). *The Nazi Olympics*. Urbana, IL: University of Illinois.

Martin, R. and Miller, T. (Eds.) (1999). *SportCult*. Minneapolis, MN: University of Minnesota.

Masteralexis, L.P., Barr, C.A., and Hums, M.A. (Eds.) (1998). *Principles and practices of sports management*. Gaithersburg, MD: Aspen.

McDonald, M.A. and Milne, G.R. (1999). *Cases in sports marketing*. Sudbury, MA: Jones and Bartlett.

McKay, J., Messner, M.A., and Sabo, D. (Eds.) (2000). *Masculinities, gender relations, and sport.* Thousand Oaks, CA: Sage.

McNamee, M.J. and Parry, S.J. (Eds.) (1998). *Ethics and sport.* London: E and FN Spon.

Messner, M.A. (1992). *Power at play: Sports and the problem of masculinity.* Boston, MA: Beacon Press.

————. (2002). *Taking the field: Women, men, and sports.* Minneapolis, MN: University of Minnesota Press.

————. (2005). Still a Man's World? In *The handbook of studies on men and masculinities,* ed. Kimmel, M.S., Hearn, J., and Connell, R.W., 313–325. Newbury Park, CA: Sage.

Messner, M.A. and Sabo, D. (1994). *Sex, violence and power in sports.* Freedom, CA: The Crossing Press.

Miller, L. (1997). *Sport business management.* Gaithersburg, MD: Aspen.

Miller, T. (2001). *SportSex.* Philadelphia, PA: Temple University Press.

Morgan, W.J. (1994). *Leftist theories of sport: A critique and reconstruction.* Urbana, IL: University of Illinois Press.

Mullin, B.J., Hardy, S., and Sutton, W.A. (1993). *Sport marketing.* Champaign, IL: Human Kinetics.

Murphy, B.O. and Zorn, T. (1996). Gendered interaction in professional Relationships. In *Gendered relationships: A reader,* ed. Wood, J.T., 213–232. Mountain View, CA: Mayfield.

Murphy, S.M. (Ed.) (1995). *Sport psychology interventions.* Champaign, IL: Human Kinetics.

Nelson, M.B. (1991). *Are we winning yet?: How women are changing sports and sports are changing women.* New York: Random House.

————. (1994). *The stronger women get, the more men love football: Sexism and the American culture of sports.* New York: Harcourt Brace.

————. (1998). Introduction in Smith, L. (Ed.) *Nike is a Godess.*

O'Donnell, L.B., Hausman, C., and Benoit, P. (1992). *Announcing: Broadcast communication today,* 2nd ed. Belmont, CA: Wadsworth.

O'Leary, J. (Ed.) (2001). *Drugs and doping in sport: Socio-legal perspectives.* London: Cavendish.

Olbermann, K. and Patrick, D. (1997). *The big show: Inside ESPN's SportsCenter.* New York: Pocket Books.

Parks, J.B. (1998). Influence of age, gender, and context on attitudes toward sexist/nonsexist language: Is sport a special case? *Sex Roles: A Journal of Research* vol. 38 (March): 477–494.

Parks, J.B., Zanger, B.R., and Quarterman, J. (Eds.) (1998). *Contemporary sports management.* Champaign, IL: Human Kinetics.

Pitts, B.G. and Stotlar, D.K. (1996). *Fundamentals of sports marketing.* Morgantown, WV: Fitness Information Technology.

Prebish, C.S. (1993). *Religion and sport: The meeting of sacred and profane.* Westport, CT: Greenwood.

Price, J.L. (Ed.) (2001). *From season to season: Sports as American religion.* Macon, GA: Mercer University Press.

Quirk, C. (Ed.) (1996). *Sports and the law: Major legal cases*. New York: Garland.

Rail, G. (Ed.) (1998). *Sport and postmodern times*. Albany, NY: SUNY.

Real, M.R. (1996). *Exploring media culture: A guide*. Thousand Oaks, CA: Sage.

Roche, M. (2000). *Mega-events and modernity: Olympics and expos in the growth of global culture*. London: Routledge.

Rogers, S.F. (Ed.) (1994). *Sports dykes: Stories from on and off the field*. New York: St. Martin's.

Rosentraub, M.S. (1997). *Major league losers: The real cost of sports and who's paying for it*. New York: Basic.

Rowe, D. (1995). *Popular cultures: Rock music, sport, and the politics of pleasure*. London: Sage.

———. (1999). *Sport, culture and the media: The unruly trinity*. Buckingham: Open University Press.

Russell, G.W. (1993). *The social psychology of sport*. New York: Springer-Verlag.

Sage, G.H. (1990). *Power and ideology in American sport: A critical perspective*. Champaign, IL: Human Kinetics.

Salter, D.F. (1996). *Crashing the old boys' network: The tragedies and triumphs of girls and women in sports*. Westport, CT: Praeger.

Sandoz, J. (Ed.) (1997). *A whole other ball game: Women's literature on women's sport*. New York: Noonday Press.

Sandoz, J. and Winans, J. (Ed.) (1999). *Whatever it takes: Women on women's sport*. New York: Farrar, Straus, and Giroux.

Schlossberg, H. (1996). *Sports marketing*. Cambridge, MA: Blackwell Business.

Scraton, S. and Flintoff, A. (Eds.) (2002). *Gender, sport and sexuality*. London: Routledge.

Scully, G.W. (1995). *The market structure of sports*. Chicago, IL: U. Chicago Press.

Senn, A.E. (1999). *Power, politics, and the Olympic Games*. Champaign, IL: Human Kinetics.

Shank, M.D. (1999). *Sports marketing: A strategic perspective*. Upper Saddle River, NJ: Prentice Hall.

Sheehan, R.G. (1996). *Keeping score: The economics of big-time sports*. South Bend, IN: Diamond Communication.

Shropshire, K.C. (1996). *In black and white: Race and sports in America*. New York: New York University Press.

Simon, R.L. (1991). *Fair play: Sports, values, and society*. Boulder, CO: Westview.

Singer, R.N., Hausenblas, H.A., and Janelle, C.M. (Eds.) (2001). *Handbook of sports psychology*. New York: John Wiley & Sons.

Smith, L. (Ed.) (1998). *Nike is a goddess: The history of women in sports*. New York: Atlantic Monthly Press.

Staudohar, P.D. and Mangan, J.A. (Eds.) (1991). *The business of professional sports*. Urbana, IL: University of Illinois Press.

Stein, M. and Hollwitz, J. (Eds.) (1994). *Psyche and sports*. Wilmette, IL: Chiron.

Stotlar, D.K. (1993). *Successful sports marketing*. Madison, WI: Brown and Benchmark.

Suggs, W. (2005). *A place on the team: The triumph and tragedy of Title IX*. Princeton, NJ: Princeton University Press.

Talbot, M. (Ed.) (2001). *Gender, power and culture: A centenary celebration of women in the Olympic Games*. Aachen, Germany: Meyer and Meyer Sports.

Theberge, N. (1981). A critique of critiques: Radical and feminist writings on sport. *Social Forces* 60 (2): 341–353.

Tomlinson, A. (Ed.) (2001). *Gender, sport and leisure: Continuities and challenges*. Aachen, Germany: Meyer and Meyer Sports.

Trujillo, N. (1991). Hegemonic masculinity on the mound: Media representations of Nolan Ryan and the American sports culture. *Critical Studies in Mass Communication* 8 (September): 290–308.

U.S. Olympic Committee (1996). *Olympism: A basic guide to the history, ideals, and sports of the Olympic Movement*. Glendale, CA: Guffin Pub.

VanderZwaag, H.T. (1998). *Policy development in sports management*. Westport, CT: Praeger.

Vinokur, M.B. (1988). *More than a game: Sports and politics*. New York: Greenwood.

Wann, D.L. (2001). *Sport fans: The psychology and social impact of spectators*. New York: Routledge.

Wascovich, T.R. (1993). *Sports marketing guide*. Cleveland, OH: Points Ahead.

Weitz, R. (Ed.) (2003). *The politics of women's bodies: Sexuality, appearance, and behavior*. New York: Oxford University Press.

Wenner, L.A. (Ed.) (1998). *MediaSport*. New York: Routledge.

Whannel, G. (1989). *Media, sports and society*. Newbury Park, CA: Sage.

———. (1992). *Fields in vision: Television sport and cultural transformation*. London: Routledge.

———. (2002). *Media sport stars: Masculinities and moralities*. London: Routledge.

Wiggins, D.K. (1997). *Glory Bound: Black athletes in a White America*. Syracuse, NY: Syracuse University Press.

Wilson, J. (1994). *Playing by the rules: Sport, society, and the state*. Detroit, MI: Wayne State University Press.

Wise, S. (1994). *Social issues in contemporary sport: A resource guide*. New York: Garland.

Wong, G.M. (1994). *Essentials of amateur sports law*. Westport, CT: Praeger.

Yasser, R., J.R. McCundy, and C.P. Goplerud (1990). *Sports law: Cases and Materials*. Cinannati, Ott: Anderson.

# PART I

# Sport Language Per Se

# CHAPTER 1

# Sportswomanship: The Cultural Acceptance of Sport for Women versus the Accommodation of Cultured Women in Sport

*L. Marlene Mawson*

"Good sport" is a term given to the competitor exhibiting valued social behaviors while engaged in a sporting contest, thought to be aware of the sociocultural values of fairness, civil courtesy, and ethical behavior. Early social-psychologists theorized that these social values are developed from personally and socially preferred modes of conduct (Rokeach, 1969), guidelines for right and wrong, good or bad, and appropriateness or inappropriateness being standards of ethical behavior based on social values. Adhering to social values and ethical standards of conduct, the "good sport" is said to display *good sportsmanship*, a term difficult to objectify. It is a relative term, since ethical values in sport vary according to the type of sporting contest, the place, the time era of the event, and the orientation of the competitors. Generally, sportsmanship means a commitment to play according to the written rules and the spirit of the rules, and acting responsibly, fairly, and respectfully toward opponents (Rudd and Stoll, 1998).

A "spirit of the rules" extends beyond written game rules, including ethical standards of behavior, or guidelines dictated by social values governing the condoned behaviors of participants. Traditionally, these socially based ethics of behavior during play have been different for women and men. "Sports*woman*ship," a word coined by the author, refers to ethical behaviors ascribed for women engaged in sport and behaviors representative of femininity in society; as such, it requires both an ethical competitive behavior as well as "ladylike" conduct consistent with cultural norms for females.

Subtle changes in sportswomanship expectations have been evidenced over time, as influenced by women's sociocultural advancements in American society from the nineteenth century through the twentieth century. The "cultured women who engage in sport" may be seen from one end of a spectrum of all American women who participate in sport competition, and the "sportswoman in the culture" may be viewed at the opposite extreme on that same spectrum. The "cultured woman in sport" is the individual whose sport participation contributes to her feminine sociocultural values. The "sportswoman," on the other hand, is an athlete first and foremost, fitting her athleticism to the social code within which her gender binds her behavioral options. Unfortunately for her, the dominance and power required in sport tends to reflect somewhat of a masculine image on her as an athletic sportswoman.

A research analysis of various components of sport participation by women is useful in understanding the full meaning of the social ethics and values dictated for sportswomanship. Comprehending its parameters is important for explaining changes over time of the sociocultural standards and behavioral codes for women as sports participants. This analytical perspective could explain ways to resolve the double standard of acceptable ethical sport behaviors between women and men.

## Sporting Women

Sport has universally held the connotation of being a masculine endeavor, its participation requiring aggressiveness and competitiveness, both deemed male social-personality traits. Early on, males enjoyed social and political dominance as they were recognized as "citizens," while females were not even accorded recognition as "persons" with individual rights under the U.S. Constitution until the 19th Amendment was passed in 1920. Thus, American sport was generated from a patriarchal perspective with masculine-oriented ethical standards that exist to this day (Eitzen and Sage, 1993).

The invasion of sporting events into the American culture for social pleasure and status had its roots in the colonies' mother country. By the eighteenth century, the American business economy and political directions softened Puritan convictions about using leisure time in sporting pursuits, and men began to increase their participation in sporting events for socialization (Van Dalen and Bennett, 1971). It was invention of the bicycle in the 1880s that revolutionized the social acceptance of physical activity and sport for all American women, and not only the socially elite (Bulgar, 1998).

The persistent exclusion of females from school sports deprived young girls from being socialized in traits presumed to bring success to males in American life (Sage, 1998). In the last quarter of the nineteenth century, relaxed moral and social standards for women allowed them increasing opportunities to enjoy sport as both spectators and participants. Amelia Bloomer introduced the ballooning pantaloon, gathered at the ankle, which allowed women to straddle a bicycle and avoid entangling long skirts in the rotating wheels. This new fashion apparel for women provided freedom of movement for other physical activities as well. Soon, the bloomer shortened (although long stockings covered the leg below), until its length was above the knee. With a garment that permitted active movement without undue exposure of the legs, the cultured women could now engage in more vigorous sport activities (Spears and Swanson, 1995). The development in 1893 of women's rules for basketball, and the introduction of field hockey in 1901, provided new frontiers of vigorous sport competition for women (Bulgar, 1988).

Sport competition itself demanded physical superiority, social sanction, and political backing, as well as funding. Women were perceived to be physically inferior to men, to whom they were socially, legally, and financially subordinate. Passage of the 1920 suffrage amendment to the U.S. Constitution allowed women to become equal under the law, although the acceptance of male domination regarding their participation in sports included the belief that females were not considered suited for the mental challenges of aggression and violence inherent in sport competition (Schneider, 2000).

Changes in the socially prescribed feminine image in the early 1900s dictated attitudes and practices of ladylike behavior. The "Gibson Girl" ideal dominated the standard of female beauty between 1895 into the 1920s in America, and the ideal woman was socially witty and sophisticated as well as physically adept at golf, tennis, cycling, swimming, and equitation—an ideal expected among women in the upper social strata. After World War I, the feminine apparel of Victorian long tresses was abandoned. Women donned shortened skirts, wore bobbed hair, and were nicknamed "flapper girls." However, the relaxed dress code did not notably change the social and behavioral restrictions on competitive sport for women (Rader, 1990).

A dark age for women's sport began with Mrs. Lou Henry Hoover's "Holy War on Women's Athletics," waged after the American Athletic Union (AAU) accepted the invitation for women to enter the 1922 Olympics for the first time. As the wife of Herbert Hoover (then Secretary of Commerce), she was asked to head a women's subdivision of the (men's) National Amateur Athletic Federation (NAAF) (Beazly and Hobbs, 1988). In 1923, she called an historical conference in Washington DC, at which a cross-section of invited women leaders of sport and athletics agreed to uphold a platform consisting of mass sport for all women, controlled by women, and protected from exploitation. These women leaders actively protested the entry of women into the 1922 and 1926 Olympic Games. The philosophy supporting the 1923 platform of the Women's Division of the NAAF was adopted by the National Section on Women's Athletics (NSWA) of the American Physical Education Association, which also opposed varsity competition in schools and colleges for girls and women. Alternatively, while rejecting competition for elite female athletes, NSWA advocated physical activity participation for all girls regardless of physical skill, offering a variety of sports to the masses in an educational environment without spectators. These women leaders took as their motto: "A sport for every girl, and every girl in a sport" (Ainsworth, 1975).

This 50-year era in the mid-twentieth century was without highly skilled sport competition for girls and women in public schools and colleges. With the current sport environment for women, it is difficult to imagine that most females in the 45 to 95-year age-range at the turn of the twenty-first century were never offered school-sponsored interscholastic competitive sports for elite athletes due to the social values imposed on women. Radical sociocultural changes occurred in the latter 1960s for American women. With congressional Civil Rights legislation came a national societal focus on "individual rights" more than social responsibility, and an emphasis on "individual freedom" more than commitment to others. Women's liberation advocates sought freedom from the oppression of male ideologies as they challenged the "glass ceiling" curtailing women's potential career opportunities. The Civil Rights movement became the catalyst to provide an alternative to "women's place" being in the home, and for contesting the social restrictions that men had imposed on them for years (Beazley and Hobbs, 1988).

The decade of the 1970s revealed great gains in competitive opportunities for girls and women across the nation. Title IX of the Education Amendments Act of 1972 promised equality of opportunity for both sexes in school sponsored programs at federally funded institutions; with its legal insertion into the U.S. Federal Register in June of 1973, it served through the 1970s as a legal threat to the male bastion in school sports. As women excelling in AIAW Championships and girls competing in state high school championships displayed their superb athletic abilities during their brief unbridled freedom from men's control of sport, they continued to gain in numbers of participants and in shattering athletic performance records (Rader, 1990). Still, Title IX presented itself as a legal threat for some (Miller, 2001).

The reawakening of women's competitive sport during the last quarter of the twentieth century was also supported by a social awareness of physical fitness, as the narrow-waisted, socially influenced body image of the ideal nineteenth century woman was coming to match a healthy physiological fitness image. A flexible, lean, and physically strong feminine body became the projected popular image for the fashion model by the 1980s, and the ideal woman's physique became similar to that required of the highly skilled athlete. The cultured woman engaging in sport was beginning to simulate the physically active sportswoman in the culture (Schneider, 2000). Women's fashion apparel of the 1980s, regardless of involvement in social events or in sport, evolved into bright-colored, stylish, sports clothing and specialized sport shoes. The appearance of cultured women in sport became more closely approximated to a sportswoman than did her social behavior. The cultured woman still remained somewhat submissive in sport competition, while the athletic sportswoman was more likely to express her assertiveness. However, women's role in sport began to change faster than sport changed (Coakley, 1994).

## DEFINING THE TERM "SPORTSMANSHIP" AS A CONCEPT

A number of theorists have attempted to explain the attributes of sportsmanship, some defining it as simply embracing "fairness and adherence to the rules" (Chambers, 1984), or equating it with "building character" (Clifford and Feezell, 1997). Researchers within the last decade have sought an understanding of sportsmanship based on "moral behavior and moral reasoning" (Beller and Stoll, 1993), some debating whether these morals are derived from values processing (Shields and Bredemeier, 1995).

### Fairness in Sport

Playing fairly within the rules includes adherence to the spirit of the game, even when there are no rules prohibiting taking advantage of an opponent when possible, there being an equitable enforcement of the "spirit of the rules" in highly contested sports (Chambers, 1984). It may be that the "fairness within the spirit of the game" expected in good sportsmanship is impossible in today's intensively competitive sport environment. For most organized sport teams, the primary goal is winning by taking advantage of skills and strategies not restricted by the rules, or not called by the officials (Hopkins and Lantz, 1999). When spontaneous play becomes organized sport competition, the emphasis of the opponents change from fairness, to valuing skill and victory (Olsen, 1988).

### Individual Character and Sport

Development of character, as a meritorious outcome of sport participation and practicing sportsmanlike behaviors, has been an old myth stemming from British school sports. From the perspective of Shields and Bredemeier (1995), the development of character through sport is inclusive of the concept of "sportspersonship," as they believe character is the outcome of sport competition when competitors embrace four principles during competition: compassion, fairness, sportsmanship, and integrity. The competitor must first assess the sport competition environment before appreciating and valuing a considerate and compassionate regard for the opponent; that is, understanding how the competitor might feel if treated in a way similarly to which s/he would treat the opponent during play. Upon recognizing the necessity of participating against a viable opponent for compelling competition, the values of competitive fairness can be defined. When choosing to value respect for the skill and dignity of opponents, as well as for one's self, a sportsmanship orientation is delineated. Finally, by exhibiting behaviors during competition within one's personal values and dignity, a self-image of integrity is developed, and one's moral character with regard to sport can be shaped accordingly.

### Moral Reasoning and Behavior in Sport

Moral reasoning and moral behaviors have been the focus of much of the sportsmanship research conducted within the past decade, morality being based on culturally universal values, than resulting from beliefs or attitudes (Shields and Bredemeier, 1995). Beller and Stoll (1993) describe cultural relativism as unquestioned values and beliefs which change by degree and circumstance within a culture or society, while ethical relativism is the normative judgments made about particular customs and/or people within that culture or society.

Vallerand and Losier (1994) have described sportsmanship as consisting of three elements toward moral reasoning and behavior: (1) sportsmanship orientation, meaning self-perceptions relevant to the sportsmanship dimensions; (2) sportsmanship development, the process for emerging sportsmanship perceptions; and (3) sportsmanship behavior, the manifestation of sport-related behavior. The concept of sportsmanship as moral reasoning must be known and understood in order for it to be evidenced in sport participants' behaviors; as over time, self-determined motivation may have the greatest influence on how sportsmanship in interpreted.

## DIFFERENTIATING "SPORTSMANSHIP" AND "SPORTSWOMANSHIP"

The dichotomy between "sportsmanship" as an exemplary sport behavior for males, and "sportswomanship" as the behavioral model for females, is easily distinguishable over the nineteenth and most of the twentieth century. Although sociocultural values and opportunities may have deterred many young women from continuing to participate in sport beyond their adolescence, researchers have determined that some gender-specific social-psychological explanations may influence young women's choice to engage in competitive sport. Sport researchers began to systematically study the changing ethical behaviors of girls and women in the late 1980s and 1990s, as female athletes became more intensely involved in year-round sport training and sport seasons.

Duda (1997) has reported that differences in sustained persistence in sport participation may not be solely affected by social norms; more likely, it is related psychologically to gender differences in task and ego orientation with regard to competitive sport goals. Kavassanu and Roberts (2001) described results consistent with Duda's research. Women collegiate basketball athletes in their study were found to have higher moral values than their male counterparts, and they had higher task orientation but lower ego orientation than male collegiate basketball players. Olsen (1988) measured differences in sport attitudes and aggressiveness between high school boys and girls basketball teams; as in other research results, it found that girls were more task-involved and had higher sportsmanship values, while boys were more ego involved, more aggressive, and had lower sportsmanship values—leading her to conclude that, as the competitive intensity and skill level in sport participation increases, the motivation to win increases, thus causing fairness to be compromised. Stephens (2000) studied pre-adolescents in organized soccer youth teams, finding that, although both boys and girls were influenced by team behavior norms, girls displayed less aggression, which could be explained as their perceived lack of competence or motivation.

## Unsportsmanlike Behavior

In recent years, athletes have displayed a decline in sportsmanlike behaviors, possibly due to a laxity in personal responsibility for moral values in the society. Research by Hopkins and Lantz (1999) has revealed that the longer sport participants are engaged in sport, the greater is the degeneration of sportsmanship behaviors. They found defensive soccer players had a lower sportsmanlike attitude than did offensive players in a youth soccer league, indicating their greater intent to gain an unfair advantage over their opponent. Those involved in highly skilled competitive play are less likely to demonstrate sportsmanlike behaviors, as the study showed that nonathletes demonstrated better sportsmanlike attitude than collegiate soccer athletes.

Elite athletes have been found to be even less sportsmanlike than athletes who play in less competitive games, providing evidence that as involvement in highly skilled sport increases, less emphasis is placed on sportsmanship values (Shields and Bredemeier, 1995). However, Kavassanu and Roberts (2000) suggest it may not be sport competition causing the decline in moral behavior, but the ego orientation required of highly skilled sport participants could be indicative of persons who display lower moral values with regard to competition. Spectators of all ages and motivations have demonstrated a decline in sportsmanlike behaviors when associated with sport competitors. Stewart (1996) reported from results of a survey that parents are not focused on emphasizing sportsmanship in youth sports, as only 36 percent of mothers and 25 percent fathers expected sportsmanship to be an outcome of their child's participation in sport.

Gillentine (1995) collected attitudes and moral reasoning of 150 interscholastic high school coaches, finding no differences in attitude or moral reasoning regarding sportsmanship among coaches, regardless of competitive level, years of coaching experience, education, sport, or gender; however, there is potential for coaches to compromise sportsmanlike behavior by using tactics such as intimidation of players or opponents through criticism or praise, coaching demeanor, dress, and reputation, all of which contribute to the attitude players have toward moral values in sport. Athletes also may demonstrate unsportsmanlike intimidation through directed insults to opponents, purposeful injuries in contact sports, and psyching-out the opponent with threatening remarks or over-aggressive behaviors (Lumpkin, Stoll, and Beller, 1999).

## SPORTSPERSONSHIP FOR THE TWENTY-FIRST CENTURY

Recently, behaviors of sportswomen have become much closer to the aggressive and assertive gestures men have expressed during competition, so future references to sport behaviors for all athletes may become more appropriately termed "sportspersonship." It may be speculated from the reported research studies that gravitation from high ethical behaviors traditionally displayed during sport competition among females has degenerated to moral behaviors more closely aligned with those of male athletes, due to the rise in skill level by women engaged in elite levels of sport, where social norms have been disregarded and where ego orientation takes as great a precedence for women athletes as for men.

The establishment of one's value of sport success is based on personal desire, social expectations within the context of the competition, and the process of choosing what is valued in sport participation; then, prizing these qualities, one should act accordingly when engaged in competition. After a series of research studies of athletes, coaches, and parents attitudes and behaviors about sport behaviors during competition, Shields and Bredemiere (1995) referred to these competitive behaviors as describing "sportspersonship," determining that they stem from individual and cultural "values." Furthermore, they contend it requires maintenance of moral allegiance against competing values, defining it as "An intense striving to succeed, tempered by commitment to a 'play spirit', such that ethical standards will take precedence over strategic gain when the two conflict" (p.194). Sportspersonship, they believe, is based on valuing the belief that one's conduct while engaged in sport competition is personally or socially preferable to an opposite or converse conduct.

Sportswomen have begun to overcome an immense social barrier in breaking into the prestigious world of men's sport. The 1996 Olympic Games were declared the "Women's Games," as U.S. women's teams excelled in winning gold medals in more sports than did men, and the success of the women's Olympic basketball team served as the springboard for the recent spectator support of women's professional basketball. In the 2000 Olympic Games, women continued to excel, as evidenced by the gold medal won by the U.S. women's soccer team, which also won the World Cup. These athletes have served as models for all women, regardless of age (Cole, 2000).

It now appears that, in the twenty-first century, when an elite woman athlete displays the ethical sportspersonship values of fairness, adherence to rules and courtesy during fierce, aggressive sport competition against opposing highly skilled women, her behavior will be socially accepted as an esteemed, feminine woman in the American society. Inferences drawn from reported research leads to an increasing similarity of sportspersonship behaviors between men and women, as women have become more highly skilled athletes and male coaches have strategically influenced women athletes' perception of sport ethics. However, until feminine social roles completely embrace sport behaviors, so that a sportswoman is accepted socially for displaying her competitive traits, as is a sport athlete, sport ethics will remain inconsistent for both men and women.

Whenever there is acceptance of women athletes as displaying socially acceptable feminine behaviors while engaged in sport, the newly defined term "sportspersonship" may eventually become the more appropriate reference to the socially expected behavior norm in sport for both women and men. Meanwhile, the residual conviction that women's ethical standards in sport competition should be of a higher morality than evidenced in men's sport, continues to enforce the reality that "sportswomanship" still connotes a different standard of behavior than "sportsmanship."

REFERENCES

Acosta, R.V. and Carpenter, L.J. (1994). The status of women in intercollegiate athletics. In *Women, sport and culture*, ed. Birrell, S. and Cole, C.L., 111–118. Champaign, IL: Human Kinetics.

Ainsworth, D.S. (1975). The history of physical education in colleges for women. In *A History of physical education and sport in the United States and Canada*, ed. Ziegler, E.F., 167–180. Champaign, IL: Stipes Publishing Co.

Beazley, W.H. and Hobbs, J.P. (1988). "Nice girls don't sweat": Women in American sport. In *The sporting image*, ed. Zingg, P.J., 337–352. Lanham, MD: University Press of America.

Beller, J.M. and Stoll, S.K. (1993). Sportsmanship: An antiquated concept? *Journal of Physical Education Recreation, and Drama* (August): 74–79.

Bulgar, M.A. (1988). American sportswoman in the 19th century. In Zingg, *Sporting image*, 85–105.

Chambers, R.L. (1984). *Sportsmanship in a sporting America: Tradition, ideal, reality* (Dissertation, Temple University) Microfiche PE 2773F.

Clifford, C. and Feezell, R.M. (1997). *Coaching for character*. Champaign, IL: Human Kinetics.

Coakley, J.J. (1994). *Sport in society: Issues and controversies*, 5th ed. St. Louis: C.V. Mosby Co.

Cole, C.L. (2000). The year that girls ruled. *Journal of Sport and Social Issues* 24 (1): 3–7.

Duda, J.L. (1997). Goal perspectives and their implications for an active and health life style among girls and women. *Women in Sport and Physical Activity Journal* 6 (2): 239–253.

Duquin, M.E. (1981). Creative, social reality: The case of women and sport. In *Sociology of sport: Diverse perspectives*, ed. Greendorfer, S.L. and Yannakis, A., 77–82. West Point, NY: Leisure Press.

Eitzen, D.S. and Sage, G.H. (1993). *Sociology of North American sport*, 5th ed. Madison, WI: W.C. Brown.

Gillentine, J.A. (1995). Comparison of the sportmanship attitudes and/or moral reasoning of interscholastic coaches (Unpublished Dissertation, University of Southern Mississippi) Microfiche GV 200 PSY 1845.

Hopkins, E. and Lantz, C.D. (1999). Sportsmanship attitude differences between defensive and offensive youth soccer players. *The Physical Educator* 56 (4): 179–186.

Kavassanu, M. and Roberts, G.C. (2001). Moral functioning in sport: An achievement goal perspective. *Journal of Sport and Exercise Psychology* 23 (1): 37–54.

Lumpkin, A., Stoll, S.K., and Beller, J.M. (1999). *Sport ethics: Applications for fair play*. Boston: W.C. Brown/McGraw-Hill.

Miller, T. (2001). *Sportsex*. Philadelphia: Temple University Press.

Olsen, L.K. (1988). *Relationship of task and ego involvement to sportsmanship and aggression tendencies* (Unpublished Dissertation, Purdue University) Microfiche GV 200 PSY 1449.

Rader, B.G. (1990). *American sports: From the age of folk games to the age of televised sports*, 2nd ed. Englewood Cliffs, NJ: Prentice-Hall.

Rokeach, M. (1969). *Beliefs, attitudes and values*. San Francisco: Jossey-Bass.

Rudd, A. and Stoll, S.K. (1998). Understanding sportsmanship. *Journal of Physical Education, Recreation and Dance* 69 (9): 38–42.

Sage, G.H. (1998). Does sport affect character development in athletes? *Journal of Physical Education, Recreation and Dance* 69 (1): 15–18.

Schneider, A.J. (2000). On the definition of "women" in the sport context. In *Values in sport*, ed. Tamrsjo, T. and Tamburrini, C., 123–138, London: E & FNSPON.

Shields, D.L. and Bredemeier, B.J. (1995). *Character development and physical activity*. Champaign, IL: Human Kinetics.

Spears, B. and Swanson, R.A. (1995). *History of sport and physical education in the United States*, 4th ed. Madison, WI: W.C. Brown.

Stephens, D.E. (2000). Predictors of likelihood to aggress in youth soccer: An examination of coed and all-girls teams. *Journal of Sport Behavior* 23 (3): 311–325.

Stewart, C.C. (1996). Parents and sportsmanship: Contemporary expectations. *The Physical Educator* 53 (Spring): 51–55.

Stewart, C.C. (1997). Parent-coach understanding: Another look. *The Physical Educator* 54 (Spring): 96–104.

Vallerand, R.J. and Losier, G.I. (1994). Self determined motivation and sportsmanship orientations: An assessment of their temporal relationship. *Journal of Sport and Exercise Psychology* 16 (3): 229–245.

VanDalen, D. and Bennett, B.L. (1971). *A world history of physical education*, 2nd ed. Englewood Cliffs, NJ: Prentice-Hall, Inc.

# CHAPTER 2

# Language, Gender, and Sport: A Review of the Research Literature

*Jeffrey O. Segrave, Katherine L. McDowell,*
*and James G. King III*

One of the recent successes of the feminist agenda has been to show that organized sport serves as a powerful cultural arena for constructing and perpetuating the ideology and practice of male privilege and dominance, sport assuming a profound role in the production and maintenance of male hegemony, contributing to historical patterns of male empowerment and female disadvantage. Women's sport is often trivialized and marginalized, and female athletes themselves frequently stereotyped as feminized women rather than competitive athletes.

One of the mechanisms that tends to inferiorize women in general is language, a critical component of the social scaffolding upon which unequal gender relations are erected and perpetuated. The language of sport in particular can contribute to their cultural devaluation. The purpose of this paper is to review and categorize research on the language of sport and gender, offering a sociolinguistics describing differences in the ways in which many different people speak differently about men's and women's sport and male and female athletes, and the ways in which all sorts of people differentially use the language of sport in a wide variety of social contexts.

## THE LANGUAGE OF SPORT

Among the many linguistic conventions contributing to the cultural devaluation of women in sport may be included masculine generics, gender marking, naming practices, descriptive linguistics, the metaphorical language of sport, the language of sport in cultural discourses, and subcultural language.

### Masculine Generics

The use of the masculine generic involves the linguistic presumption of maleness, a referent both to males and, generically, to all human beings. In their content analysis of 16 televised men's and women's college basketball games, Blinde, Greendorfer, and Shanker (1991, p.105), for example, found that one of the major differences in the verbal commentaries that accompanied the games was the constant use of male terminology inappropriately applied to the women's games: "Women athletes were called 'defensemen,' and well-coordinated teams possessed a 'workmanlike' orientation."

### Gender Marking

Another way in which women's sport is linguistically minimized and inferiorized is through the process of asymmetrical gender marking, a process in linguistic terms whereby the male is characterized as an unmarked category and the female as a marked one. By consistently defining and identifying women's athletic events as "women's" athletic events while men's athletic events are defined as simply athletic events, women are marked and identified as "other" and men as the norm, the universal. As Messner, Duncan, and Jensen (1993, p.127) note, gender marking women's athletics renders the women's game as "the other, derivative, and by implication, inferior to the men's."

Several studies have identified asymmetrical gender marking as a commonplace component of the gendered language of mass-mediated sport (Blinde, Greendofer and Shankar, 1991; Cohen, 1993; Fishwick and Leach, 1998; Halbert and Latimer, 1994; Higgs and Weiller, 1994; Koivolu, 1999; Messner, Duncan and Jensen, 1993). Whether referring to the women's Wimbleton final as the "Ladies Final," whereas the men's is simply "The Final," or labeling women's teams names such as Lady Friars, Lady Rams, or Lady Gamecocks, women's inferiority is implicated and intensified.

### Naming Conventions

Names, as linguists have demonstrated, are critical in the construction of social reality. By assigning names to things, we impose a pattern and meaning that allows us to manipulate our experiences. Like language in general, naming is neither a neutral nor random process but is, rather, a linguistic operation that encodes biases and prejudices, and those who have the power to name and rename retain a powerful cultural prerogative. With regard to naming practices, the inferiorization of women's sport and women's athletic performances is accomplished through conventions whereby women athletes are subjected to a variety of trivializing forms of address, including the use of patronizing and demeaning terms such as "girls," "sweetie," "princess," "doll," and "young ladies," informal use of first names, and/or inappropriately girly names for teams.

### Descriptive Linguistics

The marginalization of women's sport is accomplished through a variety of discursive tactics that we categorize under the following headings: the aesthetics of women's sport, the adolescent ideal, the male as norm, the linguistic framing of difference, and descriptive and narrative ambivalence.

#### The Aesthetics of Women's Sport

One of the linguistic conventions commonly employed to trivialize and denigrate women athletes is focusing remarks on factors typically unrelated to athletic performance, especially physical appearance and sexuality. By concentrating on looks and sex appeal rather than athletic performance, women are not only symbolically denied athleticism but they are also forced to conform to standard, stereotypical, and ultimately constraining ideals of femininity. In perhaps the most obviously blatant example of discursive sexism, Davis (1997) demonstrates how *Sports Illustrated*'s swimsuit issues have helped erect a monolithic conception of heterosexual femininity through linguistic idealizations of beauty.

Continual references to lesbianism also can discredit women's sport and divert attention away from the prowess and achievements of female athletes (Duncan and Messner, 1998; Kane and Lenskyj, 1998). The Women's Professional Football League has encountered many insinuations about lesbianism; one of its players, Stefanie Neroes, even being asked in a radio interview if she had ever ended up in the "69" position after being tackled (Lacy, 2001). As Duncan and Messner (1998) put it, "An easy way to discredit female athletes is to cast aspersions on their sexuality so their accomplishments can be dismissed as abnormal, freakish, deviant" (pp.183–184). Gloria Steinem (1992) has noted, "All patriarchal cultures idealize, sexualize, and generally prefer weak women" (p.217).

*The Adolescent Ideal*

Women's sport and women themselves are also trivialized by the descriptive infantilization of the female athlete, with language reducing them to adolescent, even prepubescent, status (Chisholm, 1999; Duncan and Brummett, 1987; Hilliard, 1984). In her analysis of the 1992 winter Olympics, Daddario (1994) identified three types of infantilizing comments: those that emphasized the childlike qualities of female athletes; those that reduced the adult status of female athletes by a disproportionate emphasis on their familial roles, especially their roles as mothers and daughters; and those that portrayed female athletes as other oriented, athletes who competed for someone else rather than for themselves.

*Male as Norm*

Not only does a preoccupation with nonathletic matters become a significant feature in the linguistic characterization of female athletes, but female athleticism is often mediated through debilitating comparisons to male athleticism (Blinde, Greendorfer, and Shankar, 1991; Jones, Murrell and Jackson, 1999). As Theberge (1997) argues, although women who compete in male-appropriate sports pose a significant challenge to the complex historical connections between gender, physicality, and power, the challenge is often muted by the linguistic construction of women's participation and success as simply an alternative to the version of the sport that "really counts," the male version. By constructing men's sport as the standard, and male athleticism as the dominant, indeed *defining*, expression of physical ability and accomplishment, the language of sport becomes a subtle means through which men's separation from and control over women becomes naturalized and institutionalized. By expressing the male as norm and, sometimes *only*, perspective, the language of sport in effect can bury women's sport and inferiorize it in strictly male ways.

*The Linguistic Framing of Difference*

The language of sport also contributes to a social construction of difference whereby females and femininity are constructed and hence perceived as "other than" males and masculinity. By juxtaposing descriptions of men's and women's sport, and male and female athletes, the language of sport naturalizes a gender hierarchy that translates easily into male supremacy (Hall, 1996). At the most obvious and immediate level, more is written about men's sport than women's sport, and more often, in newspapers, magazines, news bulletins, school newspapers, and web sites (Cramer, 1994; Crossman, Hyslop, and Guthrie, 1994; Lee, 1992; Matheson and Flatten, 1996; Rintala and Birrell, 1984; Tuggle and Owen, 1999; Urquart and Crossman, 1999), and typically male athletes are more praised than their female counterparts (Duncan, 1990; Halbert and Lattimer, 1994; Nelson, 1991; Sagas et al., 2000; Shifflett and Revelle, 1994; Wann et al., 1998).

Further, the linguistic construction of difference is also accomplished through a variety of other more subtle techniques, including: differential expectations and emphases in terms of athleticism, physicality, and performance (Birrell and Cole, 1990; Jones, Murell, and Jackson, 1999; Tuggle and Owen, 1999); the differential use of verbal descriptors to transmit information about sport (Duncan et al., 1994; Eleuze and Jones, 1998); differential treatments of character flaws (Daddario, 1994; Hilliard, 1984); the construction of the psychological "otherness" of women athletes (Kane and Parks, 1992; Klein, 1988); the "denial of power" for women in team sports (Duncan and Hasbrook, 1998); the differential framing of success and failure on the basis of gender and gender stereotypes (Daddario, 1994; Fishwick and Leach, 1998); the masculinization of male athletes in historically "feminine" sports (Adams, 1998); and an emphasis on women's personal lives (Kissling, 1999).

Taken collectively, these linguistic conventions construct gender difference as gender hierarchy. Not only are women perceived as "other than," they are concomitantly perceived as "less than." Women athletes are thus denied both status and legitimacy, and sport is privileged as a male preserve.

*Descriptive and Narrative Ambivalence*

Sports writers and announcers also commonly undermine women's sport by using ambivalent language, or language that comprises quite contradictory and conflicting messages (Duncan, 1986; Duncan and Hasbrook, 1988; Duncan et al., 1994; Eleuze and Jones, 1998; Kane and Parks, 1992; Lee, 1992). For example, Duncan (1990, p.71) found that Olympic sportswomen were also described in contradictory terms—on the one hand as "powerful, precise, courageous, skillful, purposeful and in control" and yet at the same time, as "cute, vulnerable, juvenile, manipulating, and toy- or animal-like." Duncan and Hasbrook (1998) have argued that structured ambivalence in the description of women's sport is worthy of critical attention because it most likely reflects a wider cultural ambivalence reflecting attitudes toward the incursion of women into traditionally male territory.

# THE METAPHORICAL
# LANGUAGE OF SPORT

Numerous commentators (Betts, 1974; Jensen and Sabo, 1994; Segrave, 1997; Tannenbaum and Noah, 1959) have noted that the language of sport—the patois, patter, and banter used daily by sportswriters and sportscasters, sports analysts, and sports fans, even sportsmen and women themselves—is a rich, metaphorical construction. It is also a language that reflects the sexist nature of sport.

From a purely quantitative perspective, Duncan et al. (1994) report, in their content analysis of televised men's and women's tennis and basketball games, that commentators used twice as many martial metaphors and power descriptors when discussing men's tennis as compared to women's tennis and three times as many when reporting men's compared to women's basketball. Whether team names, mascots, or nicknames, the conventions exist. From a more qualitative standpoint, Segrave (1997) has noted that the three main metaphorical conventions upon which the language of sport typically relies—namely, the metaphors of violence (teams "kill," "murder," "destroy," "slaughter" and "bury"); sex (athletes "penetrate," "drive," and "score"); and the machine (athletes "rev up," "burn up the track," "work well," "produce the goods," and "turn out the results")—instantiate the masculinist nature of sport. In other words, the various metaphors chosen to mediate the messages of sport or to paint the images that construct the cultural picture of sport privilege conventional and historically derived conceptions of masculinity. The metaphors traditionally associated with cultural conceptions of femininity are conspicuously muted.

## The Language of Sport in Cultural Discourses

Not only is the language of sport itself a metaphorical construction, but so also is the language of sport used as metaphor in other cultural discourses. In fact, "sportspeak", as Robert Lipsyte (1975) once called it, has become the root metaphor of a variety of cultural discourses, especially those activities that involve the problematic nexus of self-interest and social responsibility, namely the discourses of politics, sexual relations, and business. It applies to sport relative to politics, war, sexual relations, business, games, and any number of other sports-related arenas.

## Subcultural Language

The language of the sport subculture often serves as a male script that encourages the subordination and exclusion of women at the same time as it enhances male bonding and privilege. Polsky (1969) argues how the "poolroom" because an "escape hatch" from the "world of feminine values," while Johnson and Finlay (1997) have found that the particular way men talk about sport also serves as an effective exclusionary tactic, showing how men gossip about soccer as a way of creating a sense of male solidarity.

Language is also an important feature of the youth sport subculture, contributing to the socialization of boys into their appropriate gender roles. In his penetrating participant observation of Little League baseball teams in five middle-class communities, Fine (1987) shows how boys learn a language of lust that typifies a worldview consistent with traditional conceptions of male dominance and female submissiveness. A language of lust also typifies the sport subcultures of more mature, male athletes, the language of male bonding serving as a particularly fertile environment for the development of more abusive and violent attitudes toward women.

## LANGUAGE AS SOCIAL ACTION

The denigration and devaluation of women is a universal component of patriarchy and, as a dimension of American culture, it is rooted in women's politico-economic status and reflected in custom and convention, pornography and literature, occupational segregation, and discriminatory hiring practices—and in language, including the language of sport. The mere changing of sexist to non-sexist language will not immediately alter structural and structured inequality, but it can certainly help. As other institutional barriers to women's participation in sport are being confronted and dismantled, so too are linguistic expressions and conventions being challenged and replaced with language reflecting new visions of women in sport.

There are some good signs. Many media commentators and reporters are consciously striving to counter the apologetic with a more assertive discourse and to present women's athletics more fairly (Clausen, 2001; Duncan et al., 1994; Sandoz, 2000); there are heartening signs about equitable sports information for both genders on web sites, and recent studies have indicated that the context of sport, despite its conservative, masculinist orientation, does not negatively affect willingness to support nonsexist language any more than a non-sport workplace context. Taken collectively, these changes are a sign that the feminist assault against sexist language has indeed found fertile ground in the culture of sport.

There are still those who would argue that the study of language is "trivial," a distraction from "the real issues," even a side issue or a luxury. But words do, in fact, mold our cultural ideas and assumptions and give value and structure to the world in which we live. Whether framed from feminists, post-structualists, and/or humanists, language, as some linguists have put it, "speaks us." The language of sport not only reflects gender inequality but actually contributes to its construction and maintenance in both sport itself and ultimately in social settings that transcend sport. As a component of a vastly complex set of formal and informal practices encoding issues of gender, physicality, power, labor, and ideology, the social semiotic of the language of sport affirms and perpetuates discriminatory gender relations and is, therefore, worthy of our continued critical attention—perhaps even more so at a time when retrograde antifeminist discourses abound in the popular literature (McBride, 1995; Messner, 1997; Pfiel, 1995).

## REFERENCES

Adams, M.L. (1998). *Separating the men from the girls: Constructing gender difference in figure skating.* Paper presented to the International Sociology of Sport Association, Montreal, Canada.

Betts, J.R. (1974). *America's sporting heritage: 1850–1950.* Reading, MA: Addison-Wesley.

Birrell, S. and Cole, C.L. (1990). Double fault: Renee Richards and the construction and naturalization of difference. *Sociology of Sport Journal* 7: 1–21.

Blinde, E.M., Greendorfer, S.L., and Shankar, R.J. (1991). Differential media coverage of men's and women's intercollegiate basketball: Reflections of gender ideology. *Journal of Sport and Social Issues* 15: 98–114.

Chisholm, A. (1999) Defending the nation: National bodies, U.S. borders, and the 1996 U.S. Olympic women's gymnastic team. *Journal of Sport and Social Issues* 23: 126–139.

Clausen, P. (2001). The female athlete: Dualisms and paradox. *Women and Language* 24: 36–41.

Cohen, G.L. (1993). Media portrayal of the female athlete. In *Women, in sport: Issues and controversies,* ed. Cohen, G.L., 171–184. Newbury Park, CA: Sage.

Cramer, J.A. (1994). Conversations with women sports journalists. In *Women, media, and sport: Challenging gender values,* ed. Creedon, P.J., 159–180. Thousand Oaks, CA: Sage.

Crossman, J., Hyslop, P., and Guthrie, B. (1994). A content analysis of the sports section of Canada's national newspaper with respect to gender and professional and amateur status. *International Review for the Sociology of Sport* 29: 123–131.

Curry, T.J. (1991). Fraternal bonding in the locker room: A profeminist analysis of talk about competition and women. *Sociology of Sport Journal* 8: 119–135.

Daddario, G. (1994). Chilly scenes of the 1992 winter games: The mass media and the marginalization of female athletes. *Sociology of Sport Journal* 11: 275–288.

Davis, L.R. (1997). *The swimsuit issue and sport: Hegemonic masculinity in* Sports Illustrated. Albany: State University of Albany Press.

Duncan, M.C. (1986). A hermeneutic of spectator sport: The 1976 and 1984 Olympic Games. *Quest* 38: 50–77.

———. (1990). Sports photographs and sexual differences: Images of women and men in the 1984 and 1988 Olympic games. *Sociology of Sport Journal* 7: 22–43.

Duncan, M.C., and Brummett, B. (1987). The mediation of spectator sport. *Research Quarterly* 58: 168–177.

Duncan, M.C., and Hasbrook, C.A. (1998). Denial of power in televised women's sports. *Sociology of Sport Journal* 5: 1–21.

Duncan, M.C., and Messner, M.A. (1998). The media image of sport and gender. In *Media sport*, ed. Wenner, L.A., 170–185. New York: Routledge.

Duncan, M.C., Messner, M., Williams, L., and Jensen, K. (1994). Gender stereotyping in televised sports. In *Women, sport, and culture*, ed. Birrell, S. and Cole. C., 249–272. Champaign, IL: Human Kinetics.

Eastman, S.T., and Billings, A.C. (1999). Gender parity in the Olympics: Hyping women athletes, favoring men athletes. *Journal of Sport and Social Issues* 23: 140–170.

Elueze, R. and Jones, R.L. (1998). A quest for equality: A gender comparison of BBC's TV coverage of the 1995 World Athletic Championships. *Women in Sport and Physical Activity Journal* 7: 45–55.

Fine, G.A. (1987). *With the boys: Little League baseball and the preadolescent culture.* Chicago: University of Chicago Press.

Fishwick, L. and Leach, K. (1998). *Game, set, and match: Gender bias in television coverage of Wimbledon 1994.* Paper presented to British Leisure Asso., Leeds.

Halbert, C. and Latimer, M. (1994). "Battling" gendered language: An analysis of the language used by sports commentators in a televised coed tennis competition. *Sociology of Sport Journal* 11: 298–305.

Hall, M.A. (1996). *Feminism and sporting bodies: Essays on theory and practice.* Champaign, IL: Human Kinetics.

Higgs, D.T. and Weiller, K.H. (1994). Gender bias and the 1992 Summer Olympic Games: An analysis of TV coverage. *Journal of Sport and Social Issues* 18: 234–256.

Hilliard, D. (1984). Media images of male and female professional athletes: An interpretative analysis of magazine articles. *Sociology of Sport Journal* 1: 251–262.

Jensen, S. and Sabo, D. (1994). The sport/war metaphor: Hegemonic masculinity, the Persian Gulf War, the New World Order. *Sociology of Sport Journal* 11: 1–17.

Johnson, S., and Finlay, F. (1997). Do men gossip? An analysis of football talk on television. In *Language and masculinity*, ed. Johnson, S. and Meinhof, U.H., 130–143. Oxford: Blackwell.

Jones, R., Murrell, A.J., and Jackson, J. (1999). Pretty versus powerful in the sports pages: Print media coverage of the U.S. women's Olympic gold medal winning teams. *Journal of Sport and Social Issues* 23: 183–192.

Kane, M.J. (1988). Media coverage of the female athlete before, during, and after Title IX: *Sports Illustrated* revisited. *Journal of Sport Management* 2: 87–99.

Kane, M.J., and Lenskyj, H. (1998). Media treatment of female athletes: Issues of gender and sexualities. In *Media Sport*, ed. Wenner, E.D., 186–201. New York: Routledge.

Kane, M.J., and Parks, J.B. (1992). The social construction of gender difference and hierarchy in sport journalism—few new twists on very old themes. *Women in Sport and Physical Activity Journal* 1: 49–83.

Kissling, E.A. (1999). When being female isn't feminine: Uta Pippig and the menstrual communication taboo in sports journalism. *Sociology of Sport Journal* 16: 79–91.

Klein, M.L. (1988). Women in the discourse of sports reports. *International Review for the Sociology of Sport* 23: 138–151.

Koivolu, N. (1999). Gender stereotyping in televised media sports coverage. *Sex Roles* 41: 589–604.

Lacy, L. (2001). Women tackle a league of their own. *Lesbian News* 26: 26–28.

Lee, J. (1992). Media portrayals of male and female Olympic athletes: Analyses of news–paper accounts of the 1984 and 1988 Summer Games. *International Review of the Sociology of Sport* 27: 197–219.

Lipsyte, R. (1975). *Sportsworld: An American dreamland*. New York: Quadrangle Books.

Lumpkin, A., and Williams, L.D. (1991). An analysis of *Sports Illustrated* feature articles, 1954–1987. *Sociology of Sport Journal* 8: 16–32.

Matheson, H. and Flatten, K. (1996). Newspaper representation of women athletes in 1984 and 1994. *Women in Sport and Physical Activity Journal* 2: 65–83.

McBride, J. (1995). *War, battering, and other sports: The gulf between American men and women*. Atlantic Heights, NJ: Humanities Press.

Messner, M.A. (1997). *Politics of masculinities: Men in movements*. Thousand Oaks, CA: Sage.

Messner, M.A., Duncan, M.C., and Jensen, K. (1993). Separating the men from the girls: The gendered language of televised sports. *Gender and Society* 7: 121–137.

Nelson, M.B. (1991). Sports speak: Breaking the language barrier. *Women's Sport and Fitness Magazine* (April): 70–71.

———. (1994). *The stronger women get, the more men watch football*. New York: Harcourt & Brace.

Pfiel, F. (1995). *White guys.* London: Verso.

Polsky, N. (1969). *Hustlers, beats, and others.* New York: Anchor.

Rintala, J. and Birrell, S. (1984). Fair treatment for the active female: A content analysis of *Young Athletes* magazine. *Sociology of Sport Journal* 1: 231–150.

Sagas, M., Cunningham, G.B., Wigley, B.J., and Ashley, F.B. (2000). Coverage of university softball and baseball websites: The inequity continues. *Sociology of Sport Journal* 17: 198–205.

Sandoz, J. (2000). Victory? New language for sportswomen. *Women and Language* 23: 33–37.

Segrave, J.O. (1994). The perfect 10: "Sportspeak" in the language of sexual relations. *Sociology of Sport Journal* 11: 95–113.

———. (1997). A matter of life and death: Some thoughts on the language of sport. *Journal of Sport and Social Issues* 21: 211–220.

Shifflett, B. and Revell, R. (1994). Gender equity in sports and media coverage: A review of NCAA News. *Journal of Sport and Social Issues* 18: 144–150.

Spender, D. (1980). *Man made language.* Boston: Routledge & Kegan Paul.

Steinem, G. (1992). *Revolutions from within.* Boston: Little, Brown and Company.

Tannenbaum, P. and Noah, J. (1959). Sportguese: A study of sports page communication. *Journalism Quarterly* 36: 163–170.

Theberge, N. (1997). "It's part of the game": Physicality and the production of gender in women's hockey. *Gender & Society* 11: 69–88.

Tuggle, C.A. and Owen, A. (1999). A descriptive analysis of NBC's coverage of the Centennial Olympics: The "Games of the Woman"? *Journal of Sport and Social Issues* 23: 171–182.

Urquart, J. and Crossman, J. (1999). *The Globe and Mail* coverage of the Winter Olympic games: A cold place for women athletes. *Journal of Sport and Social Issues* 23: 193–202.

Wann, D.L., Schrader, M.P., Allison, J.A., and McGeorge, K.K. (1998). The inequitable newspaper coverage of men's and women's athletics at small, medium, and large universities. *Journal of Sport and Social Issues* 22: 79–87.

# CHAPTER 3

# "Throw Like a Girl" Doesn't Mean What It Used To:* Research on Gender, Language, and Power

*Faye Linda Wachs*

Language is suffused with relations of power and privilege. The ways in which ideologies of race (Moore, 1976), class (Bourdieu, 1984), sexuality (Pharr, 1997), and gender (Fay, 1994) are perpetuated and reflected in language have been well documented. Relations of power and privilege are reified in language. Understanding the complexity of the social world requires a comprehension of how language both reflects and produces such relations. Unpacking these relations is difficult, as language becomes both the object of study and the tool used to study it.

Gendered power relations provide one example of this complexity. The linguistic binary male-female underscoring social interactions presumes, presupposes, and defines a culturally agreed upon set of "natural differences." Questions asked about bodies generally presuppose a set of culturally defined "sex differences" infused with relations of power and privilege, suffused with the weight of historic rhetoric. Nearly every (gendered) act described carries with it sets of meanings, associations, denotations, and connotations presupposing a gendered subject. Are challenges possible? What types of

* The title refers to a slogan featured on the favorite game day shirt of one experienced participant, Kathy.

negotiations are required? The social world of coed softball provides an appropriate microcosm for examination. Because gender is overtly legislated in coed softball, it must be repeatedly marked; understanding negotiations of markings, namings, and presentations of performance may shed light.

## The Power of (Gendered) Language

Language shapes and defines how people structure and interpret experience, mediating experience and culture (Foucault, 1972; Lakoff, 1976; Miller and Swift, 1976). Because language structures a "realm of the fathomable," it necessarily shapes interpretations of experiences and the nature of experience itself. Because one learns a gendered language, gendered ideologies permeate thought, interpretation, practice, and forms resulting from such practices. While English lacks the gendered suffixes of other Western languages, a linguistic binary emerges in its usage. Many adjectives are gendered, applied almost exclusively to one gender (Lakoff, 1976; Miller and Swift, 1976); for example, "pretty" is generally only applied to woman. Relations of power and privilege are such that it would be insulting to apply that adjective to a man.

Given the relational nature of gender in Western culture (Connell, 1987, 1995), linguistic bifurcation is hardly surprising. Nor is it surprising that, given the history of gendered power relations, definitions of what constitutes masculinity tend to be positive attributes, while definitions of "what a woman is" are often her negative attributes (crying, weakness) (Bourdieu, 1998; Collins, 1993). There are many more negative words to describe women (e.g., slut, tart, whore, strumpet, bitch, slattern) than for men (Miller and Swift, 1976). In other cases, attributes are ascribed due to relational comparisons, a woman being what a man is not (Collins, 1993; Henley, 1977; Miller and Smith, 1976). In sports, traditional binaries have maintained male physical superiority; women's sports therefore could provide a real challenge to gendered power relations. Studies of sports broadcasts reveal tendencies among commentators to discuss men's emotions in individualistic terms, while women's emotions are linked to their ability to work as a team, framing winning as "for" others (Duncan, Messner, and Cooky, 2000). Attributions for success are linked to individuals in men's games, to the team or no-one in women's (i.e., "Johnson drives to the hoop" versus "the ball goes in") (Duncan and Hasbrook, 1988). But it is not simply that such associations exist, but that such associations are *presupposed* at the most fundamental level.

In sports, presuppositions often arise in the link between gender and ability. To feminize a male athlete's ability is an insult, whereas, to masculinize a female athlete's performance is complimentary. Calling a "boy/man" a "girl/woman" or any of the other monikers referencing a woman's anatomy is insult (Fine, 1987).

The expression "Throw like a girl" remains a critique of ability. By contrast, Leslie Heywood (1998) reports that when she demonstrated her lifting prowess she went from Leslie to Lester—which she and her lifting partners viewed as a compliment. Sexualized relations of dominance and oppression intermix such that part of the denigration of men involves feminizing their sexuality, making them "gay." What underlies such tendencies is the notion that men are more physically competent, especially at sports. Women who demonstrate too much ability have been policed by language games, labels like "mannish" used to discourage their sport participation and, of course, the stigma of lesbianism underlies this naming (Cahn, 1994; Hargreaves, 1994; Hult, 1994).

## NAMES, TITLES, AND GENDER

Linguistic conventions surrounding names and titles clearly reflect how gendered relations of power and privilege infuse language. For example, the "male universal" norm remains in the sports world, particularly noticeable where there are analogous men's and women's events. The National Collegiate Athletic Association (NCAA) tournament is presumed to be a men's tournament, while the women's tournament is marked as such (Duncan and Hasbrook, 1988; Duncan, Messner and Cooky, 2000, Duncan et al. 1994; Kane, 1998; Lakoff, 1976). Further, women's teams are often marked with feminized nicknames, while male teams hold the general mascot name (i.e., Lady Gamecocks, Wildkittens, Lady Lions) (Eitzen and Baca Zinn, 1989). Though this practice is decreasing over time, it remains a barrier to equality for women's sports.

Coed sports present an interesting counterpoint. Within such a context, what types of gender marking practices appear? How is gender difference and male dominance maintained in light of performances by bodies challenging such conceptions?

## METHODOLOGY FOR "PLAYING THE FIELD"

For my doctoral dissertation, I performed participant observation of adult coed softball leagues in Southern California from the beginning of the spring 1996 season in April through the end of the summer 1997 season in September. Follow-up observations were made in

1998, 1999, and 2000. During the initial study period, I was an active participant on four teams in four different leagues and an observer of one league in the Greater Los Angeles area, and follow-up observations were made in four of the leagues. Leagues were selected to reflect a wide range of abilities; hence, some teams played very competitive ball, while others played at a more "recreational" level. Several men's games were also observed for comparison. Unfortunately, the women's league selected for study folded both seasons I attempted to observe. Other women's leagues played at the same times as the coed leagues under observation.

While many studies focus on professional and amateur sports, the focus on recreational sports allows studying practices of "ordinary" people. Participants tended to be upper working class and middle class, between the ages of 18 and 45 (though some older players did participate), and reflected the ethnic/racial diversity of Southern California. A range of professions was represented. Teammates were doctors, nurses, architectural engineers, accountants, lawyers, managerial workers, receptionists, film editors, transportation consultants, office workers, graduate students, and a host of other professional.

Observing in a field in which one is also a participant creates a number of dilemmas, but seeking out critiques from colleagues in both fields (sociology and softball) provided invaluable assistance. This paper reflects the comments of participants, managers, and occasional spectators at games in all five leagues. Pervasive tendencies are the focus, and I attempted to represent the general practice, while avoiding making generalization from anomalous occurrences.

## DATA AND ANALYSIS— PLAYING WITH THE GIRLS

### Men and Girls

Among the participants in all the leagues studied, an interesting tendency emerged. Lakoff's 1976 study of gender and language found the term "girls" often used to refer to adult women; a quarter century later little has been done to alter this convention. "Girls" and "women" were used interchangeably by participants and managers referring to female athletes. In my field notes from every game were numerous examples of variations of these phrases: "Which girl do I follow?" "Which guy do I follow?" "Which girl is up next . . ." "Which man is on deck?" In addition to the pleasant alliteration of the double gs of girls and guys, there is something deeper at work. Many women displayed high levels of gender sensitivity and awareness of the battles over gendered ideology that take place on the field (Wachs, 2002). Many of these women also consistently called themselves or their teammates, "girls." So what is going on?

### We're not "Ladies!!"

To get a better sense of why women choose to be *girls* in this setting, one could look at what women do not like to be called. Interestingly, the terms "lady" or "ladies" were the most consistently abhorred gendered descriptors. Resistance to this term demonstrates a rejection by athletes of its connotations. Speedy, a long-time veteran outfielder, snorted, "Ladies . . . We're not having tea and crumpets" Veteran catcher/outfielder Michelle added, "Lady is what I was supposed to be whenever someone wanted me to stop doing what I was enjoying doing."

In a world where men and women increasingly perform the same set of skills, Mary Jo Kane's (1995) description of overlapping continua of ability, size, strength, and the like, rather than oppositional difference, is obvious. Hence, physical incompetence is something done or enacted, or written on the body, not something "naturally" linked to one sex. The term "lady" naturalizes this incompetence and dependence and therefore is the most resisted.

Understandings of the link between emphasized femininity and sexuality, in addition to class, are factors in the rejection of certain gendered terms like "lady," the linkages between heterosexism and sexism being well documented (Pharr, 1997). The term implies availability to and dependency on men. In her study of women's ice hockey, Nancy Theberge (1995) found many women in her study self identified as lesbian or queer and that both they and straight participants worked to create an open and tolerant environment. Similarly, many of the women in the leagues I studied also self identified as lesbian or queer, although no men openly did. Heterosexual teammates were generally at least sensitive to issues involving discrimination because of one's sexual orientation.

A lady is heterosexual. A girl, by contrast, is prepubescent, before adult norms of emphasized femininity or ladyhood are learned. Though a girl may remain under the authority of her father, she may be freed from enacting adult sexualized norms necessarily requiring women's subordination. This queering of the discourse by most of the participants observed here reflects both the long history of recreational spaces in which women were more able to challenge, violate, and ignore norms of both gender and sexuality. At the same time, because such norms are ubiquitous, they are never fully banished. The problematization of the valuation of the masculine and devaluation of the feminine in sport is reflected in the renaming of women who can play.

### Renaming Athletes

Interestingly, many women who performed and had traditionally feminine names were renamed. Two different types of renaming occurred: In the first case, performance or ability was highlighted through the masculinizing of the name. Second, women with traditionally feminine names, and especially those perceived as "upper class" were given new names by teammates. The masculinization of women's names (Heywood, 1998) provides a potent example of how ideologies of masculine ability permeate even the consciousness of skilled female athletes.

### Chicks Rule

In some cases, women chose to "reclaim" terms sometimes viewed as derogatory. In the following scenario, a derogatory term is used to celebrate female success and ability. Once, we were overmatched as a team, playing the defending champions. Late in the game we were down by over ten runs. After Kathy singled, Eric grounded out. I followed with a single, the next man hit a fly ball for another out. When our next woman singled to score Kathy, a woman on their team, Steph, cheered, "Chicks rule!! All of the women are getting on and the men are getting out!! Chicks rule. Chicks rule."

Celebrations of female ability have represented resistance to ideologies of female inability and challenged ideologies of male superiority and gender difference. Steph, despite being an opponent, specifically resisted concepts of female inability by marking and claiming the field as a site of female ability. Given the myriad ways in which female performance was undermined to protect ideologies of male physical superiority (Wachs, 2002, 2003), noting female ability, especially in light of male failure, provides a potent context for resistance. Ironically, by marking gendered ability, ideologies of female inability are reified because demonstrations of female ability are defined as noteworthy. Similar debates surround the use of formally derogatory terms by people of color and sexual minorities (Boyd, 1997).

The contradiction in simultaneously reifying and challenging ideologies of female inferiority marks the third wave of feminist theorizing (Heywood and Drake, 1997). Again, class relations intermix with gender relations on the softball diamond. While the upper class lady is consistently resisted, working class "chick" is not problematized, despite the larger culture's view of "lady" as a non-derogatory term and "chick" as more likely to evoke negative images. Clearly, this demonstrates participants' understanding of the intersections of gender and class such that although working class women are excluded from emphasized femininity because of their class status, being excluded can also mean freedom from certain gender expectations—in this case, physical incompetence. Additionally, while a "lady" is "bred to please," a chick has some agency: she pleases herself.

### Baby Girls

Demonstrations of female ability were sometimes undermined even when celebrated. The following situation provides an emblematic example of just such a case: It was a close game, oscillating between us up by one and them up by one. With two outs and two on, the opponents had a chance to put some runs on the board. The woman batting was in her mid-twenties. She sported a "club kid" look with long pigtails and baggy clothes, the shape of her body totally obscured by billows of cloth. She is a very talented player and was hitting well that day. Her teammate, Mike, a former player on our team, really wanted to beat us. From his position coaching first base he encouraged his teammate. "Come on baby girl, come on baby girl. We need a hit here." It is not the first time I have heard the expression "baby girl" used to spur a teammate on. When she got that important hit, he celebrated, "Yay. Way to go, baby girl . . . Way to go . . ."

### Guys and Dolls—Why even Distinguish by Gender?

The following final scenario reveals the growing tendency to discount gender as an important reference point. During a west Los Angeles league game, teammates Brittney and Abbey assessed the abilities of an opposing team. Watching the opposition, Brittney remarked appreciatively, "Those guys can play." Abby replied, "The girls are good too." Befuddled, Brittney replied, "I meant their whole team . . . I meant guys like everyone." "Oh," Abby replied looking a bit confused and surprised. "I just figured you said guys, so you meant the men."

Coed softball requires that gender be continuously legislated (Wachs, 2002). The paradox produced by attempting to legislate equality through defining difference remains problematic in coed environments (Scott, 1996; Wachs, 2002). Such designations undermine evidence of overlapping continua of performance transcending gender (Kane, 1995; Wachs, 2003). However, gender markings make distinctions even when many participants recognize that it is not relevant. Further, because in many cases the universal male norm is used to refer to mixed gender groups (i.e., mankind), in environments where gender is actively controlled, confusion can be created.

Participants attempted to use *guys* as a gender-neutral term, retaining the problem of it being a universal norm arising from the male. Though over the past 20 years the use of gendered universals has fallen out of favor (Martyna, 1983), with slang terms like "guy," norms remain unclear. This can leave women in situations in which to acquiesce to the male norm can erase women's presence; though, invoking the presence of both genders calls up ideologies of female physical difference and inferiority. And so, we are left with "girls?"

### *What I Meant and What I Said*

Obviously, the choice of the term "girls" arose in these sporting examples for a number of reasons. In the first case, participants recognized conflations of womanhood with "lady" as containing an assumption of physical inferiority, especially at sports. "Woman" as a corollary term has not only conflations of gender and inability, but a history of facilitating, rather than participating in, leisure (Cross, 1990).

But it is more complicated. As barriers for womens' entry into a variety of fields are eroding, beliefs of physical difference remain and continue to structure and limit opportunities for both genders. The struggle on the diamond reflects tensions present in the larger culture, as binary differences are challenged through a range of performances. Still, one must ask: does self-definition or the reclamation of a term empower the speaker or change the meaning? Is girl power *power*? Or is it self-delusional masking of patriarchal bargains? Or is it subverting these bargains? Yes, yes, and yes.

Clearly, the women on the diamond were not alone. Western media reveals a host of competing ideologies of femininity. The guerilla art group the Riot Grrls, Girl Power mantras, and other cultural icons have arrived at the same terming in the political minefield of a gendered language that already presumes female subordination. But what baggage do we bring with us in the use of this term? Although my research lent clear support to continua of overlapping abilities by gender (Kane, 1995), the marking of gender reasserted binary conceptions of gender and ability, allowing some to frame one's performance as "good for a girl" thereby avoiding comparisons to male performances (Heywood, 1998). Ultimately, it is the maintenance of such structures that protects existing relations of power and privilege. The problem, however, becomes: how does one create a coed situation in which gender "has nothing to do with it," when it has everything to do with it. "Girls," while potentially problematic, at least moves us toward an idea of equity, even though it paradoxically requires the use of a term that formerly indicated powerlessness. Clearly it is time to find some new terms.

What these shifts in language indicate are the myriad ways in which gendered roles can become irrelevant. Influxes of women into many professions previously dominated by men, such as law, medicine, and engineering reflect such changes (Kimmel, 2000). While a backlash often leads to a struggle to reassert gendered norms, change is occurring. The question becomes, where do we go from here?

## References

Bourdieu, P. (1984). *Distinction*. Cambridge: Harvard University Press.

——. (1998). *Masculine domination*. Stanford: Stanford University Press.

Boyd, T. (1997). *Am I black enough for you*. Indiana University Press.

Cahn, S.K. (1994). *Coming on strong: Gender and sexuality in Twentieth-century women's sport*. New York: The Free Press.

Collins, P.H. (1993). Toward a new vision: Race, class, and gender as categories of analysis and connection. *Race, sex and class* 1 (1): 25–45.

Connell, R.W. (1987). *Gender and power: Society, the person and sexual politics*. Cambridge: Polity Press.

——. (1995). *Masculinities*. Cambridge: Polity Press.

Cross, G. (1990). *A social history of leisure since 1600*. State College: Venture Publishing, Inc.

Duncan, M.C. and Hasbrook, C. (1988). Denial of power in televised women's sports. *Sociology of Sport Journal* 5: 1–21.

Duncan, M.C., Messner, M. and Cooky, C. (2000). *Gender in televised sports: 1989, 1993, and 1999*. Los Angeles: Amateur Athletic Foundation Report.

Duncan, M.C., Messner, M., Jensen, K., and Wachs, F.L. (1994). *Gender stereotyping in televised sports*. Los Angeles: Amateur Athletic Foundation Report.

Eitzen, D.S. and Baca Zinn, M. (1989). The de-athleticization of women: The naming and gender marking of collegiate sport teams. *Sociology of Sport Journal* 6: 362–370.

Fay, E.A. (1994). *Eminent rhetoric: Language, gender, and cultural tropes*. Westport, CT: Bergin & Garvey.

Fine, G.A. (1987). *With the boys: Little League baseball and preadolescent culture*. Chicago: University of Chicago Press.

Foucault, U. (1972). *The archaeology of knowledge*. London: Routledge.

Hargreaves, J. (1994). *Sporting females: Critical issues in the history and sociology of women's sports*. New York: Routledge.

Henley, N.M. (1977). *Body politics: Power, sex, and nonverbal communication*. Englewood Cliffs, NJ: Prentice-Hall.

Heywood, L. (1998). *Pretty good for a girl*. New York: The Free Press.

Heywood, L. and Drake, J. (1997). *Third wave agenda*. Minneapolis, MN: University of Minnesota Press.

Hult, J.S. (1994). The story of women's athletics: Manipulating a dream 1890–1985. In *Women and sport: Interdisciplinary perspectives*, ed. Costa, S. and Guthrie, S. Champaign, IL: Human Kinetics.

Kane, M.J. (1988). Media coverage of the female athlete before, during, and after Title IX: *Sports Illustrated* revisited. *Journal of Sport Management* 2: 87–99.

———. (1995). Resistance/transformation of the oppositional binary: Exposing sport as a continuum. *Journal of Sport and Social Issues* 19: 191–218.

Kimmel, M.S. (2000). *The gendered society reader*. New York: Oxford University.

Lakoff, R. (1976). *Language and women's place*. New York: Octagon Books.

Lerner, G (1979). *The majority finds its past*. New York: Oxford University.

Leslie, A. (1986). A myth of the southern lady. *Sociological Spectrum* 6: 31–49.

Martyna, W. (1983). Beyond the he/man approach: The case for nonsexist language. In *Language, gender & society*, ed. Thorne, B., Kramarae, C., and Henley, N. Rowley, MA: Newbury House Inc.

Messner, M., Duncan, M.C., and Jensen, K. (1993). Separating the men from the girls: The gendered language of televised sports. *Gender and Society* 7: 1, 121–137.

Miller, C. and Swift, K. (1976). *Words and women*. New York: Anchor Press.

Moore, R. (1976). *Racism and the English language*. New York: Council on Interracial Books for Children.

Pharr, S. (1997). *Homophobia: A weapon of sexism*. Little Rock: Chardon Press.

Pringle, R. (1988). *Secretaries talk: Sexuality, power, and work*. London: Verso.

Scott, J. 1996. *Only paradoxes to offer*. Cambridge, MA: Harvard University Press.

Theberge, N. (1995). Gender, sport, and the construction of community: A case study from women's ice hockey. *Sociology of Sport Journal* 12: 4, 389–402.

Thorne, B., Kramarae, C., and Henley, N. (1983). *Language, gender and society*. Rowley, MA: Newbury House Publishers, Inc.

Wachs, F.L. (2002). Leveling the playing field: Negotiating gendered rules in coed softball. *Journal of Sport and Social Issues* 26: 3, 300–316.

———. (2003). "I was there . . .": Gendered Limitations, Expectations, and Strategic Assumptions in the world of coed softball. In *Athletic intruders: Ethnographic research on women, culture, and exercise*, ed. Bolin, A. and Granskog, J. Albany, NY: SUNY Press.

# PART II

# Historical Perspectives

# CHAPTER 4

# "A Glow of Pleasurable Excitement": Images of the New Athletic Woman in American Popular Culture, 1880–1920

*Nancy G. Rosoff*

Images shape our perceptions and beliefs, offering insight into the kinds of behaviors considered appropriate and acceptable. In the late nineteenth and early twentieth centuries, textual descriptions as well as visual images of athletic women appearing in print media served both to shape and to reflect gender ideology. Would-be athletes could learn the techniques of various sports and also how to dress appropriately for participation in athletic activities from a variety of publications, including such resources as instruction manuals, newspapers, and popular periodicals like the *Ladies' Home Journal* (LHJ) (Damon-Moore, 1994). Acquiring information about the skills required for a sport allowed women to develop competence and confidence in new activities, while descriptions of suitable attire gave them strategies to pursue their new activities in comfort. Instruction in the rules and skills of sports contributed to the physical emancipation of women, while advice about appropriate apparel disguised women's cultural emancipation in conventional styles.

Physical training of women in this period challenged the boundaries of expected behavior by giving them new skills and strength. Their increased athletic activity played an intrinsic role in challenges to gender restrictions represented by the new athletic woman. Potential participants in athletic activity learned how to engage in such pursuits and how to dress for them through a variety of popular culture sources. The language used to instruct and encourage women to such pursuits played a vital role in the development of new gender ideals.

Readers of popular periodicals between 1880 and 1920 gained familiarity with a wide variety of athletic endeavors and learned proper techniques for several sports. Several issues of *LHJ* featured descriptions of and instructions for athletic activities, as did the pages of the *New York Times* and *Harper's Bazaar*. Often accompanied by illustrations, these articles went beyond those documenting the presence and accomplishments of athletic women to educate readers in proper skills for specific sports. Advertisements also used images of athletic women, casting them in a positive light. Print media descriptions of women's athletic activity deployed language encouraging women to participate in such ventures, helping to shape healthy athleticism as an ideal.

Beginning in 1890, Ellen Le Garde (1890) became a columnist for *LHJ*, contributing articles about athletic activities intermittently for several years, advocating athletic activity for girls and women. She offered readers information about several sports, and encouraged them to pursue outdoor activities such as walking, tennis, rowing, badminton, and swimming. "Sports for girls in the open air are not so limited in number as mention of the subject would suggest." Le Garde advised that, "Not alone is bone and muscle made; you are learning, girls, how to handle and carry your bodies." As she explained, "Every game in which you take part requires skill, dexterity, coolness, and courage with presence of mind. Cultivate and play all the sports you can in the open air, and they will make you a fitter type of perfect womanhood" (p.3). Not only would readers develop the skills of the games they played, argued the author, they would also acquire personal attributes essential for the ideal woman. Significantly, sports and fitness figured as fundamental components in Le Garde's construction of "perfect womanhood." She encouraged readers to acquire and exercise athletic skills, suggesting the myriad benefits that would ensue when they did.

Annie Ramsey (1891), another *Journal* author, offered readers advice on mountain climbing and noted the prerequisites for a successful venture: "Powers of endurance, of quick recuperation, strong lungs and heart, and a keen sense of the beauty of Nature must all be yours, or no amount of preparation can make your walks a delight." Advising potential climbers to condition themselves by climbing up and down a hilly road, gradually increasing the distance, she reminded readers that "training must, however, be continuous: walking one day and resting the next is useless." Once readers were ready to take on the mountain, Ramsey recommended a steady pace, and warned her readers "no matter how tired, *never sit down* to rest." She reminded them that getting started would be the hardest part, but perseverance would lead to triumph over inertia. Once underway, Ramsey suggested making few stops until luncheon, after which climbers should rest before beginning their descent. "Do not drink at every spring—and *do not eat the snow.*"

Other sports, such as bicycling and basketball, required learning specific skills. Although experience would prove the best teacher, many women could have gained at least rudimentary knowledge of such activities by reading about them in newspapers and magazines. Bicycling had become tremendously popular by the 1890s. "All the world seems to be awheel," proclaimed the lead of an article in the *New York Times* (The Ubiquitous Wheelwoman, 1895). Women could acquire a basic knowledge of bicycles and bicycling from reading the popular press (Garvey, 1995). Some athletic clubs and gymnasiums offered riding academies for their members, where women could learn to ride without undertaking the additional hazards of the road until they had gained sufficient skill to take such risks.

Basketball, another sport for women that developed and blossomed in the 1890s, afforded them yet another opportunity to develop skills and self-assurance. Several of the women's colleges became hotbeds for the new game. Team members gave up candy and desserts, practiced frequently, went to bed early, and took cold baths each morning, earning the ecstatic envy of their classmates, whom they represented in the inter-class contests that marked early college competitions (Basket Ball at Smith College, 1896). Fanny Garrison (1899), granddaughter of famed abolitionist William Lloyd Garrison, played basketball at Smith College; she wrote to her family that, "We are now in training. I shall have to confess to find getting to bed by half-past nine rather hard. And, of course, now that sweet things are to be avoided, I have had innumerable chances to enjoy them."

Women began to play basketball almost immediately after its creation by James Naismith in 1891, and the game became very popular in women's colleges. According to Senda Berenson (1903), director of the gymnasium and physical culture at Smith from 1892 to 1911, an "Enthusiasm for games, this natural outlet of the play instinct created a need for a game that should require team work, organization, scientific development—in short, should be a game for women such as football is for men. And out of a clear sky came basket ball" (p.2). Berenson worried, however, that the rough, physical style of play initially associated with basketball would prove problematic for female players; consequently, she created modified rules and established zones of play from which players could not stray. Her modifications became the basis of a distinct set of rules for women's play agreed upon at a conference held at Springfield College and published by the Spalding Company.

Ellen Emerson (1900), granddaughter of Ralph Waldo Emerson, had not initially favored Berenson's rules. She had written to her mother that, "We played our first game of basket-ball under the new collegiate rules that Miss Berenson & Bryn Mawr & Radcliffe people got up & we liked it pretty well & in time it may prove the best way, but it is hard to give up our old game for the sake of uniformity." Another Smith student, Eleanor Upton (1906), offered a more fervent endorsement of the new rules. Visiting her friend Bertha at Mount Holyoke and watching a game between two of the classes there, Upton wrote: "They play a terrible hard game at Holyoke—I wonder the girls can stand it. It is just like the boys' game—no lines drawn, everybody can run anywhere and anybody can throw a goal. As it is played at Smith," she explained, "the players are kept in three groups and when the ball is somewhere else they have nothing to do but be on the lookout for it to come their way."

The rules created by Berenson and her colleagues made their way into popular culture through stories for girls, including a series that featured Jane Allen, of Wellington College, who moved, in subsequent books, from the sub-team to right guard to center. According to author Edith Bancroft (1917), "Jane Allen's spirited play was often commended," even while she played only on the practice team (p.290). Jane gained expertise in the previously unfamiliar aspects of the game by sending for and studying the official basketball guide.

Whether they took the form of rulebooks, magazine or newspaper articles, instruction manuals, or fictional accounts, publications detailing the techniques of particular sports proved immensely useful to women who sought to participate in athletic activities at the turn of the century. The media informed them how to play various games, provided role models who played the game, and often suggested strategies that would bring success. Related articles suggested how women should dress in order to engage in particular athletic endeavors, and many of the clothing suggestions that appeared in periodicals followed the practical turn of the instructional pieces.

Most of the attention about women's sporting fashions focused on bicycling. The central, and well-known, controversy revolved around whether bloomers should be worn (Marks, 1990). Proponents of cycling offered two solutions to this dilemma: the divided skirt or wearing bloomers underneath a traditional skirt. Fashion advice for bicycling followed pragmatic strains. Ellen Le Garde (1891) explained simply that, "Two conditions are needed for a perfect costume for the bicycle. Looseness, to permit the freedom to the many muscles constantly in action, and a color scheme somber and dark" (p.8). Comfort and safety marked the design of most bicycling attire. The Ladies' Cycling Club of New York drew attention when it was formed in 1891 for their somewhat unorthodox organizational scheme, as members of the club used democratic procedures to determine meeting times and their schedule for riding excursions. "Anyone can call a meeting at any time, and there are no fines for non-attendance. It is an association of equal rights, and all is happiness, contentment, and amiability" (The Ladies' Cycling Club, 1891). At the same time club members gained notice for their unconventionally collective decision-making process, their uniform was intentionally unremarkable: "A yachting cap, a tailor-made waist, tight-fitting, and a straight skirt of walking length. The color throughout is dark blue, and the material serge. The skirt is lined with blue flannel, which, as explained, keeps it down and prevents its flying in the wind and catching in the wheel."

Mary Sargent Hopkins (Dress for Wheelwomen, 1894) of Boston offered her views on proper cycling attire in an interview in the *New York Times*, assuring readers that there was "Not the slightest need of any radical departure from conventionality when a woman takes to wheeling. Her bicycling dress need be no more peculiar than her shopping gown." Arguing against the notion that wearing knicker-bockers or bloomers resulted in more freedom for the rider, she claimed that their close fit prevented ease of movement. Women could "Move much more comfortably and freely in smooth, well-fitting hosiery and tights, and a skirt which does not cling and is properly lined and shaped" (p.18).

Sometimes, conventional behavior was imposed on women. In 1895, the school board of College Point, Long Island (Object to Women Cyclists) decided bicycle riding by young women was improper, declaring that, "When the riding was done by a young woman school teacher the practice had a tendency to create immorality among the children of both sexes placed under such teacher's immediate charge." They prohibited women teachers from riding their bicycles to and from the school. One member of the board expressed the fears of many when he proclaimed that, "[I]t is not the proper thing for the ladies to ride the bicycle."

The media during this time included articles offering advice about how to dress for such sports as golf and tennis, stressing comfort and practicality, with more than a passing nod to questions of fashion. Suggestions for golf clothing (Dress for the Golf Links, 1894, p.18) focused on its relative simplicity and loose fit that allowed ample room for a wide swing: "If golf is to be fashionably played, it of course must be fashionably dressed." The ideal golf costume combined a stylish appearance with a pragmatic cut: "Simple, short, rather scant skirts are used, with belted waists or vests and jackets . . . loose suede or canvas shoes that have sufficiently heavy soles to stand rough wear, for the links are by no means smooth tennis lawns." Sometimes, the authority of fashion had to succumb to the reality of athletics; for example, one golf costume made of white serge, decorated with red bands, would ideally require white shoes to make it complete. However, the article acknowledged, "A golf course is no place for white shoes, nor will they exist there as such long."

Those who offered fashion advice to golfers could not ignore pragmatic considerations such as what shoes to wear. Frances Griscom (1903) suggested "A sensible pair of shoes, large enough to be absolutely comfortable, and with very low heels . . . One must have rubber or hobnails on the soles to keep from slipping. It is a great aid in playing not to slip" (p.161). The ideal clothing for golf did not restrict a player's movement, and allowed her to take significant steps toward physical emancipation. "The question of corsets is one which a woman can decide for herself," explained Genevieve Hecker (1904), a national champion in the early twentieth century, noting that "They play no more important part in determining good golf than does the weight or color of a player's skirt" (p.30).

J. Parmly Paret (1900), a tennis player and frequent dispenser of advice about sports, explained that, "A short skirt is absolutely necessary in order to run about the court with any freedom. A loose waist," he continued, "preferably a shirt-waist, is also necessary to give freedom to the use of the arms, and it is much wiser to play without corsets, if possible, although it must be admitted that few women do so." Tennis champion Molla Bjurstedt (1916) reinforced the importance of pragmatic dress for athletic activity, noting, "I like a very simple dress—with the idea of being clothed and not gowned."

Some experts noted the importance of attire specifically designed for athletic activity. Englishwoman Constance M.K. Applebee (1903), who single-handedly spread field hockey throughout the eastern United States, explained that, "The game cannot be safely or well played in ordinary dress." In fact, she chastised those who "Cheerfully play holding up a train in one hand, feebly wielding the stick with the other," expecting that "the stiffness, colds, and exhaustion that follow in the wake of the would-be athlete who ignores the importance of 'dress' will, somehow, escape them" (pp.211–213). Applebee suggested wearing a loose shirt-waist with a plain skirt over matching knicker-bockers in distinctive club colors, the skirt short enough to allow free movement around the field.

By 1920, photographs of teams included in *Spalding's Field Hockey Guide* (Abbott, 1915) showed the influence of contemporary fashions, as several teams included players sporting flapper-style headbands and bobbed hair. The rules allowed for shorter skirts, which improved mobility.

Annette Kellerman (1915), a champion swimmer, emphatically expressed the need for clothing that did not restrict one's motion. "Don't wear any more clothes than you need. They hinder your movement and make the body much heavier. Don't, above all, wear a corset or tight belt, for these hinder the circulation" (p.10). Although her suggestions pertained to swimming costumes, they applied equally well to what women should wear for any athletic activity. In Hints on Mountain Climbing, Annie Ramsey (1891) commented upon the restrictive nature of the corset, writing that, "In climbing, half the secret of a woman's inability lies in the fact that her chest and abdomen are so confined that she cannot breathe properly, and is exhausted by the struggle to do so" (p.2). She advised the loosest feasible garb to allow for the greatest possible movement.

Advertisements also suggested to women that they should be able to move more freely when they engaged in athletic activity. The Ferris Brothers Company developed a looser version of the corset that allowed "Full expansion of the lungs, at the same time giving the body healthful and graceful support" (For Bicycle Wear, 1897). Their ads stressed the hygienic aspects of the product as well as the comfort and unrestricted movement its wearers would enjoy. "It adjusts itself to every bend of the body," read the copy of an advertisement for the Bicycle Corset Waist (Style No. 261), "permitting absolute freedom of movement and full respiration so essential to good health and good riding" ("perfect Comfort"). Another advertisement characterized "The Winning Girl [a]t golf or any other feminine sport is the girl who is dressed for comfort and freedom."

Corset waists manufactured by Ferris Brothers were designed to meet a variety of athletic needs. Advertisements developed for the company's products explicitly linked a looser means of support to athletic activity and good health as well as to comfort and hygiene. The ads pointed to their suitability for athletic endeavors, showing models engaged in bicycling, gymnastics, tennis, and golf. The corsets provided support without the restrictions imposed by wearing their rigid predecessors. One ad showed a woman dressed in the Good Sense Athletic Waist holding a golf club. "For the devotee of physical culture; for the tennis and golf players; for the college girl, and all women who appreciate the value of healthful exercise," it proclaimed, the "Ferris Good Sense Athletic Waist is an indispensable factor of Beauty and Health." And the Athletic Corset Waist "is especially designed for women who enjoy outdoor sports." The advertisements stressed the mobility and freedom provided to wearers of various Good Sense Waists, promising "Freedom of motion, freedom of respiration—the freedom of absolute comfort."

Nearly twenty years later, an advertisement for Lady Sealpax—the New Athletic Underwear for Women, linked appropriate undergarments to athletic activity. With a spirited game of basketball pictured in the background, two young women dressed for the game extolled the virtues of Lady Sealpax: "It gives me so much freedom I feel as if I could play better than before" (My, but this Lady Sealpax is a Blessing, 1918). A companion ad explained that the "Athletic cut armhole, yielding elastic back-band, roomy athletic drawer and ventilated waistband, are features that make *Lady Sealpax* the logical underwear for the active women of today" (Isn't It Great, Jane?, 1918). Through both their texts and illustrations, these advertisements equated appropriate attire with physical freedom.

Advertisers also used celebrity endorsements to attract attention to their wares. The actress Sarah Bernhardt extolled the virtues of the Hulbert Cycling Suit, noting that, "It adjusts itself very quickly before mounting a bicycle, and then gives such complete freedom of movement, and leaves to the woman all her natural grace" (What Sarah Bernhardt Says, 1896). They used images of healthy, strong women engaging in athletic activities to sell their products, not only creating a market, but also documenting and endorsing the emergence of the new athletic woman as an ideal.

The clothing worn for sporting activities symbolized the changes in women's lives. Le Garde (1890) noted the connection between clothing that allowed for freedom of movement while maintaining the appearance of propriety. "With the thought of common sense in dress manifest all around us, a girl's costume for athletic sports can be loose, and still lady-like," she explained. "A divided skirt below, a wide, light-weight skirt over it, reaching just below the ankles, and a loose blouse, would be all that practicability would demand" (p.3). In many senses, the outward appearance of women served as a disguise for the changes that increased athletic activity engendered.

The greatest changes for women, however, were not on the superficial level of outward appearance; rather, the loosening or removal of one's corset to participate in sports symbolized the sweeping cultural changes in gender roles. Athletic activities enabled women to try on new roles as they donned the specific attire required for participation in sporting pursuits. By participating in sports, many women of this generation developed self-confidence and determination, attributes that would characterize the new woman. Instruction manuals, stories, periodical articles, rulebooks, and advertisements helped the new athletic woman to create herself, enabling her to know how to participate in athletic activity by providing descriptions of the necessary skills and proper attire for such undertakings. Moreover, the language used in this advice literature functioned as the underpinning for this new construction of gendered ideals. As women became more and more familiar with sports through these vehicles of popular culture that demystified the unfamiliar, they became increasingly able to take steps toward a healthy active life.

### References

Abbott, S.B. (Ed.) (1915). *Spalding's official basket ball guide for women*. New York: American Sports Publishing Co., 1915. <http://clio.fivecolleges.edu/smith/berenson/5pubs/spaldings/?page = 1>.

Applebee, C.M.K. (1903). Field hockey. *Athletics and out-door sports for women*. Ed. Lucille Eaton Hill. New York: The Macmillan Company. 205–226.

———, (Ed.) (1921). *Spalding's field hockey guide*. New York: American Sports Publishing Co.

Bancroft, E. (1917). *Jane Allen of the sub-team*. New York: Saalfield Publishing Company.

———. (1918). *Jane Allen: Center*. New York: Saalfield Publishing Company.

Basket ball at Smith College: Exciting contest between the sophomores and the freshmen. *New York Times* (March 23, 1896): 3.

Berenson, S. (1903). The significance of basket ball for women. In *Basket Ball for Women*, ed. Senda Berenson. New York: American Sports Publishing Company. <http://clio.fivecolleges.edu/smith/berenson/5pubs/bball_ women>.

Bjurstedt, M. (1916). *Tennis for women*. Garden City: Doubleday, Page & Company.

Damon-Moore, H. (1994). *Magazines for the millions: Gender and commerce in the Ladies' Home Journal and the Saturday Evening Post, 1880–1910*. Albany: State University Press of New York.

Dress for the golf links: What may be worn on the course of "drives" and "lies" (1894). *New York Times* (June 24): 18.

Dress for wheelwomen: Bloomers and knickerbockers "unsuitable and unnecessary." (1894). *New York Times* (October 20): 18.

Emerson, Ellen to mother, May 6, 1900, Class of 1901 Letters, Smith College Archives, Northampton, MA.

For Bicycle Wear. (1897). *Ladies' Home Journal* (April): 35.

Garrison, Fanny to family, February 24, 1899, Class of 1901 Letters, Smith College Archives, Northampton, MA.

Garvey, E.G. (1995). Reframing the bicycle: Advertising-supported magazines and scorching women. *American Quarterly* 47 (March): 66–101.

———. (1996). *The adman in the parlor: Magazines and the gendering of consumer culture, 1880s to 1910s.* New York: Oxford University Press.

The Girl Who Loves Good Health (1899). N.W. Ayer Collection, Archives Center, National Museum of American History, Smithsonian Institution, Washington, DC.

Griscom, F.C. (1903). "Golf." *Athletics and out-door sports for women.* Ed. Lucille Eaton Hill. New York: The Macmillan Company.

Hecker, Genevieve [Mrs. Charles T. Stout] (1904). *Golf for women.* New York: Baker & Taylor Company.

Isn't it great, Jane? (1918). *Smith College Weekly* (May 15): 10, College Archives, Smith College, Northampton, MA.

Kellerman, A. (1915). The girl who wants to swim. *Ladies' Home Journal* (July): 10. The ladies' cycling club. *New York Times* (September 24, 1891): 9.

Le Garde, E. (1890). "Out-door sports for girls." *Ladies Home Journal* (June): 3.

———. (1891). How to dress for bicycle riding. *Ladies' Home Journal* (June): 8.

Marks, P. (1990). *Bicycles, bangs, and bloomers: The new woman in the popular press.* Lexington: University Press of Kentucky.

My, but this Lady Sealpax is a blessing. (1918). *Smith College Weekly* (April 17): 10. College Archives, Smith College, Northampton, MA.

Object to women cyclists: College Point school trustees say they must not ride to and from their duties. (1895). *New York Times* (June 15): 1.

Paret, J.P. (1900). Good form in women's tennis. *Harper's Bazar* (June 9): 344.

Perfect Comfort. (1898). *Ladies' Home Journal* (August): inside front cover.

Ramsey, A.R. (1891). Hints on mountain climbing. *Ladies' Home Journal* (August): 2.

The ubiquitous wheelwoman: She may ride modestly and acceptably if she will. (1895). *New York Times* ( July 7): 21.

Upton, Eleanor to mother, March 18, 1906. Class of 1901 Letters. Smith College Archives, Northampton, MA.

What Sarah Bernhardt says about her Hulbert cycling suit. (1896). *Ladies' Home Journal* (June): 25.

CHAPTER 5

# A Woman in a Man's World: "Annie Laurie," One of America's First Sportswriters

*Mike Sowell*

Winifred Black, who wrote for the San Francisco *Examiner* under the byline "Annie Laurie" (Belford, 1986), infiltrated an all-men's club in 1892 to become the first woman to cover a prize fight for an American newspaper. She also wrote about football and interviewed heavyweight boxers. Although Black is recognized as one of America's best reporters from an era when few women made it into the newsroom, her role as one of the first women to write sports has received little attention. This chapter is an analysis of her sports coverage for the *Examiner*, and how it compared to the "sports writing" that was just coming into being in the 1880s and 1890s. Her stories are analyzed for her style of writing in contrast to her male counterparts, her use of the interview as a story form, and her use of sports to comment on gender roles in American society.

On Memorial Day in 1892, two featherweight boxers in San Francisco battered one another for 41 exhausting rounds, at which point neither could continue with the fight. When the bout was suspended, many in the sold-out crowd of spectators at the Pacific Athletic Club gymnasium jeered, although it was clear that both men were physically spent. Their faces were disfigured and swollen, their legs unsteady. One man had a broken right hand. For most of the spectators, it was a disappointing ending to an otherwise exciting evening. For Winifred Black, it was a revelation. Hidden in a perch overlooking the arena, Black, who wrote for William Randolph Hearst's

San Francisco *Examiner* under the pen name "Annie Laurie," had infiltrated the all-men's club to become the first woman to cover a prize fight for an American newspaper (Creedon, 1994, p.70). In doing so, she discovered a world that, until that night, had been hidden from her. "I have seen men," she wrote. "Not as women see them, but as men see them . . . Men have a world into which women cannot enter. They have a being that women cannot understand. I learned all this at the prize-fight" (Laurie, 1892, p.9).

Exploring new worlds was nothing new to Black, one of America's most famous journalists during a career that began on the *Examiner* in 1889 and spanned 47 years. She first made a name for herself by posing as a vagrant and then exposing the brutal treatment of the poor in San Francisco's public hospital. She hid under a table in President Benjamin Harrison's private train in order to gain a personal interview with him, making her only the second woman to interview a president (Belford, 1986). And in 1900, she dressed as a man in order to report firsthand on the aftermath of a devastating tidal wave in Galveston, Texas.

Like her more famous counterpart, Elizabeth Cochrane, who wrote for Joseph Pulitzer's New York *World* under the byline "Nellie Bly," Black was a "stunt journalist," injecting herself into stories, often by going undercover in writing about college football teams, interviewing professional fighters, and being the first woman to "cover" a prize fight; as such, she displayed a style of writing that was distinct from her male counterparts at a time when sportswriting was in its infancy.

The specialized brand of reporting that came to be known as sportswriting was just coming into being in the 1880s and 1890s. Black never was considered one of these new "sporting writers," but her stories are significant nonetheless. As a woman occasionally venturing into this new territory during this time, her sports stories in the San Francisco *Examiner* from 1889 to 1895 were different from those of her male counterparts not just because of what she wrote but how she wrote it. As Annie Laurie, she wrote for all readers, particularly women, who normally were not privy to the male bastion of sports. In so doing, Black approached sports with the unique perspective of one who was not part of this culture of competition, physical aggression, and domination.

## The Early Days of Sportswriting

In search of new "stunts" to entertain and inform her readers early in her career at the *Examiner*, it was appropriate that an enterprising journalist like Winifred Black would venture into another novelty of the newspaper world of the late nineteenth century: the sports beat. For much of the 1800s, daily newspapers published only occasional reports of sports events, most often horse racing. Newspaper editors generally "looked on athletics as the province of the weeklies" (Nugent, 1929, p.335), and when they did cover an event like a prize fight or a yacht race, the assignment was given to "nonspecialists on the city desk" (Juergens, 1966, p.119), telegraph operators, or promoters.

But as spectator sports, particularly baseball, began to grow in popularity after the Civil War, newspapers began devoting more space to coverage of these events. In part, this increased coverage resulted from the efforts to boost circulation through the sensational reporting that appealed to the masses rather than the upper classes. As Louis M. Lyons (1971, p.38) wrote in his history of the Boston *Globe*, "[S]ports . . . next to crime, made the most exciting news of the late seventies and early eighties." It was not until after World War II that women began gaining widespread acceptance into the field of sports writing.

## "Annie Laurie" on the Sports Beat

Winifred Black (aka "Annie Laurie") occasionally turned her attention to sports during her tenure at the *Examiner* from 1889–1895. Her first such articles were celebrity interviews with heavyweight boxers Peter Jackson and James Corbett prior to their prize fight in San Francisco on May 21, 1891, examining them as people and wondering what attracted them to such a violent sport. A year later, Black took her readers inside the boxing arena when she "covered" a prize fight from her hidden vantage point, writing of her experiences on June 5, 1892, again displaying a fascination with the violent scene both in the arena and the audience. Her next foray into sports, was spending the day with the Stanford and University of California-Berkeley football teams prior to their annual game (October 28, 1894).

She portrayed the athletes she wrote about not as savage brutes but as engaging young men with curious battle scars that said much about how they approached life. All of her stories are examples of Black's short, crisp writing style, which was unique in the way she skillfully wove her personal observations into a dialogue with her subjects. She took advantage of being one of the few women in the field of journalism, writing, "A woman has a distinct advantage over a man in reporting, if she has sense enough to balance her qualities" (Elwood-Akers, 1989, p.865), and she used this advantage to elicit responses that her male counterparts did not or perhaps could not.

As she watched boxing action, for example, Black began to recognize its beauty. Although she had been skeptical of all the talk she had heard about the "science" of the sport, she admitted: "I expected to see them fight like tigers, but they sparred like clever athletes" (Laurie, 1892, p.9). Still, the match had its brutal moments, as when Johnnie Murphy appeared on the verge of knocking out his opponent. Although Billy Murphy "staggered" under the rain of blows, Black watched in fascinated horror, writing, "I could not bear to see it, but I could not look away" (ibid). Later, covering the universities of Stanford and California football teams preparing for their annual showdown in what then was the new but rapidly growing sport of college football, she spent a day with each of the two teams, afterward announcing, "I've joined the glorious army of football cranks, and I don't care who knows it" (Laurie, 1894, p.17). ("Crank" was the popular term for fan and, judging by her story, Black met the qualifications.)

Much of Black's attention was directed at the training tables of the two teams and the players' strict diets, which included oatmeal water and tapioca pudding at both camps. The rivalry between the two teams was evident even in the foods they ate. While dining with the Berkeley players, Black made the comment, "They don't allow salad at Stanford." In watching the teams practice, she realized, "[I]t took marvelously quick wit, as well as a good strong physique, to be a football player" (ibid). By now, she was a celebrity in her own right, but in the closing of her story she wistfully remarked that her time with the football players had made her realize what it must be like to live the life of a campus hero: "I carried the memory of their bright alert faces home with me, and I wished when I came into the noisy, tired city full of worried people that I was a college boy and that I was going to be in the big fight on Thanksgiving Day" (Laurie, 1894, p.17).

## IMPLICATIONS

When women began moving into sports writing in increasing numbers in the 1970s and beyond, Betty Cuniberti was one of the trailblazers, covering the Oakland Raiders football team for the San Francisco *Chronicle*. Looking back on the resistance that she and others faced to women sports writers, she commented: "No one has ever given me one good reason why women shouldn't cover sports . . . Sports is a world for men and women, as spectators as well as participants" (cited in Mills, 1988, p.234). Winifred Black proved this point decades before the many outstanding women reporters who made it onto the sports beat in the latter part of the twentieth century.

Black did not write sports full time, but when she did choose to write about athletes and their contests, she proved herself to be comparable to the best of the men who entered this specialized field that was just developing when she began her career at the San Francisco *Examiner*. Early sports writing in American newspapers was uneven, ranging from what today is an "indecipherable jargon" (Fullerton, 1928) to the gifted prose of a Grantland Rice or Ring Lardner. The best sportswriters both in the 1890s and modern times are those who capture the emotion of the games and the personalities of the players.

"Annie Laurie" did this in her sports stories, which often succeeded in placing the reader at the scene or in making the various athletes seem much more human than they appeared elsewhere. Repeatedly, she elicited responses from her subjects that her male colleagues failed to get because she asked questions they might not think to ask. Men accepted it as a given that in boxing you try to hurt your opponent. Black wanted to know how a man felt when he inflicted such pain on another man.

In this regard, she seems to exhibit a trait that modern women sportswriters share. Annette John-Hall, who covered sports for the Oakland *Tribune* and *Rocky Mountain News* in the 1970s and 1980s, recalled a time she suggested a story idea to a male coworker about a young struggling player. While he started the story with three paragraphs of statistics, "I would have written about the guys' knee surgery and his frustration at sitting on the bench," recalled John-Hall, adding that she and her female colleagues "bring to the craft a more human perspective" (cited in Mills, 1988, p.229).

It has been written that the best sports writers are those who just happen to write about sports. Winifred Black was an outstanding writer and reporter, and she proved it even when her subject was sports. Not only did her writing style contrast to her male counterparts, but she also used sports to comment on gender roles in American society of the era. Sports often has been called a mirror of our society; if this is true, the male sportswriters of the late nineteenth century can give us only a partial view of the country as it was. For a more complete reflection, we can look at the words of "Annie Laurie" in her role as one of the first women on America's sports beat.

### References

Belford, B. (1986). *Brilliant bylines.* New York: Columbia University Press.

Creedon, P.J. (1994). Women in toyland: A look at women in American sports journalism. In *Women, media and sport: Challenging gender values,* ed. Creedon, P.J., 67–107. Thousand Oaks, CA: Sage.

Elwood-Akers, V. (1989). Winifred Black. In *Biographical dictionary of American journalism*, ed. McKerns, J.P., 865. New York: Greenwood Press.

Fullerton, H. (1928). The fellows who made the game. *Saturday Evening Post* (April 25): 18–19, 184–188.

Juergens, G. (1966). *Joseph Pulitzer and the New York World*. Princeton, NJ: Princeton University Press.

Laurie, A. (1892). Annie Laurie at a prize fight. *San Francisco Examiner* (June 4): 9.

———. (1894). Annie Laurie a crank. *San Francisco Examiner* (October 28): 17.

Lyons, L.M. (1971). *Newspaper story: One hundred years of the Boston Globe*. Cambridge, MA: Belknap Press of Harvard University Press.

Mills, K. (1988). *A place in the news: From the women's pages to the front pages*. New York: Dodd, Mead.

Nugent, W.H. (1929). The sports section. *The American Mercury* (January): 329–338.

# CHAPTER 6

# White *Sauvage-ry*: Revisiting the Collegians and Coeds of Old *Siwash* College

*Jane M. Stangl*

## PRELIMINARY STORIES—SPORTING FACT AND FICTION

The hero born of the sport fiction genre offers readers an insightful rendering of the making of American males; a boys-to-men developmental process that speaks as much to yesterday's novelty athlete as it does today's. This chapter unearths an All-American pastime—not in the pastoral sense of baseball, but in the primordial and grounded game of the gridiron. Here, football, sport literature, manly men, soft women, and social outsiders converge to offer us insights into our storied pasts. These stories, however distant and removed from contemporary audiences, remain attached to the social fabric of our present lives. Through rhetorical twists, embellished spins, and linguistic appropriations, the genre of sport fiction offers an unnerving home to the notion that our current lives consist as much of fiction as facts, and remind us that old sport stories are like any other narrative: Stories that in and of themselves are never complete, and rarely end with the closing of a book.

Tom Brown, Dink Stover, and Frank Merriwell, were all fictionalized sport heroes who engendered the literate turn of the century subculture, setting the stage for the rise of the athletic school boy as cultural hero. Arguably as popular in the late 1800s were Walter Camp's real All-Americans (1909), honoring the legendary Yale football coach, considered the father of American football. Yalies Stover and Merriwell especially served as protagonists who worked to ensure the importance of sport fiction's place in the mindset of the turn of the twentieth-century American male. Their characters and ensuing storylines articulated a relationship about cultural ideals that were particularly American, particularly male, and particularly white. As popular novels, their content underscored a social desire for the pious and disciplined young hero—a popular hero far removed from tomfoolery and the frontier, yet a compliant hero, enmeshed in the possibilities of social progress and mobility. In short, he was a school sport hero, an idealized young man (Messenger, 1981), an athlete, and often a footballer.

The heroes' creators, Tom Hughes, Owen Johnson, and Gilbert Patten, relied on sport fiction as their forum, used in conjunction with the rising popularity of football to imprint its literary placement in the cultural imaginary (Messenger, 1981; Oriard, 1993). Although not of the same literary class as canonized popular peers such as Nobel winner William Faulkner, writer Nathaniel Hawthorne, or novelist James Fenimore Cooper, their names became notable in their own right and contributed to a growing list of legendary authors who used sport to relay their message—Ralph Henry Barbour, Mark Twain, Jesse Lynch Williams, F. Scott Fitzgerald, and Ring Lardner, among them. However, lost among the big-time writers, but not on those acquainted with cultural humorists, nor those familiar with popular periodicals of the day such as *McClure's*, *Collier's*, *Outlook* and the *Saturday Evening Post*, was a writer of lesser fame: George Helgesen Fitch, who served as national president of The American Press Humorists (c. 1913), a group that included national press writers Peter Finley Dunne, Frank L. Stanton, and George Ade.

In the early 1900s, George Helgesen Fitch (1877–1915) wrote 20 fictitious stories about the football and fraternal antics of young male ruffians at a college he named *Siwash* (italicized herein to emphasize its lingua franca roots, tied to the derogatory application of Native Americans). *Siwash* College, won the hearts of the general public through edited versions of Fitch's tales as they appeared in the *Saturday Evening Post* from 1908 through 1913, and later as serial pieces entitled respectively, *The Big Strike at Siwash* (1909), *At Good Old Siwash* (1911), and *Petey Simmons at Siwash* (1916). Respected nationally as a humorist and journalist, especially in Illinois and Iowa, Fitch's *Siwash* stories worked to capture the buffoonery and characterizations of collegiate fraternizing and football. His protagonist was trite and regressive when compared to the more sincere Dink Stover sort, and Messenger (1981) defined Fitch's work as a "comic series of bumpkin misadventures" (p.342). Yet, Fitch's work sought to satirize the sports hero's sincerity and, unlike previous authors, his burlesque approach made a mockery of collegian behavior.

Although Fitch's literary prowess is not the central theme of this chapter, the fact that his stories were a success calls attention to their prominence and, more importantly, to the fictionalized constructions of the ideal footballer. Also, Fitch's tales offer a peculiarity of the sport fiction genre not only because of their buffoonery and satire, but more so because of their name and notoriety as the "*Siwash* stories." This attachment to naming and the usage of language is significant as it highlights the unconscious adaptability of social circumstances to broader social outcomes. It contributed to Chinook jargon, wherein it disparagingly signified Indians of any tribe. By the 1940s, however, the term was popularized within U.S. culture and came to be associated with the small college scene, specifically, provincial inland colleges. As fiction, the behaviors exhibited at the "old coll."—Fitch's reference to *Siwash* College—subtly exuded assimilationist efforts of ethnic groups, yet also elicited assumptions about gender and sex that buttressed the naturalized differences already deeply entrenched in the dominant cultural codes of the time.

This chapter unpacks Fitch's narratives in their social and historical context by examining how the association of *siwash* with the small college scene unearths a hegemonic male preserve that spun a white heterosexual bourgeois ideology around simplistic notions of difference. It is also intended to provide critical insights into the masculinized and colonized effects salient in team-naming practices, where fact and fiction coalesce to construct a relational image feeding on myths about Native Americans valorized by notions of white masculinity. By deconstructing these communicative fictions, Fitch's stories call to question the socially privileged college setting of the past, as historically satirical accounts deepen our understanding of athletic privilege and the process of team-naming in the present.

## COMING TO TERMS WITH OLD *SIWASH*

In order to understand the relevance of Fitch's fiction to its current application around issues of difference and team-naming, returning to the roots of the word "*siwash*" is critical. It has taken on at least two distinct and separate meanings over the course of 150 years, as well as a range of enigmatic interpretations. *Siwash* was deemed a corruption of the French *sauvage*, meaning uncivilized, wild—largely in association with Indians (Partridge, 1950). By the 1940s, the term came to be associated with "a small college regarded as typical of its class," at least according to Fitch inquirer Martin Schmitt (1957), who noted that lexicographers apparently credited *Time* magazine with introducing the word in 1947, and the Chicago *Maroon* with making this application respectable in 1948. Still alternative definitions from the 1940s retain *siwash*'s previous and pejorative application—notably, dictionaries of slang suggest that a *siwash* is an Indian not up to the white man's standards, being inefficient, inferior, unenterprising and contemptible (Berrey and Van Den Bark, 1945; Chapman, 1986; Davis, 1981).

While Fitch understood that his audience consisted of people interested in the affairs of colleges, humorously or otherwise, he also knew that many readers had transposed his writing onto their own personal college experience, so *Siwash* College could be "anyman's" college. His *Siwash* was quite removed from an ideal; indeed, its preferred reading as humorous conjecture and frivolous innocence as applied to college life stood in stark contrast to a savage environment. Read critically, the *Siwash* stories conjure up a brutish environment where taunting, teasing, and put-downs were prevalent interactions; thus, as *siwashes*, savages, or renegades, the question worthy of attention is: Just who was the "anyman" of the "old coll"?

Fitch's *Siwash* was the home of football and fraternizing, where Scandinavian immigrant Ole Skjarsen played the backwards, northwoods, football hero protagonist—a behemoth, a pile-driver, a subhuman cast out of an ethnologist's diorama. His counterpart was Petey Simmons, and the supporting cast—Allie Bangs, Hogboom, and Keg, were surrounded by other "bright lights" of the college, men with "masculine minds" (Fitch, 1911, 1916).

It is the foray through these mythical "masculine minds" that ironically lends credence to the ever-present concern that homosocial male environments are fertile grounds for the exploitation of oppressed groups (see Bryson, 1990; Crossett, Benedict, and McDonald, 1995; Dunning, 1986; Frintner and Rubinson, 1993). By uncovering the past of Old *Siwash* as anyman's college, the reader is provided with a precursor to the contemporary matters of male domination, and whether satirically intended or not, it is no joking matter (see Lyman, 1987; Powell, 1911). Reading *Siwash* offers an aging vocabulary of football's underlings, but it remains a vocabulary that suggests as much about the brutality and violence of the fratriarchies of yesteryear as it references today's connections between sport, fraternities, and violence (Hagedorn, 1926; Loy, 1995).

## Football and Fraternities—Home
## to the *Siwash* Man

Football served as the center of *Siwash*'s universe. Three stories about football followed *The Big Strike at Siwash*, Fitch's seminal piece introducing readers to *Siwash* College and Ole Skjarsen's gridiron feats: "Skjarsen's First Touchdown," "Frappéd Football," and "Sic Transit Gloria All-America." They illustrated problematic themes surrounding football prevalent in the 1890s/early 1900s, including its brutality and violence, but also cultural opposition to the rising importance of athletics (Moore, 1984).

Elementary as football and fraternities were, their fusion and conflation created an exclusive male bastion of *Siwash* College and arguably a bastion of white savagery, as men were often rude, violent, and barbaric as evidenced in stories about fraternity life. "Initiating Ole" and "Curing By Suggestion" serve as examples of *Siwash*'s double meaning: While one story addresses the heinousness of initiation rituals, the other tears down the egos of the fraternal members previously built up. Humility and submission become rites of passage, as the group is ultimately given primacy. *Siwash* as savage was suggestive of the behavior going on inside *Siwash* as a college. This inward living environment is important in that it reflects the agenda of what Loy (1995) calls, "agonal fratriachies"—a collective of lads bent on doing as they please and having a good time. These clusters of males are bound and often motivated by the interest of the group, and ultimately become dominating as collectives. An initial look at *Siwash* through the construction of *Siwash* men, noting first the making of their minds, then examining *Siwash*'s outsiders, serves to amplify the ego-centricity, narcissism, and superiority of the young white men at the center of this infamous college.

## Mingling with a Real Masculine Mind

Football and fraternity life at *Siwash* directed the majority of readers' attention toward all-male social engagements. In these settings, the *Siwash* man was meant to mingle with similar peers, the idea being that through these engagements, men would undoubtedly acquire the socially desirable traits of manhood and masculinity. A simple perusal of the *Siwash* stories makes it apparent that men's sphere of influence is the primary social construct of college living. Of the 20 stories in the series, 15 involved specifically male engagements, the remaining five focusing largely on men enticing women, mostly in a perceived romantic sense—women being viewed as valued possessions, future necessities.

Though Fitch's stories may have been satirical takes on the collective antics of men, by using the term *Siwash*, he implicated an even more contentious social construction than that of the collegiate male: He drew attention, unwittingly or not, to that of the Native American Indian. Contextualizing *Siwash* as savage, from savage as Indian is a construction not without consequence, and while Fitch's use of the term suggested humor, it also worked to inject humor's antithesis and thus trivialize a prevailing cultural tome by suggesting an acceptability of Indian stereotype as savage-like.

Persistent throughout the *Siwash* pieces is the subtext of "otherness," a misnomer intended to focus on those outside acceptable social standards imposed by "normal" populations of footballers, fraternity members, and the proper coed sort. Ole Skjarsen is the classic embodiment of this "othered" character, even if many outsiders are criticized consistently as flawed by *Siwash* standards. Or, consider his satirical construction of fraternities with names like the Chi Yi Sighs and the Delta Kappa Whoopsilons.

## The Preservation of *Siwash*

We have noted how multiple particularities written into Fitch's narratives serve to support the construction of *Siwash* as a white male preserve. The male gender, the very concept of maleness and being a man, especially an Anglo-Saxon man, were so central to the function of *Siwash* that a much larger relational process was created than Fitch may have originally intended, or may be presumably concluded by those who read his work. As Bederman (1995), Kimmel (1996), Messner (1992) and numerous others have argued, the rise of sport as a social institution in the late nineteenth and early twentieth centuries had much to do with men's class and racial relationships with other men, or men's relationships with women. *Siwash* culture fused sport with gender, social class, and race relations; through this a lens, it was most evident that *Siwash* College stood in as an important, albeit fictitious, site for the construction of hegemonic solidarity.

Sport, especially football—embedded in physicality, aggression, strength, and skill, bolstered the notion of hegemonic masculinity by linking it with the competitive achievements of a team. As scholars of football and masculinity have argued, football was a crucial undertaking for learning how to be a man (Connell, 1995; Messner, 1992).

Difference, when articulated as non-male and nonwhite, is evidenced by the repeated referrals to women as coeds and "other" social outsiders. Women at *Siwash* remained on the periphery, as their presence and entry into this male sanctuary threatened its solidarity. Furthermore, the presence of "others" in general offered the opportunity for *Siwash* men to rehearse, reaffirm, and amplify their distinction as separate, privileged beings. This persistent noting of difference also served to reproduce a male hegemony that included racial and ethnic antipathy. Ethnicity at *Siwash* was obvious through the character of Skjarsen's whiteness, some whites were whiter than others. Mythical construction of Indianness perpetuated a common misperception about racial designations related to Native Americans, where color assumed primacy over other social markers. Scholars such as Fogelson (1998) and Thornton (1998) note the distinctions, asserting that some argue that Indians are not a race at all but a citizenry; while others see Indianness as ethnicity or a product of European colonialism—ancestrally tribal. But defining Indianness is about defining identity, and the sine qua non for Native American identity is legally bound by blood, land, and *community*.

So, how does this complex web of ideology and social preservation impact our need to understand *Siwash* College? Respected social thinkers, from C. Wright Mills (1959) to Renato Rosaldo (1993) and others have argued that one's social circumstance and place in history and culture are shaped by where people are and what they are doing in that space and time. Hayden White (1987) makes this point even more poignant, asserting, "Every representation of the past has specifiable ideological implications" (p.199). Fitch is no exception: As an author he effectively reproduced a culture he intimately understood, and through that replication engaged ethnocentrically biased and Eurocentric modes of representation about social life, especially the projected social life of white men.

Regarding maleness and difference, this concept took on fanatical proportions with the support of Theodore Roosevelt who, according to Hoxie (1995) believed that, "The white races had a duty to raise less powerful nonwhite nations to a better standard of living" (pp.106–107). Central to Roosevelt's dominant thesis on the manliness of American (white) men was an oppositional corollary: the Indian as brutal and quite unmanly (Bederman, 1995; Stangl, 1999).

During the time period in which the *Siwash* stories were written, the culture was caught between excesses of richness and intemperance, and the desire to constrain and reform this behavior. *Siwash* College, under Fitch's construction, served predominantly to reinvent and reinscribe notions of cultural difference. The themes prevalent in the construction of *Siwash* served especially to reproduce and preserve whiteness and maleness, largely by engaging a dominant cultural rhetoric, but also by appropriating a lost term. Herein, the men of *Siwash* represented a race that was implicitly white, and a race whose gender was implicitly male.

## Naming the Past without Regard for the Future

What emerges as an understated, yet potent, part of Fitch's narratives is just what happened to Old *Siwash* over time. By 1920, at least five years after Fitch had passed and 20 years prior to the stories' rise to film status, Fitch's alma mater, Knox, had invoked the spirit of *Siwash* more literally. The seemingly manly men of Fitch's tales became the real men of Knox's gridiron and eventually their athletic fields, and the college assumed this historic misnomer as its nickname. Culturally, by this point in time numerous colleges had already inscribed images of Indians to their college alter ego (King and Springwood, 2001). Yet, Knox infused no visual imagery, no logo, no icon, no chief dancing at halftime, nothing but the term itself to signify the "old coll." Though one may argue that Old *Siwash* will never offer currency to a commodified culture without a signifier or logo, it is the memories of Fitch and his famed tales that make this naming story unique in terms of application, even more unique in terms of its dependency on cultural imaginary. Unfortunately, Old *Siwash* was no less unique when it came to indulging the cultural appetite for difference through savagery and, arguably, it was as blatant in its misappropriation of Indianness as any other college donning war bonnets, tomahawks, chiefs or headdresses. Fitch's fiction did more than "play Indian": It vividly embellished Indianness (Deloria, 1998).

Fitch's *Siwash*—his projections about gender relations, his notions of ethnic others, his assumptions about assimilation, and his persistence in engaging concepts related to nature and culture, place the college directly amidst a cultural fusion that expressed and ultimately distinguished between those who fit within its dominant college culture and those who did not. Social exclusivity, privilege, and solidarity were powerful forces not easily undermined in the days of *Siwash*'s fictional creation, when regression through savagery seemed an essential undercurrent to social rising. Regardless of Fitch's style or *Siwash*'s literary genre, at many levels this work sought to out-savage the savages, outwit the dupes, and physically pummel the weak. For the most part, it replicated not only prevailing assumptions about the culture of colleges, but also the make-up of the United States.

Of the boys made men during this phase of American life, the prevalent ethos was that of a warrior ethic, one that intoned through militarism, expansionism, and colonialism, ideas about maleness that engaged deceptive behavior and reckless acts of pillaging. In this time frame, boyhood to manhood ultimately meant domination. Fitch's boys of *Siwash* were built of the disturbing illusion where fiction conflated with the social fact that learning to be a man meant acquiring some status and power. But, by burying in the past the sport fiction from which this illusion arises, we become subjects of the present only, and social historical conditions become lost. We abide ourselves to the heroes of a more visual culture, and readily let go of those constructions that lived without imagery or logo, but certainly not without meaning. In their day, the *Siwash* stories were remarkably reflexive tales about the rhetorical and linguistic meanings of being a white male in a college setting—one that was ironically caricatured with and against a setting in which many collegians still reside to this day.

## REFERENCES

Bederman, G. (1995). *Manliness and civilization.* Chicago: University of Chicago Press.

Berrey, L.V. and Van Den Bark, M. (1945). *The American thesaurus of slang.* New York: Thomas Y. Crowell Company.

Bryson, L. (1990). Challenges to male hegemony in sport. In *Sport, men and the gender order*, ed. Messner, D. and Sabo, D., 173–184. Champaign, IL: Human Kinetics.

Camp, W. (1909). Heroes of the gridiron. *Outing* 55 (November): 131–142.

Chapman, R.L. (Ed.) (1986). *The new dictionary of American slang.* New York: Harper and Row.

Connell, R.W. (1995). *Masculinities.* Berkeley, CA: University of California Press.

Crosset, T.W., Benedict, J.R., and McDonald, M.A. (1995). Male student athletes reported for sexual assault: A survey of campus police departments and judicial affairs offices. *Journal of Sport and Social Issues* 19: 126–140.

Daugherty, F. (1940). Hollywood looks back to the early 1900's: George Fitch's Siwash yarns in preparation for screen. *Christian Science Monitor* (February 9): 9.

Davis, R. (1981). *Western words: A dictionary of range, cow, camp and trail.* Norman: Oklahoma University Press.

Deloria, P.J. (1998). *Playing Indian.* New Haven, CT: Yale University Press.

Dunning, E. (1986). Sport as a male preserve: Notes on the social sources of masculine identity and its transformation. *Theory, Culture, and Society* 3: 79–90.

Fitch, G. (1909). *The big strike at Siwash.* New York: Doubleday, Page & Company.

———. (1910). *At good old Siwash.* Philadelphia: Curtis Publishing Company.

———. (1916). *Petey Simmons at Siwash.* Boston: Little, Brown & Company.

Fogelson, R. (1998). Perspectives on Native American identity. In *Studying Native America: Problems and prospects*, ed. Thornton, R., pp. 40–59. Madison, WI: The University of Wisconsin Press.

Fritner, M.P. and Rubinson, L. (1993). Acquaintance rape: The influence of alcohol, fraternity membership and sports team membership. *Journal of Sex Education and Therapy* 19 (4): 272–284.

Hagedorn, H. (Ed.) (1926). *The works of Theodore Roosevelt.* Vol. XIII. New York: Scribner.

Hoxie, F.E. (1995). *A final promise: The campaign to assimilate the Indians, 1880–1920.* Cambridge: Cambridge University Press.

Kimmel, M. (1996). *Manhood in America.* New York: The Free Press.

King, C.R. and Springwood, C.F. (Eds.) (2001). *Team spirits.* Lincoln, NB: University of Nebraska Press.

Leitch, B.A. (1979). *A concise dictionary of Indian tribes of North America.* USA: Reference Publications.

Litvin, M. (1991). *I'm going to be somebody!* Woodston, KS: Western Books.

Loy, J.W. (1995). The dark side of agon: Fratriarchies, performative masculinities, sport involvement, and the phenomenon of gang rape. In *International sociology of sport: Contemporary issues*, ed. Bette, K. and Rutten, A., 263–281. Stuttgard, Germany: Naglschmid.

Lyman, P. (1987). The fraternal bond as a joking relationship. In *Changing men*, ed. Kimmel, M.S., 148–163. Newbury Park, CA: Sage Publications.

Messenger, C.K. (1981). *Sport and the spirit of play in American fiction: Hawthorne to Faulkner.* New York: Columbia University Press.

Messner, M. (1992). *Power at play: Sports and the problem of masculinity.* Boston, MA: Beacon Press.

Mills, C.W. (1959). *The sociological imagination.* London: Oxford University Press.

Moore, J.H. (1984). Football's ugly decades, 1893–1913. In *The American sporting experience*, ed. Reiss, S.A. New York: Leisure Press.

Oriard, M. (1993). *Reading football: How the popular press created an American spectacle.* Chapel Hill, NC: University of North Carolina Press.

Partridge, E. (1950). *A Dictionary of the underworld—British and American.* New York: Macmillan Company.

Powell, E.P. (n.d. c. 1911). *Unity.* (George Helgeson Fitch Papers, Manuscript Collection, Seymour Library Archives). Knox College, Galesburg, Illinois.

Reed, T. (Producer). (1940). *Those were the days.* (Motion Picture). United States: Paramount Pictures.

Rosaldo, R. (1993). *Culture and truth: The re-making of social analysis.* Boston: Beacon Press.

Stangl, J.M. (1999). Naming and social privilege: A century of (mis)appropriating *Siwash* (Doctoral dissertation, University of Iowa, 1999). *Dissertation Abstracts International* (60)12A, 321.

Thornton, R. (1998). The demography of colonialism and "old" and "new" Native Americans. In *Studying Native America: Problems and prospects,* ed. Thornton, R., 17–39. Madison, WI: The University of Wisconsin Press.

White, H. (1987). *The content of the form: Narrative discourse and historical representation.* Baltimore, MD: Johns Hopkins University Press.

PART III

# Print Media Representations

# CHAPTER 7

# She Got Game, but She Don't Got Fame

*Susan Burris*

*Sports is entertainment. The age where people say sports is like entertainment is over. Sports is entertainment. It's billion-dollar entertainment.*

—David Falk (Cited in Benes, "Fame Jam")

Sports agent David Falk, as cited above, has asserted that a sporting event is now more than just a game. Sports is an entertainment industry, and the constant media exposure has inflated the cultural significance of this industry, as sports have seeped into the fabric of our mainstream culture, reflecting the perception that sports matter to us. During the 1990s, the National Basketball Association (NBA) positioned itself as one of the most important institutions at the turn of the century in terms of American popular culture. Many members of the media declared the NBA the best modern sport, and subsequently its athletes were proclaimed by many as the best, most important athletes of this period. The NBA saturated our media more than football or even baseball, our national pastime.

Although the NBA's popularity soared, the newly formed Women's National Basketball Association (WNBA) struggled to maintain its initial popularity. Even as we entered a new century, when women had attained more status, sports fans were quick to dismiss the WNBA. Many believe the lack of acceptance of women's sports is rooted in the perception that women are not good athletes. As lesser athletes, the thinking goes they are boring to watch; yet, women are neither lesser nor boring athletes. Women's sports teams have a limited fan base because they have not been marketed well. The WNBA does not seem to know how to sell its product. Part of the problem is that we are unwilling to market women in the roles of athletic personas who we typically see portrayed by male athletes: the dominator; the playboy; or the lovable, big clown. The public is not ready to see women in these roles, contributing to the stagnation of the WNBA. This essay explores the effects of rhetorical texts that help shape our perceptions of professional basketball players and the women of the WNBA.

## THE RISE OF THE NBA

Kids hung out on courts in the 1990s, letting their baseball mitts and footballs gather dust, and they did not even unwrap their hockey sticks. No doubt about it: Basketball was king. Certainly, socioeconomic shifts in our culture have made it easier for clusters of kids and adults to grab a ball and play hoop, rather than orchestrating a small army to play football or baseball. Basketball ruled, and Michael Jordan was king of the court.

In 1984, David Stern became commissioner of the NBA, and over the course of a decade, the 50-year old league experienced unprecedented expansion and astronomical revenue growth, its licensing alone producing at least $1 billion annually (Benes, 1996). NBA stars were everywhere: guests on talk shows, Magic Johnson even hosting his own show. They sold products, dated supermodels, and became very familiar to us. According to *Sports Illustrated*'s Frank Deford (2000), "Attendance and TV ratings and the mainstream endorsements that stars garner tell us how popular a sport is."

Michael Jordan was the NBA's new age superstar, a marketing prototype. Broadcasters and sports writers clogged their commentaries with claims that the NBA attracted the best athletes, and fans were led to believe that it offered the best sports competition available. The style was domination. Jump. Slam. Steal. Pound. The NBA became macho.

## PROFESSIONAL WOMEN'S BASKETBALL IS RE-REBORN

Naturally, women saw an opportunity during the perceived basketball boom to create a vehicle for women to play professionally within the United States. Women's teams already existed overseas and flourished.

Periodically, professional leagues had emerged here, but they always collapsed quickly. For example, the Liberty Basketball Association started competition in February 1991 and folded immediately in March of that year. With the public's newfound commitment to basketball during the late 1990s, people felt more confident about the creation of the American Basketball League (ABL), followed quickly by the birth of the WNBA.

The new women's leagues sought to feed America's insatiable appetite for the sport, thinking that if fans truly loved basketball, the WNBA would be a natural winner. However, the league would all too soon find out that it was not basketball that fans loved, but it was the superstars of the NBA. No superstars in the WNBA meant few fans. The NBA game exacted an image of a basketball player who represented a modern athlete with power and speed. To Americans, professional basketball exclusively meant powerful men, so when the WNBA was born, it was not surprising that the public rejected the feminized version of modern, masculine basketball. It seemed impossible for women to be able to construct a "professional" presentation of basketball.

Still, two women's leagues formed. The ABL learned that reconstructing a society's definition of sport was a formidable task. Setting reasonable, modest goals it nevertheless had a short, unstable life, completing its inaugural season with the Columbus Quest defeating the Richmond Rage 77–64 for the title. A crowd of 6,313 celebrated the event, but with winning teams like the Quest drawing only 6,000 plus fans, the ABL did not stand a chance (ABL Co-founder Optimistic, 1999). The local college football team, which happened to be one of the most popular in the country, drew over 100,000 on a bad day. Ohio State football managed to recruit and promote a new crop of superstars every year, but it seemed unlikely that the Quest could market its professional athletes with such skill. Columbus fans just were not interested in the product.

In December 1998, in the middle of its third season, the ABL announced bankruptcy. The WNBA watched with mixed emotions. With the ABL out of the way, the two leagues did not have to fight over resources, but those associated with the WNBA must have asked, "Will we be next?" This brought new meaning to the WNBA's slogan "We Got Next."

The WNBA started in 1997 with eight teams, doubling to 16 by 2000. It did not take long for it to experience growing pains. By 2000, the average attendance dropped and so did television ratings. According to records compiled by the *Sports Business Journal*, attendance during the 2000 season dropped about seven percent from 1999; by contrast, Major League Baseball attendance went up about four percent ("Attendance," 2000). These percentages may seem insignificant, but they translate into dollars, and for a new league like the WNBA, the attendance and viewership numbers define its future.

As the WNBA stormed the courts, the league bombarded the media with messages. However, after a loud start, the league seems to have quieted down. If the league is to grow, or even maintain its position, it needs to market its players. The American public needs to *want* to buy this product. Fans don't *need* another professional sport, as they are already flooded with options. However, if marketing creates a desire for us to buy the product, people may be tempted.

## THE IMPORTANCE OF MARKETING WOMEN'S BASKETBALL

When women's sports struggle to gain a fan base, the first claim made to explain the lack of enthusiasm is that "women can't play." Women's games are "boring." Women athletes simply are not as "fun" to watch. Certainly, women play *differently*, but the bigger concern deals with marketing and the rhetorical messages embedded in the public presentation of images used to market WNBA players. Americans do not think they like women's sports, because the media has not convinced them that they should. The rhetorical presentation of women in sports dictates the public's acceptance of women as entertaining athletes. Sporting events are a product and, with enough buzz, the consumers may buy the WNBA.

Commodification of desire sells the product, and, according to popular culture scholars Sonia Maasik and Jack Solomon (2000, p.124), "The desire itself becomes the product that the advertising is selling." The NBA tells us, "We love this game!" The campaigning increases our awareness of the NBA, and the rhetorical message encourages us to believe that most people not only like, but love, the NBA, preying on our desire to fit in and creating a collective desire to be a part of the NBA. The WNBA needs to create a desire for its product, but the league has not yet figured out how to sell its athletes and create a buzz.

When the ABL and the WNBA offered similar products, the public bought the WNBA because the desire for the WNBA was stronger than the ABL. Critics, however, claimed the ABL was a better brand of ball, with many journalists claiming that the ABL clearly offered the superior product (Knapp, 1996). The ABL appeared to have more talent, with most of the 1996 USA Olympic team spread throughout the league, but the ABL only averaged 3,536 fans per game (Smith, 1998, p.330). Playing with a "men's" ball (rather than the smaller collegiate ball), a "men's" 2-and 3-point range shot, and a shot clock, it seemed the ABL had the better product, so why did it fold so quickly? People probably did not want the athleticism of the ABL, because they wanted to be part of the notoriety of the WNBA, which received more publicity. What the WNBA lacked in competition, it made up for in cash, creating a marketing buzz. With the NBA bank-rolling its female counterparts, the WBNA claimed, "We Got Next" so loudly, that the ABL seemed to play at a whisper.

With the ABL out of the way, the WNBA seemed to have an open market to sell its game. Five years later, it still had not made its way into mainstream popular culture. The WNBA even had its own version of Michael Jordan and the Bulls in Cynthia Cooper and the Houston Comets, with Cooper dominating the court like Jordan. In fact, she ruled over a dynasty. Cooper, who retired at the end of the 2000 season, was the WNBA's marquee name. She led the Houston Comets to four titles in four years, something not even matched by Jordan. Yet, to refer to her as the marquee player is a stretch. Retiring at 37, Cooper spent most of her basketball career in near obscurity, despite two NCAA titles, two Olympic medals, four WNBA titles, four finals MVPs, and two regular season MVPs. Today, despite her dominance on the court, she can stroll through an airport virtually unnoticed, go to the movies, or grocery shop with little disturbance. It is difficult to be the marquee player if there is no marquee. The league did not succeed in transforming her into a mainstream celebrity, and the league never really knew how to package her persona for the public.

The league planned to focus on younger players like Rebecca Lobo and Lisa Leslie, but Cooper dominated them. The league had not expected this, and was not prepared to market her cleverly. Should she be packaged as the "old lady" of the league? That did not sound very attractive. How about the "big sister"? That was not sexy either. The "playgirl"? The "girl next door"? It never figured out how to sell her image. In reality, the league tried too little, too late.

When a fan buys a ticket to a game or tunes into a broadcast, the fan is buying more than the game. The fan is buying a relationship with a personality. According to Bill Perry (2002), marketing consultant and former Cincinnati Reds employee, "The WNBA could leverage personalities to help build its brand . . .[they] could showcase not just talent, but personality—nastiest, sexist, best hard-luck story, comeback kid etc." Fans will build a relationship over time with someone in whom they believe, someone who they think is worth rooting for. The WNBA needs this type of fan devotion. People need to learn about the women and find that they like them. Likability matters.

## THE CLASSIC CHARACTERS IN SPORTS

A player's character helps determine his/her likability. The July 31, 2000 issue of *Sports Illustrated* featured a story about sports' great characters—not the superstars, but the characters who keep us tuned into sports. These are the people who give sports flavor. Most of the time, they are not Hall-of-Famers, but they are the lifeblood of sports, the underdogs, and the people who we root for. During a losing season, these are the players we come out to support. If the WNBA wants to expand its fan base, it needs to find its characters and promote them. Fans want to root for a person, not just a number on a jersey.

*Sports Illustrated's* ("The Originals," 2000) list featured:

- William (the Refrigerator) Perry of the Chicago Bears
- Bill (the Spaceman) Lee, who pitched for the Boston Red Sox
- Dick Fosbury, who popularized the high jump Fosbury Flop
- Anne White, who wore the first unitard at Wimbledon
- Eddie (the Eagle) Edwards, who was placed last in the ski jump at the Calgary Olympics
- Al Hrabosky, the Mad Hungarian who talked to himself before each pitch
- Renee Richards, formerly Richard Raskind
- Pete Gogolak, the first soccer-style NFL kicker
- Otis Sistrunk, who practiced his reckless style at "the University of Mars"
- Bo Belinsky, a high-profile playboy

The list includes two women (sort of): Renee Richards and Anne White, neither of whom gained fame by endearing themselves to the public through tough play or with contagious personalities; rather, they were sideshow attractions. The personalities of these women did not warrant a change in the public's rhetoric. Are women's sports perceived as unskilled and boring?

The NBA dominated the 1990s because it threw out the best sales pitch, featuring a number of colorful, contagious characters. A host of NBA players signed contracts to endorse everything from shoes, to sunglasses, to hot dogs.

## NIKE-ORAMA

Basketball skills were helpful, but not necessary, for an NBA player to get a lot of "face time" in the media. The player's public image mattered most. For that matter, the image did not even have to be clean cut or all-American. It merely needed to be engaging, to entertain. According to *Sports Illustrated's* Jack McCallum (1997, p.29), "What might be called the Nike-ization of the NBA is also at work here. Whatever foibles a player has, they can be expunged or magically transmogrified into positives through movies (*Space Jam*) and countless feel-good ads."

The NBA has created personalities for its players and marketed them in every corner of the world. Through constant exposure, much of the public came to think that the NBA was full of personality and amazing athletes. The repetitious rhetorical devices redefined our perceptions. We bought the image of the product. However, the WNBA cannot seem to get the public to recognize legitimate stars like Lisa Leslie, Teresa Weatherspoon, or Sheryl Swoopes. When the WNBA learns how to market its players, it will see a rise in popularity.

Now, women's basketball just does not receive the face time it needs to redefine how the public might respond to female basketball players. For proof, visit the Nike web site: www.nike.com. Except for the "Nike Goddess" link, no female personalities welcome the consumer. The omission of women here implies that men only play basketball. Nike's web rhetoric implies that men are "cool." Men are "interesting." Men are "worthwhile." Women, however, are an afterthought. From Nike's introductory page, the consumer is sold personalities. The browser meets these men and is asked to "recognize" them—literally. After the consumers are sold on the "cool" ness of these men, they can move through the links to watch these stars play basketball. Eventually, if they go through enough links they can even find Nike basketball shoes to buy, but it requires navigation. Nike's site requires that you select a country (Unites States) and then a topic (basketball). There is no gender implied here. Basketball is not inherently gender specific. The site is not labeled NBA, which would designate a gender. To Nike, basketball equates male. There are no women on the Nike Basketball site! None.

Although Nike represents only one media voice, and the WNBA's lack of media presence cannot be blamed on Nike, the absence of women on Nike's web site reflects our society's discourse of basketball players. Nike is America's contemporary voice for basketball. The effects of discourse generated by this campaign shape how we collectively define a basketball player. Examining Nike's definitional assumptions, it is evident that women do not equate as basketball players. Members of our sociocultural system do not have an opportunity to read rhetorical messages to infer that women play basketball. Within the context of Nike, we can only interpret the definition of basketball player as male.

## The Rhetorical Presentation
## of Women Athletes

It is not that women are completely ignored by the media; however, the publicity that women athletes receive is often marked by controversy. Many women wonder if their publicity, particularly cover-girl like photos, propels women's sports forward or continues to contribute to its lack of credibility. Are women presenting themselves wisely? Female athletes need to realize they have some control over how their personas are presented to the public. If female athletes want more popularity, they need to shape their public personas and control the rhetoric associated with these personas.

Historically, women are portrayed in the media as one of two general characters: a wife/mother or a sexual object. The WNBA struggles with these images. "You have to be sexy and beautiful yet be an athlete and that' s what I don't think anyone to date have been great at achieving," explained Jack McCue who manages WNBA player Chamique Holdsclaw. "I've yet to see a major cosmetics or fashion design company sign a female athlete. The problem is image" (Marketing Chamique, 1999). WNBA players seem unable to create and market personalities that the public feels safe accepting.

Is labeling professional women's athletes as wives and mothers in the media entertaining? Certainly, some women would wear this image well. Current WNBA player Sheryl Swoopes is a high-profile mom. She is feminine and athletic, and committed to her role as mother, and media coverage focuses on her role as mother first, followed by athlete. During a 1999 interview with Swoopes the topic was not on athletic performance, but on pregnancy and motherhood. The first question the interviewer asked was, "How much weight did you gain during the pregnancy . . . ?" The next question: "What has surprised you most about motherhood?" While some questions did appear to address other concerns, such as the team's prospects heading toward the playoffs, the interview soon came back to "Do you feel changed by parenthood?" (A Parent and a Player, 2001). Male athletes field few questions regarding their fathering techniques.

Obviously, any emphasis on the athlete's performance is diminished by such extensive references to parenthood. Beyond the few female athletes who have managed to emphasize traditionally feminine qualities, media coverage has been found to trivialize, marginalize, and caricaturize women.

Our discomfort is reflected in the lack of attention women receive in the form of sponsorship for their athletic accomplishments. Nike took small steps to associate its product with female basketball players. In 1996, current WNBA player and Olympian Dawn Staley became the first woman featured on a giant Nike billboard. Nike followed by giving Sheryl Swoopes her own shoe, Air Swoopes. Years later, most Americans still cannot recognize these women. Giving Swoopes a shoe is one thing; marketing her persona is another. The average American cannot tell you about Swoopes' personality. This is because, as *Sports Illustrated's* L. Jon Wertheim (2002, p.64) states, "The players are still not perceived as celebrities." The perception of knowing WNBA players has yet to permeate our media. Crump (2002) was discouraged by the lack of progress made by the WNBA player as compared to her experience as a professional basketball player over 20 years ago. "Today's woman athlete has more money and certainly does get some TV time, but for the most part, they are lost to the consciousness of the average American because the potential fans don't see the female athletes on billboards, in ads, and on mainstream talk shows, etc." The WNBA needs to evolve beyond simply introducing women who play basketball; the league to needs to publicize women *as* sport, *as* professional basketball players. This in turn may increase the popularity of the league, because Americans love to transform athletes into celebrities.

## The Future of the WNBA

The WNBA is a great product, but if the public does not think the product is valuable, it may not buy it. Advertising is much more than letting the public know a product is available; it is persuading people to *want* the product. It is hype. Wanting the product is more important than having the product. We need to think we just cannot live without the WNBA. Fans will make WNBA players a part of their lives, if we are told through repetitive, rhetorical mass-media messages that we should like them. There is a host of engaging characters to market.

One of the WNBA's most unique strategies was to serve as the players' employers, rather than the individual teams. In theory, this should allow the league to market creatively the players and control the messages associated with them. According to Val Ackerman (as cited in Brown 2002, p.12), president of the WNBA, the league is making "steady" progress, albeit "cautiously." Perhaps too cautiously, as L. Jon Wertheim (2002, p.59) used the terms "niche sport," to describe the league, and referred to its television ratings as "minuscule" and its arena attendance as "plateaued." It seems as if the WNBA should address its strategies for marketing its players. As employers in the entertainment industry, the league can succeed it if harnesses the spirit of these female basketball players and markets this spirit to the world.

The WNBA has Lisa Leslie, a model modern female basketball player. She is talented, leading the Los Angeles Sparks in scoring. She even scored 101 points in one game during high school, so we know she has skills. Moreover, she is beautiful. In 1996 she signed a modeling contract with Wilhemina Models, Inc. She can be accepted as a tall, athletic, beautiful, and powerful woman. Leslie represents the WNBA's spirit, with a will to change basketball and how the nation defines basketball players. She recognizes she has the attributes to become a celebrity, reaching far beyond the WNBA.

Despite print media's lack of interest in the WNBA, television had at least one bright WNBA moment when Lisa Leslie starred in a Bud Light commercial that demonstrated that female athletes can capture the attention of television viewers as effectively as NBA players. In the commercial, Leslie is sitting at a counter in a diner when a man next to her accidental attempts to dunk his doughnut in her coffee; humorously, she swats the doughnut across the room, and proclaims that no one dunks on her. The commercial ends with Bud Light stating that it is a proud sponsor of the WNBA. The commercial is simple, funny, and memorable. The commercial demonstrates that a WNBA player has the charisma necessary to sell a product. Unfortunately, the commercial did not air often, nor beyond WNBA games, limiting the number of people who could meet Leslie and learn to identify her as a professional basketball player. Nonetheless, the commercial serves as a model for other mass-marketing campaigns.

Another player who has the potential to change the way the WNBA is perceived is Chamique Holdsclaw. As Holdsclaw left the University of Tennessee, she was arguably the most skilled female basketball player in history. There was great anticipation about what her influence would bring to the WNBA. According to ESPN journalist Shelly Smith (1998, p.313), "Experts predicted she'd become the first woman player with true bargaining power in endorsement offers." Entering the league, she signed the biggest contract ever offered to a female basketball player by Nike. The contract pays between

$300,000 to 500,000 a year over five years (Frey, 1999). Despite the large contract, the public has seen little of Holdsclaw, so the league has not been able to capitalize on her buzz.

Even manager Jack McCue resolves himself to the problems associated with marketing a WNBA player. Holdsclaw's image needs to be manipulated and presented carefully to the public. "We want boys to look at Chamique and be able to say 'Wow she's cool' and at the same time she's a great athlete. But at the same time she's hot." He knows he needs to sex-up her image to convince the decision-makers on Madison Avenue that Holdsclaw is a good investment (Marketing Chamique, 1999). Regardless of her skills, Holdsclaw, unlike her male contemporaries, must sell some of her sexuality. NBA athletes do not worry about being "hot." According to Holdsclaw's attorney Lon Babby, "Tim Duncan and Grant Hill walk into a mature league where, if they succeed on the court, they are going to be hugely successful. With the WNBA . . . I think some of the success of the league depends on women like Chamique Holdsclaw capturing the imagination of the public. At some level, she bears a responsibility for helping to grow the league" (as cited in Frey, 1999). To a great extent, Holdsclaw's abilities to entertain and engage in a certain level of foreplay with the public will define her level of popularity within the mainstream.

Few visible female athletes reach celebrity status without flaunting some sexuality. Much of soccer player Mia Hamm's popularity can be attributed to her sex appeal, and the WNBA has a Mia Hamm-like star who is waiting for mainstream marketing opportunities. Sue Bird may be the type of WNBA player who can achieve celebrity status. By the end of her rookie season (2002) in Seattle, she was being interviewed by ESPN's Dan Patrick, and her name received mention on various sports talk shows. She has also been seen on a date with Nick Carter of the Backstreet Boys, increasing her popular culture status. Although Bird has the sex appeal to become a celebrity, in the wake of Dennis Rodman's retirement, there is an opportunity for a WNBA player to introduce herself as a Rodman-like character to the public. Although Rodman's bad boy image would not be well received in a female version, his non-conformist image would. Many of the people who adore Rodman love him because of what he represents. The public has provided evidence that there is room within the marketplace to support celebrity athletes who are traditionally attractive and those who represent freedom as well as rebellion from restrictive norms. The players of the WNBA represent these spirits.

The WNBA should invest in the images of these women, because this investment will secure the future of the league. Without the development of entertaining personas, the WBNA may die, just like its sister-leagues that came before it. The league needs to take bold risks to advance its image. At the turn of the century, sports is entertainment, and when the WNBA learns to market celebrity female athletes, fans will find the WNBA entertaining and its popularity will increase. Mass marketing campaigns will create repetitive exposure to new language that will alter how we think and feel about professional female basketball players and the WNBA. Through changes in language, marketing has the ability to transform how we define "basketball player."

### REFERENCES

ABL co-founder optimistic about women's pro basketball. (1997). Nando.net. *Associate Press*. <http://www.sportserver.com/ newsroom/ ap/bkb/1997/abl/abl/feat/archive/031297/abl27301.html>

Attendance down for WNBA. Fox Sports. <http://www.foxsports.com/ business/bites/z000816attendance1.sml>

Benes, A. (1996). Fame Jam. *Cigar aficionado*. <http://www. cigaraficionado.com/Cigar/Aficionado/people/ff597.html>.

Brown, J. (2002). Women's pro basketball wins fans all its own. *The Christian Science Monitor* (July 19): 12.

Crump, Marguerite Keeley (2002). *Milwaukee Does, Minnesota Fillies*. Free Spirit Press.

Deford, F. (2000) Reversal of fortune harms league's image. *Sports Illustrated* (November 17). <http://sportsillustrated.cnn.com/inside_game/ deford/news/2001/11/15/deford/index.html>.

Frey, J. (1999, July 17). Suddenly, the world looks up to Holdsclaw. *Washington Post*. <http://members.tripod.com/chamiqueholdsclaw/links/ links.html>

Halberstam, D. (1999). *Playing for keeps*. New York: Random House.

King, M. (2002). Lisa Leslie as a work in progress. *Sports Illustrated for Women* (May/June): 86–89.

Knapp, G. (1996). Biggest battle in women's basketball looms off the court. *San Francisco Examiner* (October 30).

Maasik, S. and Solomon, J. (2000). *Signs of Life*, 3rd ed. New York: Bedford/St. Martin's.

Marketing Chamique. (1999, June 8). *NN/SI*. <http://members. tripod.com/ chamiqueholdsclaw/column/column.html>

McCallum, J. (1997). A cut above. *Sports Illustrated* (March 10): 24–32.

The Originals. (2000). *Sports Illustrated* (July 31): 84–107.

A parent and a player. *The Official Site of the Houston Comets*. <http://wnba.com/comets/swoopes_transcript2.html>

Perry, Bill. (2002). Personal Communication (October 23).

Smith, S. (1998). Basketball. In *Nike goddess*, ed. Smith, L., 293–314. New York: Atlantic Monthly Press.

Wertheim, J.L. (2002). Fast times in the WNBA. *Sports Illustrated* (August 5): 57–65.

# CHAPTER 8

# Strong Enough to be a Man, but Made a Woman: Discourses on Sport and Femininity in *Sports Illustrated for Women*

*Cheryl Cooky*

Media discourses proclaiming "Girl Power" have exploded in recent years, Katherine Dieckmann (1996) arguing that, in response to this explosion, girls today have a variety of empowerment models from which to chose. Barbie, Mattel's infamous toy designed for young girls, has recently become a professional basketball player, the president, a doctor and an astronaut. Several years ago the popularity of Spice Girls, the pop music group imported from England whose hit single "Wanna Be" became a girl culture phenomenon, gave girls various images of femininity they could aspire to, from "Sporty" to "Posh." This empowerment for young girls, courtesy of the Spice Girls and others, has been manifested in the phrase "Girl Power" now a mantra (and marketing tool) in girl culture. Within the realm of sports, female athletes like Brandi Chastain, whose sports bra clad body was featured after the 1999 U.S. women's soccer team won the World Cup on the cover of *Newsweek* along with the announcement that "Girls Rule!" are held up for girls and young women as models of this new female empowerment.

Much of the popular media discourse on female athletes has centered on this notion of sport as a space for (potential) empowerment for young girls, a space where they can exercise their "Girl Power" regardless of their chronological and/or biological development.

However, with the exception of academic feminist analyses that have recognized the importance of studying girl culture as a site wherein gender is constructed and challenged, very few question the potential meanings of "Girl Power" for girls at this historical moment. There are only a few scholars (e.g., Geissler, 2001) who are analyzing dominant discourses on sports for the ways in which girls are or are not empowered by popular culture, the supposed source of "Girl Power." By examining one site wherein, according to dominant discourses, girls are empowered—sports, this essay will explore representations of girls/women and athleticism and the ways in which power/knowledge are infused in dominant discourses surrounding girls/women and sports.

## SEARCHING FOR THE FEMALE ATHLETE: GENDER, SPORTS, AND THE MEDIA

Whereas the 1999 U.S. World Cup Soccer victory was heralded as a triumph for girls/women's sports, we can look to other "media events" surrounding the female athlete that challenge this celebration of female athleticism and Girl Power. If we look back historically at the coverage of female athletes, the preoccupation with sexuality and the "heterosexy" imperative is nothing new. Much like contemporary findings on the media coverage of women athletes, Susan Cahn (1994) found that the coverage of female athletes in the 1920 Olympics, the first Olympic Games where women were allowed to compete, was relatively sparse. When women athletes were covered the media focused on the "heterosexiness" of the athletes more so than their performances. Cahn writes, "Athletes were clearly perceived and portrayed as attractive, erotic women . . . which alerted the readers to the sexual attractiveness and possibly the erotic power of modern female athletes" (p.47).

Despite the significant gains made by the passing of Title IX in 1972, the professionalization of women's sports such as basketball, football, and softball, and the popular cultural celebrations of Girl Power, not much has changed in terms of the quality of coverage of female athleticism. Contemporary media representations of "real" women in sport are still relatively scarce. When women *are* represented in the media, these images often trivialize, objectify, and/or marginalize women in sport and physical activity (Birrell and Theberge, 1994; Duncan and Hasbrook, 1988; Duncan and Messner, 1998; Messner, Duncan, and Cooky, 2000; Messner, Duncan, and Cooky, 2003; Kane and Lenskyj, 1998).

Our study of gender stereotyping in televised sports newscasts in Los Angeles, California (on KCBS, KNBC, KABC, and ESPN) found that women's sports represented approximately 8 percent of all sports newscasts on the networks. When sportscasters *did* focus on female athletes, their participation was often debased and trivialized (Messner, Duncan, and Cooky, 2000). These representations, or lack thereof, lead to what gender studies scholars have referred to as the "symbolic annihilation" of women (Gerbner, 1978).

This study focuses specifically on gender representations in television where both men's and women's sports are covered. At the time this article was written, a women-centered sports television program did not exist, and women are often left out in programs like ESPN's "Sports Center." There have been other media outlets devoted solely to female sports and female athletes, such as *Sports Illustrated for Women* (in this essay referred to as: *SI for Women*), which hit the newsstands in spring, 1997 with two issues that year. At the time of this initial analysis, *SI for Women* was published ten times a year and had a circulation of roughly 400,000 (Messner, 2002). Five years later, Time, Inc. decided it would no longer publish it, claiming a lack of readership to sustain the magazine. On November 4, 2002, Susan Casey, managing editor, announced that the December 2002 issue was its last issue.

Despite that decision, *SI for Women* is still an important site for understanding how gendered discourses operate in our culture. How do the representations in a magazine devoted to the coverage of women's athletics reproduce and/or challenge some of the patterns already found in the media coverage of women's athletics? How do the discourses *of SI for Women* construct the female athlete? What strategies do these discourses employ in this construction? These questions will be explored further.

## METHODOLOGY AND THEORETICAL FRAMEWORK

*SI for Women* was chosen for several reasons. First, at the time of this analysis, there was a scarcity of studies of the magazine in the academic literature, even though it was soon represented at various conferences (Cavalier, 2002; Cooky, 2001; Gordy, 2002). Each of these studies has pointed to the paradoxical positioning of the power of female athleticism and the media images of female athletes. Cavalier argues that the coverage of female athletes, which focuses on emphasized femininity, suggests a "backlash" to the gains that women have made in sports, while Gordy echoed some of these findings and suggested that the increasing attention to female athletes by mainstream media is acceptable only so long as it is consistent with the "male hegemony in our society."

Prior to the emerging research on *SI for Women*, sport studies scholars analyzed other forms of media coverage of women's athletics. For example, Margaret Carlisle Duncan (1994) employed Foucault's concept of panopticism to analyze issues of *Shape* magazine. She argued magazines like *Glamour*, *Cosmopolitan*, *Mademoiselle*, as well as health and fitness magazines such as *Shape* and *Women's Sport and Fitness*, invite women to engage in a self-conscious monitoring of their bodies. As she encouraged sport studies scholars to utilize Foucault's theories in the study of sport, this essay is a response to Duncan's call.

Second, *SI for Women* is unlike many other sports media outlets because the magazine was solely devoted to the coverage of women in sport. Although there have been other magazines devoted to women's sports such as *Real Sports* and *Women's Sport and Fitness*, *SI for Women* is the first mainstream magazine devoted to the coverage of women's sport (rather than women and fitness or women and health).

Third, the magazine was marketed for young girls/women. The fact that young girls/women comprise the market for a mainstream sports magazine is a unique phenomenon. This analysis of *SI for Women* aims, then, to offer an understanding of how the female athlete is represented in popular culture, specifically in media representations of sport and what these representations might suggest for female empowerment. It reports on a discursive analysis of *SI for Women* from spring, 1997 to November/December, 2000, when it had moved from four to six issues per year. Starting in 2001, it was published ten times a year. The first issue is also included in the analysis, not only because it is significant in that it was the first issue of *SI for Women* to be published, but also to allow for an examination of any shifts in the discourses/representations of the girl in the magazine.

### Reading Magazines

This analysis borrows from the work of the Birmingham School in analyzing media texts. Several studies have explored the ways in which girls read magazines and the meanings they attribute to the messages contained in magazines (Currie, 1999; McRobbie, 2000), exploring how notions of femininity are constructed through the discourses of girls' magazines; however, they have focused on the readings and meanings of mainstream teen beauty and fashion magazines. Current research is now exploring how young girls "read" and negotiate images of female athletes and female athleticism (Heywood and Dworkin, 2003).

Although a process including interviewing girls about the ways in which they read *SI for Women* is not part of the methodology here, some opinions of its readers have been posted to the "epinions" web site, where Internet users can either post their opinions on various issues or read others' postings. "Rocketgirl," for example, liked the way that the stories covered a variety of sports and sports personalities, even if she was highly critical of the magazine's primary focus on the production of femininity. Another reader, "tennisjen" wrote that she had difficulty embracing *SI for Women* because she grew up reading the "real" *Sports Illustrated*.

The power of meaning, we know, is within the producer of the text and the reader. So this paper focuses on the dominant discourses produced by the magazine itself, based on a Foucauldian analysis.

## Using Foucault

Some feminist sport studies scholars have turned to the theories of Michel Foucault to understand the institution of sport and women's participation within that institution (Andrews, 1993; Chapman, 1997; Cole, 1994; Duncan, 1994; Markula, 1995), as his work has been helpful in theorizing how the body can become a contested site for power relations. Discourse is produced and reproduced by individuals and is dependent on individuals for its existence, and Foucault sees the discursive and the material inextricably linked in a symbiotic relationship of the power/knowledge complex (McNay, 1994).

The notion of the body is central to feminist analyses of oppression because it is the biological differences between men and women's bodies that underpin the inequality that is (re) produced and legitimated in contemporary society. However, although women's oppression is based on "the appropriation of women's bodies by patriarchy," this is not the sole basis for women's oppression. The differences between men and women cannot be explained solely on an a posteriori effect of "natural difference." McNay (1992) sees Foucault as a way out of this dilemma, as for Foucault, sexuality is not an innate, biological fact; rather, power/knowledge relations inscribe sexuality on the body.

Expanding on Foucault's assertion in his 1978 *History of Sexuality*, (where the sexual body is seen as both the principle instrument and the effect of modern disciplinary power), feminists have shown the ways in which strategies of disciplinary control of women's bodies, such as cultural representations of femininity to corporeal methods of confinement and control, are central to the (re) production of hierarchical social relations.

## DISCURSIVE CONSTRUCTIONS OF PATHOLOGICAL BODIES IN *SI FOR WOMEN*

In *SI for Women*, women were allowed space to be athletic at the same time that they must also engage in bodily practices to maintain their feminine image. The constant surveillance required of the female athletic body was apparent in the "In Every Issue" sections of the magazine, "Your body," "Your food," and "Personal trainer," which emphasized and encouraged girls/women readers to engage in surveillance of their bodies. It provided examples of the ways in which their bodies are pathological and then offers girl/women readers strategies that can be used to "cure" the pathology. The ideal female body, as constituted in these discourses, is without flaws, adequately moisturized, buffed of dry and dead skin, blemish and acne-free, and fragrant. While sport disrupts the production of the proper female body, girls/women can reclaim their femininity *after* the game, by engaging in the recommended gendered bodily practices.

*SI for Women* was unique in that it encouraged girls/women to eat, albeit eat healthy, and exposed myths about food and weight gain. Ultimately, *SI for Women* encouraged a well-balanced diet defined by proper nutrition (vitamins, protein, and complex carbohydrates), adequate water intake, and plenty of calories to support athletic participation.

"Your personal trainer" was another section of the magazine where girls/women are encouraged to scrutinize their bodies and segment them, breaking down the body into parts, to be evaluated for fat distribution and muscle tone. Through these discourses of personal training, gendered bodies are constituted through practices that produce the feminine ideal as articulated by *SI for Women*.

## NAKED FEMALE ATHLETES AND THE "NEW FEMINISM"

As noted earlier, *SI for Women* did not offer its readers any knowledge on how to weight lift or strength train, even as it celebrated female strength. Girls/women who claim their femininity in the sporting

context can be read as an act of resistance, challenging the no
that "feminine girls" are not athletic. Indeed, some argue that fe
athletes who pose nude are representatives of the "new feminism" and
"Girl Power."

Those who resist engaging in gendered practices that produce
feminine bodies are often viewed as masculine and, as a result of their
gender transgression, their sexuality is called into question (Cahn,
1994). They are often seen and constructed through discourses as
lesbian, regardless of their self-proclaimed sexual identity. Therefore,
the naked athletic body ultimately produces the power/knowledge
complex it could potentially challenge.

## CONCLUSIONS: SPORTING BODIES
## VERSUS GENDERED BODIES

This essay has argued that, through *SI for Women*, traditional discourses
of femininity were rearticulated through sporting practices altering
the ways in which discourses of femininity have been traditionally
understood. These discourses serve to reinforce the double bind for
female athletes and readers; "real women" can participate in sport yet
participation in sport serves as a direct threat to their constitution of
femininity. It is the knowledge imparted to the reader via *SI for
Women* that girls/women learn to reconstitute this pathology into a
"healthy" (i.e., traditional) feminine bodily ideal.

As we have seen, bodies are not just sporting bodies or gendered
bodies; they are both. For example, while Lisa Leslie is positioned by
the WNBA as a marquee player, mostly because of her off-court career
as a model, she is complicit in fulfilling this role that has been discur-
sively constituted by the WNBA. In her appearances on TV interviews
and half-time shows she is seen wearing make-up, jewelry, and other
markers of traditional femininity.

Chapman (1997, p.219) argues, "The discourse of femininity thus
reinforces the discourse of sport: Producing oneself as a woman, like
producing oneself as an athlete, means engaging in disciplines of body
maintenance. Both discourses emphasize producing a specific type of
physical body or a specific 'look' as being central to being a success."
In response to feminists who claim sport is a form of empowerment
whereby women can challenge male dominance, it has been argued
that sporting practices are similar to other everyday technologies of
femininity in that both require "disciplines of bodily maintenance."

However, unlike technologies of femininity, technologies of sport
simultaneously produce gendered-docile and gendered-intractable

bodies. The technologies of sport require bodies that are strong and athletic; however, as this analysis of *SI for Women* has demonstrated, the female sporting bodies produced are not removed from the everyday practices of femininity. Indeed, one may argue that female sporting bodies require even more surveillance due to the fact that sport constitutes a pathological body (sweaty, dirty, and odorous) which requires maintenance surpassing traditional technologies of femininity. It is for this reason that sport studies scholars should encourage the general public to question how empowering discourses of sport, such as those produced in *SI for Women*, can be for girls/women. What kind of empowerment does this magazine offer for its girl/women readers? Is it an empowerment that should be celebrated and embraced, or are we just singing the same song to a different tune?

This paper has attempted to show the ways in which a discursive analysis of the media can be useful for understanding issues of gender and sport. Foucault's theories can allow sport scholars to see the tactics and strategies that are employed to re-articulate the threats women's participation in sport pose to gender hierarchies. While shifts may occur in how girls/women experience sport (ranging from complete prohibition to professional sport leagues), the discourses surrounding women's sports often re-articulate themselves in ways which maintain difference and hierarchy.

### References

Andrews, D.L. (1993). Desperately seeking Michel: Foucault's genealogy, the body and critical sport sociology. *Sociology of Sport Journal* 10: 148–167.

Birrell, S. and Theberge, N. (1994). Ideological control of women in sport. In *Women and sport: Interdisciplinary perspectives*, ed. Costa, D.M. and Guthrie, S.R., 341–359. Champaign, IL: Human Kinetics.

Bordo, S. (1993). *Unbearable weight: Feminism, western culture and the body.* Los Angeles, CA: University of California Press.

Cahn, S. (1994). *Coming on strong: Gender and sexuality in twentieth century women's sport.* Cambridge, MA: Harvard University Press.

Cavalier, E. (2002). *Media images of female athletes.* Paper presented at the Southern Sociological Society. Baltimore, MD.

Chapman, G.E. (1997). Making weight: Lightweight rowing, technologies of power, and technologies of self. *Sociology of Sport Journal* 14 (3): 205–223.

Cole, C.L. (1994). Resisting the canon: Feminist cultural studies, sport and technologies of the body. In *Women, sport and culture*, ed. Birell, S. and Cole, C.L., 5–29. Champaign, IL: Human Kinetics.

Cooky, C. (2001). *Representations of the "girl" in Sports Illustrated for Women.* Paper presented at the American Sociological Association. Anaheim, CA.

Currie, D. (1999). *Girl talk: Adolescent magazines and their readers.* Toronto: University of Toronto Press.

Dieckmann, K. (1996). The girls are alright. *The village voice.* <http://www.villagevoice.com/vis/158/dieckamnn.shtml>

Duncan, M.C. (1994). The politics of women's body images and practices: Foucault, the panopticon, and Shape magazine. *Journal of Sport and Social Issues* 18 (1): 48–65.

Duncan, M.C. and Hasbrook, C. (1988). Denial of power in televised women's Sports. *Sociology of Sport Journal* 5: 1–21.

Duncan, M.C. and Messner, M.A. (1998). The media image of sport and gender. In *MediaSport*, ed. Wenner, L.A., 170–185. New York: Routledge.

Foucault, M. (1978). *History of sexuality. Volume 1: An introduction.* New York, Pantheon.

———. (1980). *Power/knowledge: Selected interviews and other writings 1972–1977.* New York: Pantheon.

Geissler, D. (2001). Generation "G." *Journal of Sport and Social Issues* 25 (3): 324–331.

Gerbner, G. (1978). The dynamics of cultural resistance. In *Hearth and home: Images of women in mass media*, ed. Tuchman, G., Daniels, A.K., and Benet, J., 46–50. New York: Oxford University Press.

Gordy, L. (2002). *Distorted progress: Images of women in sports magazines.* Paper presented at the Southern Sociological Society. Baltimore, MD.

Haber, H.F. (1996). Foucault pumped: Body politics and the muscled woman. In *Feminist interpretations of Foucault*, ed. Hekman, S., 137–156. University Park, PA: University of Pennsylvania Press.

Hall, S. (1980). Encoding/decoding. In *Culture, media and language*, ed. Hall, S., Hobson, D., Lave, A., and Willis P., 128–139. London: Hutchinson.

Heywood, L. and Dworkin, S L. (2003). *Built to win: The female athlete as cultural icon.* Minneapolis, MN: University of Minnesota Press.

Kane, M.J. and Lenskyj, H.J. (1998). Media treatment of female athletes: Issues of gender and sexualities. In Wenner, *Mediasport*, 186–201. New York: Routledge.

Lovejoy, M. (2001). Disturbances in the social body: Differences in body image and eating problems among African American women and white women. *Gender and Society* 15 (2): 239–261.

Markula, P. (1995). Firm but sexy, strong but thin: The postmodern aerobicizing female bodies. *Sociology of Sport Journal* 12 (4): 424–453.

McNay, L. (1992). *Foucault and feminism.* Boston, MA: Northeastern University Press.

———. (1994). *Foucault.* New York: Continuum Publishing.

McRobbie, A. (2000). *Feminism and youth culture*, 2nd ed. New York: Routledge.

Messner, M.A. (2002). *Taking the field: Women and men in sports.* Minneapolis, MN: University of Minnesota Press.

Messner, M.A., Duncan, M.C., and Cooky, C. (2000). *Gender stereotyping in televised sports.* Los Angeles, CA: The Amateur Athletic Foundation.

Messner, M.A., Duncan, M.C., and Cooky, C. (2003). Silence, sports bras and wrestling porn: The treatment of women in televised sports news and highlights. *Journal of Sport and Social Issues* 27 (1): 38–51.

Orenstein, P. (1994). *School girls: Young women, self-esteem and the confidence gap.* Anchor Books: New York.

Wickman, G. (1986). Power and power analysis: Beyond Foucault. In *Towards a critique of Foucault*, ed. Gane, M., 149–177. London: Routledge & Kegan Paul.

# CHAPTER 9

# Running a Different Race: The Rhetoric of "Women's-Only" Content in *Runner's World*

*Marie Hardin and Julie E. Dodd*

When *Runner's World* (*RW*) senior editor Eileen Portz-Shovlin (2002) recounted the birth of the magazine's "Women's Running" column in 1994, she began with a story about a women's road race in Sweden the previous year. When she and a friend arrived at the starting line, she looked around at a field of 30,000 other women runners, proof of what she already knew: Women's running was a phenomenon. "We were hearing about big women's races," she reported. Participation in the "Race for the Cure" (breast cancer research) series, women's races started in 1983 also grew during the 1990s, becoming some of the largest 5K (3.1 miles) events in the country—drawing upwards of 20,000 runners (Zemke, 1998).

Thus, content in the magazine, aimed specifically at women, "made sense," according to Portz-Shavlin. In 1994, a monthly women's column was launched, using freelance contributions. "Women's Running," appeared on a full-page of the magazine in each issue, typically page 20 or 22, accompanied by drawings or photos. *RW* was flooded with contributions. The editors chose mostly those written by female freelance writers who were also running enthusiasts. In addition to having the writer's byline, each "Women's Running" column had a brief bio, with occupation and city/state of residence of the writer. It was mostly anecdotal, recounting lessons about life and sport through women's experience, with a rare column written by men.

It reached upwards of two million readers monthly, many likely seeing *RW* as the authoritative voice on running issues as it is likely the most influential media source on running. While other running magazines exist (such as *Running Times, Florida Running and Triathlon, Running Journal* and *Trail Runner*), *RW* is the highest-circulation running magazine in the United States, with a subscription base of more than 500,000 (*RW* Media Kit, 2002). Launched in the 1966 as "Distance Running News," it claims a total readership of more than two million: 57.7 percent male, 42.3 percent female, mostly married and with a median age of 36. That relates to a general running population of about ten million: 53 percent male, 47 percent female, with an average age of 27 (Demographics, 2001). According to research by American Sports Data, the percentage of women runners has increased since 1999, up from 45 percent (Demographics, 2001).

In May, 2002, however, the column stopped, part of the magazine's redesign. Portz-Shovlin (2002) said it just didn't have the mass appeal: "It wasn't how to train," she stated. "It was more just an essay on about running and what it meant to [women]." Other columns remained: Liz Applegate's "Nutrition," John Bingham's "The Chronicles," Ed Eyestone's "The Fast Lane," George A. Hirsch's "Publisher's Letter: The Inside Track," and "Joe Henderson's Journal." The last page of the magazine is devoted to a standing column: "Finish Line," open to submission by readers. "It's not that we have forgotten women," Portz-Shovlin claimed. "We know that women's running is growing." *RW* continues to be cognizant of its female readers in other ways: through a special section (laden with advertising) mailed only to female readers, for instance, and the occasional tribute to female runners in its general content. One article promoting the benefits of running for men and women encouraged women to run because "Oprah runs" (Editors, 2002, p.73).

Still, the philosophy of RW contends that female runners have the same values as those served by the general readership (read: men). Women runners are interested in reading the same types of sport articles as men, or they wouldn't be reading the magazine, is the assumption. So the "Women's Running" column is gone, even while women's running continues to grow. We ask: Did the "Women's Running" have any value for *RW* readers? After all, it wasn't about performance, but about the meaning of running and things like "the spiritual thing, the buddy thing" (Portz-Shovlin, 2002), not values typically associated with sport. Should they be? Did the column address topics that are as legitimate in a sport magazine as articles about training or strategies of competition? We believe they are. The

nen's Running" column provided a "safe space" for female
ers, a unique place where women's sports values were validated,
shed, and celebrated, where *females counted fully*. The end of
nen's Running" marks the silencing of their sporting voices
rating important ideas about sports into an otherwise male-
oriented (or, arguably, gender-neutral) magazine.

## Sport Socialization

The fact that *RW* generally orients itself toward the male reader (or
that material for women is marked as such—i.e., "Women's Running"
and "Women's" section) is the norm for sport media, which typically
reflect cultural values bound in sport socialization. Sport socialization
is a complex combination of factors by which individuals are encouraged to participate in physical activity and sport; including media
influence, they combine to socialize us to the values and practices of
the sport subculture.

Women, we argue, also are socialized to view sport as the road to
aesthetic enhancement, a key social variable for femininity (Creedon,
1994). In our culture, the use of exercise for body maintenance
(weight reduction and body toning) is acceptable, even encouraged
(Creedon, 1994; Hargreaves, 1994). For women, sport must be
intertwined with chasing the feminine ideal, not just for the sake of
competition. Thus, they run. But even running was, until relatively
recently, considered too demanding for the frailty of a female body
(*The Complete Woman Runner*, 1978). The Boston Marathon celebrated
its 100th anniversary in 1996, but has only allowed women to enter
the race officially for 24 of those years—beginning in 1972.

## Radical Feminism, Sport Socialization, and Sport Media

Radical feminism has been an important influence in theoretical
debates regarding women and sport, arguing that characteristics normally ascribed to men—and to sport, such as strength, aggression,
and competition—should be rejected. Instead, characteristics such as
cooperation and grace should, in turn, be embraced (Hargreaves,
1994; Lenskyj, 1994; Tong, 1989).

Because male values are the standard, it is understandable that
women have been sidelined in sport and, by default, in sport media;
indeed they are assumed "inferior," studies showing them generally
marginalized and sexualized (Davis, 1997; Miner, 1993). While

research focusing on running publications is scant, numerous studies relating gender to sport media have been published, as media representations of sport continue to expand (Bellamy, 1989; Birrell and Theberge, 1994; Eastman and Billings, 1999; Kane and Greendorfer, 1994; Sage, 1990).

Sportswomen have historically been underrepresented and misrepresented in overall coverage, despite increases in their opportunities and participation, a number of studies revealing disproportionate rates of coverage (Boutilier and SanGiovanni, 1983; Kane, 1988; Reid and Soley, 1979; Rintala and Birrell, 1984). For instance, several studies of *Sports Illustrated* have found that men dominate from cover to cover (Boutilier and SanGiovanni, 1983; Lumpkin and Williams, 1991; Salwen and Wood, 1994), especially significant findings because *Sports Illustrated* has been labeled the most influential sport publication (Kane, 1996). This trend is just as prevalent in other media outlets, from magazines to children's sport media (Cuneen and Sidwell, 1998; Duncan and Sayaovong, 1990; Rintala and Birrell, 1984) as well as daily newspapers. Lont (1995) aptly captures the representation of women athletes in the print media. It is more common to find a story about a male who lost than a female who won.

The one study that has examined presentation of gender in *RW* found the magazine "responsive to the female in sport" (Bryant, 1980, p.37), and that it presented females as sporting role models in both its advertising and editorial content. A study of editorial photos in *RW* between 1992 and 2001 found that the percentage of women depicted there improved through the 1990s, with women represented in almost half of its editorial photos in 2001, even if photos of women were far fewer than those of men (Hardin, Dodd, and Chance, 2001).

Most of these studies examine whether women are simply included in sport media, and if so, to what degree. Even when they are included, female athletes are typically subject to linguistic sexism (Daddario, 1994; Kinnick, 1998). Language is used to reinforce male values in sport, and to subject females (and female values) to derision. Condescending descriptors and imagery, compensatory rhetoric, emphasis on familial roles of female athletes, and the framing of female athletes as adolescents instead of adults (i.e., the term "girls") present women and their sporting values as "less than the norm" in sport (Daddario, 1994). Women's sporting accomplishments are also marginalized through "gender marking," designated not as "general interest" events or topics, but as "women's." The implication: Men's interests encompass all interests, but women's are "special interests," or inferior (Kinnick, 1998). The *RW* column, "Women's Running," is an example; notably, the title conveys that the content isn't useful for all readers, as might be other columns in the magazine.

From a radical feminist viewpoint, stories in the "Women's Running" column have served to reject male values assumed to be universal in sport; for one page a month, women's voices provided the "power in story" to which Sandoz (2000) refers relative to her question about the 1999 *Newsweek* cover, "Girls Rule," celebrating Brandi Chastain's soccer victory in the U.S. World Cup: "Where's the girl?" It is instructive to see the values that emerged as primary in this column over a three-year period (1999–2001), reflecting and validating the female sports socialization experience.

## Themes and Values in "WR" Columns

### *Relationships*

Running as a way of establishing or enhancing relationships was a major theme in *RW* "Women's Running" columns; in fact, it was the most discussed topic in the three years' issues examined for this study. Twenty-one of the 34 columns (1999–2001) focused on the theme of relationships, or included that idea as one of several themes in the column. The relationships were mostly with family members (living or deceased), but also with friends.

Several mothers discussed running in terms of their perception of their children and roles as parent. In October, 1999, Libby Howard discussed being disappointed in her daughter, Karin, as she didn't have the same sense of intensity as the mother did in the family's fitness activities; only when she became an accomplished high school cross country runner did her mother seem to accept her. Once Karin had proven she could meet her mother's view of an athletic daughter, Howard was able to accept her role: "These days, we still occasionally take family walks. In fact, just last Sunday, as we strolled through the autumn woods, Karin lagged way behind, looking at the leaves and mushrooms. And I was right there with her" (p.22).

In a January, 2001 *RW* column, doctoral student Saundra Wright remembered the runs she used to have every Saturday with her mother when she was an undergraduate: "As we ran together we realized we weren't just mother and daughter—we were equals. We were two woman with sleep-mussed hair and oversized sunglasses, sharing, confiding, and consoling one another as we matched strides mile after mile" (p.20). Some women also wrote of running bringing them closer to a deceased parent. Beddow Gibson (July, 2000), described her decision to run a course around the ballfields where she attended games and played ball as a tribute to her father who was a baseball enthusiast, helping her develop a love of the sport: "Nowhere else do I feel so close—and so enlivened by—the presence of my dad" (p. 22). Running helped Louise Davenport deal with the loss of her mother. She received that call, helped with the funeral arrangements, then set out for a run: "I felt like an actor on stage with no script or direction. Totally helpless. Nothing could erase the sad reality that my mother was gone. I had to run. It was all I knew to do" (November, 2001, p.22). Following the funeral, she ran to the cemetery: "After all the chaos surrounding the funeral—dealing with family, seeing friends, helping with arrangements—I finally found some time alone with Mom" (p.22).

Only one column focused on running shared by a married couple or partners; Meg Waite Clayton's December 1999 story being about the way competition influences relationships and sharing. Two non-runners wrote about their relationships with their partners who do run. A.J. Poulin, the only male writer of a *WR* column during this three-year study period, wrote in June, 1999 that he couldn't understand his girlfriend's passion for running but agreed to train with her to hike the Grand Canyon. As they completed the 27-mile hike and his girlfriend told him how happy and proud she was of him, Poulin understood: "Finally I realized why running is so important to her and why she insists on being called a runner. Because it's her passion, and it gives her life meaning. It's not about winning. It's about finishing. It's about *doing*" (p.24). Barbara Shaw, the wife of a runner recounted (June, 2001) her husband's predictable morning running routine—from his pre-run routine to his after-run breakfast and shower; still unconvinced to start running herself, she obviously admired her husband's determination and consistency: "That's right. I'm married to a runner. And I wouldn't have it any other way" (p.20).

Running is also a way to develop meaningful friendships and provide time for those friendships. "Moment of Truth" (February, 1999) recounted Pamela Hunt's sunrise runs in the desert with her girlfriends and the power the time running had in their bond and their sense of self: "We talk as we run, stopping our conversations only to use our breath for the hills . . . During these runs, even our failures have grace, and our past glories are as close as our shadows. We get a glimpse of the strength we are building, strength that ultimately will come from holding on to who we are" (p.20).

Michele Bender found a running-only friend to be special and important. She met Melissa (she didn't know her last name) as they ran on treadmills at the gym, and they became regular workout companions, encouraging each other's workouts and discussing their lives. "Melissa has never met my husband or my friends, so I can talk openly about them. Since she is outside of my life, she can give me objective advice," she wrote (p.22). The two have chosen to keep their friendship only through their running. "We are joined by sweat. Bound by nothing. We are running friends. I wouldn't want it any other way" (September, 1999, p.22).

### *Body Image*

The second most frequent theme in the Women's Running columns was a concern about body image, ten of the 34 columns dealing with running as a way of losing weight or maintaining weight. But in running for weight control, most women also found that running helped them develop a better perspective on themselves. The columns offered frank discussions of the pressure too many women feel to achieve the "ideal body," their perceived shortcomings in getting there, and their willingness to accept themselves anyway.

Karen Dove Barr described an after-work treadmill run on a winter night motivated by a birthday cake at the office that day: "I feel the fat cells moving through my body, preparing to take hold. So I can't skip my run" (March, 2000, p.16). Looking as good as the mother of the bride was the motivation for the mother of the groom, Carole Howard Tremblay (May, 2000), who gave up cookies and took up running to get into shape. By the time of the wedding not only did she fit into the perfect dress but found that she truly enjoyed running: "On days when I can't run, I feel as if I'm missing something important—time for myself, time to think, time to watch the sunrise" (May, 2000, p.24).

Kelly Lynne Conforti admitted in an October 2000, column that she started running in college in hopes that Jay, whom she had a crush on, would ask her to run with him. So she took up running to get in shape. He never asked her to go running (or to go out on a date), but Conforti was hooked on running: "A year ago I never would have imagined that I could live in harmony with myself, run toward my dreams, and, more important, realize my own beauty" (p.26).

Susan Barnson Hayward began exercising as "an overweight teenager" (July, 2001, p.22); her quest: "I just wanted to fit into my jeans." But as she ran as a college student and years later as a busy mother of two, she realized that beyond the weight loss was the "blessed escape," finding that running gave her time to "savor the small pleasures of life." "I am that peculiar animal, the fat runner,"

Patricia A. Patton stated (July 1999, p.26), her column focusing on her embarrassment, shame, and anger at being a slow runner, holding up the race volunteers who were waiting for "Blubberbutt" in a race where she finished last. As she agonized about her race performance, she came to a new awareness: "I realized that I do compete—not against other runners, but against a negative view of myself that has undermined every physical activity I've attempted."

Two women wrote about taking on a specific competitor during a race to improve their own body images. Melissa Ann Pline singled out one's appearance. "I had to beat her. She was too beautiful" (September, 2000, p.20). Whereas Pline wore an unmatched shorts and top, the beautiful runner's shirt and shorts "were perfectly tailored to her Barbie proportions." At the finish line, the beauty, who beat Pline in the final yards of the race, congratulated her. " 'Good race,' she said. 'You looked great.' I gaped at her, stunned by her comment. *She* thought *I* looked great. It was as if she'd placed a beauty crown on my head." And in that exchange, Pline realized the beauty of a race run well, not just a runner's appearance.

To deal with losing her youth when turning 29, Jennifer Brodie spotted an older woman to outrun in a 10K race, but was beaten by her; afterward, she discovered the older woman was a record-holder in the 65–69 age group. At first Brodie was horrified to be beaten by a woman almost 40 years older than she, but, "Then it hit me . . . Without even speaking a word, she had taught me that aging should not be feared. She showed me that as women age we can still maximize our potential, we can still be victorious, and we can still inspire. Suddenly my disappointment melted away and my heart filled with admiration" (November, 2000, p.24).

## DISCUSSION

An examination of the now-defunct "Women's Running" columns reveals they did indeed provide a "safe space" for the values of sporting females. Instead of male-defined competition and aggression, the sporting principles promoted there were cooperation- and relationship-building. These values, perhaps considered "deficit" because they are marked female, are *equally valid* to the male sporting values considered mainstream. Clearly, as these columns demonstrate, they can have a place in sport, as all the women who wrote these columns are athletes.

By emphasizing relationships and acceptance of self, these columns categorically rejected the notion of competitive sport as it has been defined under male hegemony; perhaps the women writers rejected male-defined competition because it was perceived as a threat to interpersonal relationships (Lenskyj, 1994). Losing a race turned into a blessing for the 29-year-old runner trying to cling to her youth; the woman who raced against her husband decided that competition sapped the joy from running. Other columnists recounted accomplishments in another kind of competition: against the barriers in their personal lives. An overweight woman finished the race she set out to run; another cried with joy when she and her boyfriend met a goal together.

The rejection of male-defined competition is welcome under a radical feminist analysis of sport; radical feminists seek to "challenge the assumption that friendship, connection and cooperation must all be abandoned in order to give primacy to competition and winning," Lenskyj (1994, p.11). In these columns, the traditional/male understanding of competition typically is ignored, and women's sports values are promoted.

Radical feminists reject the male-defined ideal female body, one that forces women to obsess over meeting socially constructed standards of femininity (Tong, 1989). From that perspective, these columns are encouraging, as they signify the awareness by these women of the "beauty standard," albeit insisting it would not rule their lives. The 29-year-old runner learned to accept and embrace aging; another came to see her daily run for more than chasing the beauty ideal. Perhaps the most striking example of this position is the column by Patricia Patton, an overweight runner who wrote about the embarrassment she felt running a race—not meeting the athletic beauty standard. But she ran anyway, rejecting the idea that sport is only for those who are beautiful. There is *power* in Patton's story, as Sandoz (2000) insists is in every female athlete's story. Her voice, and the others who appeared in the *RW* "Women's Running" column during its eight-year run, offered readers a chance to read and embrace an alternative sports paradigm—a glimpse into the potential for ideological change (Kane and Greendorfer, 1994). It gave them the chance "to see girls and women as magnificent in their own right, with reference only to athletic challenge" (Sandoz, 2000, p.34).

The *RW* decision to pull these columns is regrettable, but perhaps predictable for a sports magazine, viewing sports from a tradition (i.e., male competitive) perspective. "Women's Running" was different. The column was "deficit," in that it didn't conform to the traditional sports paradigm. What the editors failed to realize in their decision to eliminate it was that its different vision was not a weakness but a value. "Women's Running" provided a rare place for the female voice: inside the pages of a sport magazine.

REFERENCES

Bellamy, R.V. (1989). Professional sports organizations: Media strategies. In *Media, sports, and society*, ed. Werner, I.A., 141–162. Newbury Park, CA: Sage Publications.

Birrell, S. and Theberge, N. (1994). Ideological control of women in sport. In *Women and sport: Interdisciplinary perspectives*, ed. Costa, M. and Guthrie, S., 314–357. Champaign, IL: Human Kinetics.

Boutilier, M.A. and SanGiovanni, L. (1983). *The sporting woman*. Champaign, IL: Human Kinetics.

Bryant, J. (1980). A two-year selective investigation of the female in sport as reported in the paper media. *The Arena Review* 4 (2): 32–44.

Cimons, J. (1966). Four who dared: They changed marathoning forever. *Runner's World* 31, 4 (April): 72–79.

*The Complete Woman Runner* (1978). Mountain View, CA: World.

Creedon, P. (1994). The archetype of Artemis in sport. In *Women, media and sport: Challenging gender values*, ed. Creedon, P., 275–299. Thousand Oaks, CA: Sage.

Cuneen, J. and Sidwell, M.J. (1998). Gender portrayals in *Sports Illustrated for Kids* advertisements: A content analysis of prominent and supporting models. *Journal of Sport Management* 12: 39–50.

Daddario, G. (1994). Chilly scenes of the 1992 Winter Games: The mass media and the marginalization of female athletes. *Sociology of Sport Journal* 11: 275–288.

Davis, L.R. (1997). *The swimsuit issue and sport: Hegemonic masculinity in Sports Illustrated*. New York: State University of New York Press.

Demographics—Updated August 1, 2001 (2001). USA Track & Field Road Running Information Center Web site. March 18, 2002. <http://64.84.58.116/state/demographics.html>

Dowling, C. (2000). *The frailty myth: Redefining the physical potential of women and girls*. New York: Random House.

Duncan, M.C. and Sayaovong, A. (1990). Photographic images and gender in *Sports Illustrated for Kids. Play and Culture* 3: 91–316.

Eastman, S. and Billings, A.C. (1999). Gender parity in the Olympics: Hyping women athletes, favoring men athletes. *Journal of Sport & Social Issues* 23 (2): 140–170.

Editors (2002). We love running. *Runner's World* 37, 4 (April): 78.

Hardin, M., Dodd, J., and Chance, J. (2001). *On equal footing: The framing of sexual difference in* Runner's World. Paper presented at the national conference for the Association for Education in Journalism and Mass Communication, Miami, FL.

Hargreaves, J. (1994). *Sporting females*. London: Routledge.

Heywood, L. (1998). *Pretty good for a girl*. New York: The Free Press.

Hilliard, D. (1984). Media images of male and female professional athletes: An interpretative analysis of magazine articles. *Sociology of Sport Journal* 1: 251–262.

Howard, J. (1999). The whole world is watching: Wonder women a marvel. *Newsday* (July 9): A79.

Jones, R., Murrell, A., and Jackson, J. (1999). Pretty versus powerful in the sports pages. *Journal of Sport & Social Issues* 23 (May): 183–192.

Kane, M.J. (1988). Media coverage of the female athlete before, during, and after Title IX: *Sports Illustrated* revisited. *Journal of Sport Management* 2: 87–99.

———. (1996). Media coverage of the post Title IX female athlete: A feminist analysis of sport, gender and power. *Duke Journal of Gender Law & Policy* 3 (1): 95–127.

Kane, M.J. and Greendorfer, S.L. (1994). The media's role in stereotyped images. In *Women, media and sport: Challenging gender values*, ed. Creedon, P., 28–42. Thousand Oaks, CA: Sage.

Kinnick, K. (1998). Gender bias in newspaper profiles of 1996 Olympic athletes: A content analysis of five major dailies. *Women's Studies in Communication* 21 (Fall): 212–233.

Lenskyj, H. (1994). *Women, sport and physical activity: Selected research themes*. Gloucester, Ontario: Sport Information Resource Centre.

Lont, C.M. (1995). *Women, men and media: Content, careers, and criticism*. Belmont, CA: Wadsworth.

Lumpkin, A. and Williams, L. (1991). Mass media influence on female high school athletes' identification with professional athletes. *International Journal of Sport Psychology*, 18: 231–236.

Miner, J.M. (1993). Women in sport: A reflection of the greater society? *The Journal of Health, Physical Education, Recreation and Dance* 64 (3): 44–48.

Portz-Shovlin, E. (2002). Senior Editor, *Runner's World*. Telephone Interview. May 21.

Reid, L.N. and Soley, L.C. (1979). *Sports Illustrated* coverage of women in sports. *Journalism Quarterly* 5 (4): 861–863.

Rintala, J. and Birrell, S. (1984). Fair treatment for the active female: A content analysis of *Young Athlete* magazine. *Sociology of Sport Journal* 1: 231–250.

*Runner's World* Media Kit (2002).

Sage, G.H. (1990). *Power and ideology in American sport: A critical perspective*. Champaign, IL: Human Kinetics.

Salwen, M.B. and Wood, N. (1994). Depictions of female athletes on *Sports Illustrated* covers, 1957–89. *Journal of Sport Behavior* 17 (2): 98–107.

Sandoz, J. (2000). Victory? New language for sportswomen. *Women & Language* 23 (Spring): 33–37.

Tong, R. (1989). *Feminist thought: A comprehensive introduction*. San Francisco, CA: Westview Press.

Zemke, T. (1998). 5K runs becoming more and more popular: Pittsburgh Race for the Cure part of a national trend. *Pittsburgh Post-Gazette* (August 25): D–7.

# CHAPTER 10

# Exercising Control: Empowerment and the Fitness Discourse

*Jennifer Smith Maguire*

## INTRODUCTION

To take the body as a project, as a site of investment and work, is to take account of its form and function (Baudrillard, 1998; Featherstone, 1982; Shilling, 1993). We typically confront the *form* of the body through outer appearances—physique, surfaces, and decoration. In a consumer service economy, where physical appearances are important for occupational success and social status, investing in the body's form— through toning exercises, dieting, and cosmetic surgery—is considered a way of maximizing one's competitive edge.

The *function* of the body is typically considered through the lens of health. In a society dominated by a "cultural imaginary of health" (Greco, 1993, pp.257–258), where health and disease are framed as matters of individual will or failure, investing in the body—through cardiovascular exercise, vitamin supplements, smoking cessation, and the like—can help minimize one's health risks. Since the 1970s, the commercial fitness industry in the United States has promoted exercise as an ideal solution to both of these body projects. Fitness programs and products are promoted as a way to control both appearance and health. Exercise helps you look good *and* feel good.

Physical fitness has long been about more than just bodily vigor and endurance. In the United States, for example, it has been wed to a variety of larger causes, such as moral reform in the nineteenth century Muscular Christianity movement, national strength in Theodore Roosevelt's Strenuous Living philosophy at the turn of the century, and personal improvement and enjoyment in the burgeoning service economy of the early twentieth century (Green, 1986; Mrozek, 1989). Since the 1970s, however, the concept of fitness has increasingly narrowed to a commercialized lifestyle, an individualized project of self-improvement through the consumption of exercise programs and fitness goods. While specific exercise may be intended to improve flexibility (such as yoga), cardiovascular endurance (jogging or aerobics), and/or strength (weight training), the fitness lifestyle is represented as a general enhancement of health, appearance, and, ultimately, quality of life (Howell, 1990; White, Young, and Gillett, 1995). In short, "fitness" is not about exercise per se, but taking control of one's body and life.

This chapter examines how fitness media articulate the dual concerns of bodily health and appearance through a language of empowerment, encouraging reader/users (women in particular) to associate fitness with personal control, choice, self-improvement, responsibility, and competence. It is drawn from a discourse analysis of thirteen fitness texts from the late 1970s to late the 1990s. Eight were targeted at audiences of both women and men: *The Gold's Gym Weight Training Book* (1978); the American College of Sports Medicine's *ACSM Fitness Book* (1992 and 1998 editions); the American Heart Association's *Fitting in Fitness* (1997); *Fitness Facts* (1989) and its 1999 2nd Edition, *The Health Fitness Handbook*; and *Fitness for Dummies* (1996 and 2000 editions). Five were targeted predominantly at women readers: *Jane Fonda's Workout Book* (1981); *Nautilus Fitness for Women* (1983); *Self* magazine's *Self's Better Body Book* (1998); and 1979 and 1990 issues of *Self* magazine.

Sociological studies of women and aerobics (Hargreaves, 1994; MacNeill, 1994; Maguire and Mansfield, 1998; Real, 1999) have highlighted two conflicting aspects of their participation: On the one hand, women gaining access to a formerly male sporting domain signals an emancipatory potential; on the other, the emphasis in magazines, videos, and exercise classes on "looking sexy," rather than "getting healthy" suggests the reproduction of a repressive beauty regime. Overall, these scholars draw attention to a deep-seated tension between external motivations (typically, achieving a fit and sexy "look") and internal motivations (such as improved health, social contact, and increased energy), and the enabling and constraining features of aerobics and other fitness activities. This research confirms this ambivalence, examining how it is perpetuated at the level of language, in the fitness discourse itself.

In identifying the common, recurring themes of empowerment across different texts and years, I build on and significantly extend earlier analyses of women and fitness magazines, which have focused on very small numbers of issues or articles (Duncan, 1994; Estes, Duncan, and Miller, 1998; Markula, 2001). By using a larger sample, this research offers an analysis of the coherence of the wider fitness discourse and its ambivalent representations of empowerment.

The discussion begins with an overview of women's consumption of fitness and the historical factors which have created both a market for fitness and the "conditions of existence" (Foucault, 1991, p.60) for the fitness discourse. It then deals with the ways in which the fitness discourse is shaped by the larger issues of women's empowerment, examining the varied ways in which the notions of personal power, choice, and control are articulated in relation to fitness. Specifically, three common themes emerge from the fitness texts, connecting empowerment with physical strength, self-care, and embodied experience. The concluding section assesses how this discourse, in naturalizing a particular way of understanding fitness, establishes the limits of exercising empowerment.

## Women and the Consumption of Fitness

Predominantly, fitness consumers tend to be women, although this is more pronounced for some fitness commodities than others. Health club membership in the United States today is relatively even, according to the International Health Racquet and Sportsclub Association (see www.ihrsa.org), with 52 percent of members being women, 48 percent men. Fitness magazines, Mediamark Research Inc. reports, tend to target gender-specific audiences: for example, the majority of the 1.69 million *Men's Health* readers are men, and the majority of the 1.68 million *Shape* readers are women. However, of the four top selling fitness magazines, three expressly target women, each with a circulation of more than a million readers. As well, women make up nearly 65 percent of the total circulation of these magazines, even though the top selling publication, *Men's Health*, is ostensibly for men only.

Clearly, not all women are fitness consumers. The consumption of fitness products and services, such as fitness magazines, personal trainer services, or health club membership, tends to be circumscribed by socioeconomic status. Fitness consumers—both women and men— are overwhelmingly middle class, with a relatively high proportion of upper-middle-class professionals and managers (Epaminondas, 2002, p.1). Health club industry research, for example, reveals that the average member of a commercial club has a household income of

$69,200, and almost half of the members have incomes above $75,000. Fitness magazine readers also come from higher income brackets, with more than a quarter of readers working in professional or managerial positions.

However, the consumption of fitness is not simply an expression of the possession of the means to do so. Several factors have contributed to the creation of a group of consumers who are not only economically able to participate in the fitness market, but are also looking and hoping for ways to shape their bodies and improve their health. Three of these factors warrant discussion, as they relate particularly to women's consumption of fitness and the notion of empowerment.

First, since the early 1970s, countries such as the United States, Canada, and Great Britain have promoted "active, healthy living" as a way to prevent disease and manage the escalating costs of cancer, heart disease, and other chronic illnesses. At the same time, healthy living was given a grassroots, political element by members of the women's health movement and other advocates of de-medicalization. As a rejection of the medicalization of "conditions" such as childbirth, and the unequal power relations between doctors and patients, these health movements emphasized how taking care of oneself—by choosing a healthy lifestyle and learning about health risks—could lead to empowerment and "medical self-competence" (Crawford, 1980, p.374; cf. Fox, 1997). Publications such as the original Boston Women's Health Book Collective's *Our Bodies, Ourselves* (1973) claimed that taking control of their bodies was an essential step toward women's general liberation and empowerment.

Second, in keeping with the larger feminist movement, exercise was encouraged as a way to not only manage one's health, but also become physically empowered. Building muscle tone and strength were presented as ways to exercise one's feminism, overcoming the traditional associations of femininity with frailty. Furthermore, 1972's Title IX legislation banning sexual discrimination in sports helped to open up women's access to physical culture, fostering a dramatic increase in the number of female high school athletes and facilitating a larger attitude shift regarding women, exercise, and strength. Television in the 1970s portrayed the new, strong, and emancipated woman, capturing the tension between old and new notions of feminine power: Wonder Woman, the Bionic Woman, and Charlie's Angels drew huge audiences with their (often contradictory) combination of traditional sex appeal and feminist empowerment. Although hyper-muscled female bodies remain marginal cultural figures, muscles are no longer feminine taboos (cf. Balsamo, 1994; Bordo, 1993; MacNeill, 1994).

Third, the female market for fitness also stems from the emergence of a "new" woman consumer. Between 1970 and 1990, civilian labor force participation in the United States rose 33.9 percent for women, their increased labor force participation being concentrated in image- and appearance-conscious service work. Women made up nearly 60 percent of finance, insurance, and real estate services in 1998, and 70 percent of all personal services. At the same time, many women were delaying marriage and childbirth, diminishing the family obligations that compete for their time and money. The result was a market of women with the economic means of self-directed consumption and the occupational incentives to improve their self-presentation. Magazines such as *Self* and *Working Woman* portrayed them spending time and money on self-development (through exercise or otherwise), not as selfishness or an abandonment of womanly/wifely duties but as the enactment of a woman's newfound independence and power.

The fitness discourse has reflected these larger themes of empowerment back to women in the form of an escalating array of exercise programs and fitness products and services. Indeed, the fitness discourse is unmistakably commercial: Exercise is presented as the panacea for all manner of ills, enticing us to consume fitness goods whether our motivation is the quest for enhanced health, self-confidence, success, strength, sexuality, or all of the above.

## EMPOWERMENT IN THE FITNESS DISCOURSE

Foucault (1978, 1991) highlights the social nature of discourses, inviting us to examine the "conditions of existence" (1991, p.60) that make discourses possible and, in turn, enable and constrain particular ways of seeing, knowing, and acting. The current fitness discourse depends on material preconditions—such as the shift away from manual labor, and urban growth patterns that favor automobiles over bicycles and walking—that make getting fit a choice rather than an unintentional but inherent aspect of daily life, and the possibility of unfitness a distinct likelihood for many people. However, the particular associations between exercise and empowerment also depend on and are supported by broader contemporary feminist discourses that have equated empowerment with a woman's ability to participate as an equal player in economic, social, political, medical, and sporting arenas.

It is through the fitness discourse that symbolic links are forged between the language of empowerment and the exercising body. Three themes traverse exercise manuals and fitness magazines, privileging some aspects of the exercised body over others through affiliations with control, competence, confidence, and power. Thus, the fitness discourse not only equates exercise with empowerment, but does so in a way that naturalizes particular expectations of exercise: increased physical strength and muscle tone; decreased health risks and greater medical self-awareness; and opportunities for active embodiment— that is, to experience the body as an integrated whole.

### Physical Strength as Empowerment

Perhaps the most literal link between fitness and empowerment concerns physical strength. Once the exclusive domain of men, strengthening exercises such as weight training and bodybuilding have become increasingly popular with women. According to research by the Sporting Goods Manufacturers Association in 2000 on frequent fitness participation (defined as activities in which individuals, aged six or older, participate at least 100 times a year), the top fitness activities in the United States for women were fitness walking (10.5 million), free weights (5.8 million), treadmill (5.4 million), and running/ jogging (3.7 million).

Weight training and bodybuilding—and their associated strength gains—have gained a wider audience in part thanks to movies such as *Pumping Iron*(1977) and *Pumping Iron II: The Women* (1985), and charismatic spokesmen and entrepreneurs such as Arnold Schwarzenegger and Joe Weider. In addition, new user-friendly weightlifting systems such as Nautilus entered the exercise equipment market in the early 1970s, removing the need for weightlifting expertise and technique.

The symbolic affiliations between exercise and empowerment obscure the gap between women's physical power, and the appearance of strength: Being strong is acceptable, being hyper-muscled is not. Moreover, this gap is further naturalized through the invocation of biochemistry. Hormones are presented as a natural, neutral constraint upon physical development, thereby sidestepping the more difficult— and political—question of how social norms inhibit women's individual and social empowerment.

### Self-Care as Empowerment

In much the same way that the symbolic association between muscles and political and social empowerment is marketed to women, fitness is widely promoted as a way for people—women and men, young and (especially) old—to take control of their bodies and health.

One health issue that explicitly brings together women and exercise is body image disorder, "women becoming increasingly medicalized over the past 20 years." (Bordo, 1993; Markula, 2001). Buoyed by medical research on the positive effect of exercise on body image, the fitness media promote exercise as a way for women to reclaim their bodies from normative definitions of beauty. For example, consider the following from *Self's Better Body Book* (Billings, 1998):

> What's a better body? It's a strong, healthy body in balance with a strong, healthy mind. Forget the notion that a better body is the "perfect body." It's not. There is no universal standard of physical perfection that we all can achieve. . . . All of us, however, have the capacity to tone, firm-up, slim-down, build stamina and cardio strength and live a happier, healthier life. We all have what it takes to be as strong, healthy and vital as we can be at every age and stage of our lives. (p.5)

The shift away from dependence on expert authorities, such as doctors telling us why exercise is good for us, toward "medical self-competence" (Crawford, 1980, p.374) involves not a decline of medical authority, but its reformulation in the therapeutic helping hand of the magazine or manual. Building on the appeals to women's physical empowerment, fitness as a healthy lifestyle is thus affiliated with individual competence and responsibility. However, care of one's health and one's appearance are often elided in the fitness discourse.

### Embodied Experience as Empowerment

In addition to increasing one's physical strength and gaining control of one's health, the fitness discourse also associates exercise with an experiential notion of empowerment. That is, exercise is presented as yielding experiential rewards, such as an authentic awareness of the body and the pleasure of physical exertion. The discourse thus implies that such rewards cannot be found in the mundane routines of worka-day life; fitness is positioned as a way to get more (pleasure, energy, awareness, and so forth) from one's body and life. This active notion of embodiment—as a sensation that must be consciously produced through exercise—dovetails with the larger cultural fascination with self-awareness, self-actualization, and self-esteem that intensified over the second half of the twentieth century (Lasch, 1979; Rose, 1996).

Looking and feeling more confident are external motivations for joining the fitness lifestyle, positioned in the discourse as keys to social and occupational success. More than this, however, the fitness discourse highlights the opportunity to *feel the body* as an internal motivation for exercise. Given the increasingly sedentary patterns of desk jobs, commuting, and television watching, this notion of active embodiment resonates with the "quest for exciting significance" (Maguire, 1992, p.109; cf. Elias and Dunning, 1986) that characterizes many leisure forms.

A particular notion of pleasure is thus positioned as the hallmark of what "counts" as exercise. Cleaning the house burns calories, but does not provide the intimate experience of one's body; watching a movie may involve pleasure, but lacks the satisfaction and rewards of discipline. As the saying goes, "No pain, no gain." In other words, exercise in the context of fitness is not (only) about losing weight or having more energy, but is framed as a particular experience of one's body to satisfy desires for control, authenticity, and pleasure.

The fitness discourse confines the pleasure of exercise within a language of self-discipline. At the same time, however, it employs the discipline of exercise to legitimate other, consuming pleasures. In prescriptions of material rewards, the fitness discourse reconciles the tension between the expectation of instant pleasure—promoted so heavily in consumer culture—and the prolonged work and effort required to see (health and shape) results from exercise. If bribery is a way to motivate fitness behavior, it is significant that the bribe be shopping, linking the field of fitness to the reproduction of consumption more broadly. Bodily discipline in one sphere (exercise) becomes the alibi for indulgence in another (shopping). Instant gratification is thus reconciled, at the level of language, with the long-term self-discipline of fitness. This reward aspect of fitness motivation provides us with an important insight into the ways in which the ascetic traditions of self-denial (the Protestant work ethic) coexist with the hedonistic impulses of the Romantic ethic (Campbell, 1987). That is, self-discipline and self-gratification are not irreconcilable, but are configured in the fitness discourse as temporally and spatially separate aspects of the same lifestyle: do two more sit-ups now, so you can buy the new dress, new sneakers, or new watch later.

## Concluding Thoughts

Fitness magazines and exercise manuals represent fitness as an empowered lifestyle, instructing readers to manage their bodies so as to improve their strength, self-confidence, and appearance, and decrease their health risks. Media such as fitness magazines and exercise manuals may thus be viewed as a genre of sensibility manuals and manner guides by which individuals are educated in the problems and solutions of social status and consumer lifestyle. Such texts supply specific information on physical activity, but also claim to provide the objective, rational solutions to the problems of everyday life: how to choose between the multiplying options of the market; conduct your life so as to optimize your chances of success and happiness; reduce the risks of failure and disease, and shape a lifestyle that both conforms and stands out, earning both acceptance and distinction (cf. Rose, 1996, pp.156–157).

The fitness discourse promotes a narrowly bounded understanding of empowerment. On the whole, the ambivalence of empowerment lies in its conception as an inherently individual project of work on the body. By emphasizing the individual's ability and responsibility to take control of her life, the discourse obscures the social and structural factors that constrain an individual's chances of success, health, and social mobility. Accordingly, the fitness discourse locates the arena in which empowerment is to be enacted at the level of the individual, not the social, and constructs the signs of empowerment as matters of bodily control. Empowerment, as understood through the fitness discourse, is possible for—but *only* for—the individual body.

The degree to which the fitness discourse has accomplished the construction of this narrow, symbolic bridge between exercise and empowerment is perhaps best illustrated by a time when the world seemed quite beyond control. In the weeks immediately following the terrorist attacks of September 2001, health clubs in New York experienced a significant increase in the sale of new memberships, with one chain (New York Sports) selling more than 10,000 memberships in a single day. At a time of insecurity, doubt, danger, and risk, the body becomes all the more precious as a vestige of individual competence and control. However, such a sense of control and empowerment is inevitably fragile. For all of our best efforts, our bodies are uncontrollable entities; aging, if not injury, ensure that health and vitality are neither static nor guaranteed. The fitness lifestyle is one in which satisfaction is located less in pleasure *in the body*, and more in control *over the body*, which is always tenuous at best.

## References

Balsamo, A. (1994). Feminist bodybuilding. In *Women, sport, and culture*, ed. Birrell, S. and Cole, C.L. Champaign, IL: Human Kinetics.

Baudrillard, J. (1998). *The consumer society: Myths and structures*. London: Sage.

Billings, L. (1998). *Self's better body book*. New York: Clarkson Potter.

Bordo, S. (1993). *Unbearable weight: Feminism, western culture, and the body*. Berkeley: University of California Press.

———. (1997). *Twilight zones: The hidden life of cultural images from Plato to O.J.* Berkeley: University of California Press.

Campbell, C. (1987). *The romantic ethic and the spirit of modern consumerism*. New York: Blackwell.

Crawford, R. (1980). Healthism and the medicalization of everyday life. *International Journal of Health Services* 10 (3): 365–388.

Duncan, M.C. (1994). The politics of women's body images and practices: Foucault, the panopticon, and Shape magazine. *Journal of Sport and Social Issues* 18 (1): 48–65.

Elias, N. and Dunning, E. (1986). *Quest for excitement: Sport and leisure in the civilizing process*. Oxford: Blackwell.

Epaminondas, G. (2002). Find home, sweet home, at the new haute gym. *The New York Times* (April 28): IX, 1–2.

Estes, T., Duncan, M.C., and Miller, E.M. (1998). The discourse of empowerment: Foucault, Marcuse, and women's fitness texts. *Journal of Sport and Social Issues* 22 (3): 317–344.

Featherstone, M. (1982). The body in consumer culture. *Theory, Culture & Society* 2: 18–33.

Foucault, M. (1978). *The history of sexuality: An introduction*. New York: Vintage Books.

———. (1991). Politics and the study of discourse. In *The Foucault effect: Studies in governmentality*, ed. Burchell, G., Gordon, C., and Miller, P. Chicago: University of Chicago Press.

Fox, R.C. (1997). The medicalization and demedicalization of American society. In *The sociology of health and illness: Critical perspectives*, 5th ed., ed. Conrad, P. New York: St. Martin's Press.

Goldberg, V. (1975). Body building: Is it an art, a sport or sheer exhibitionism? *The New York Times* (November 30): 264.

Greco, M. (1993). Psychosomatic subjects and the "duty to be well": Personal agency within medical rationality. *Economy and Society* 22 (3): 357–372.

Green, H. (1986). *Fit for America: Health, fitness, sport and American society*. New York: Pantheon Books.

Hargreaves, J. (1994). *Sporting females: Critical issues in the history and sociology of women's sports*. New York: Routledge.

Howell, J. (1990). *Meanings go mobile: Fitness, health and the quality of life debate in contemporary America*. (Unpublished doctoral dissertation, University of Illinois at Urbana-Champaign).

Lasch, C. (1979). *The culture of narcissism: American life in an age of diminishing expectations*. New York: W. W. Norton & Company.

MacNeill, M. (1994). Active women, media representations, and ideology. In Birrell and Cole, *Women, Sport, and Culture*.

Maguire, J. (1992). Towards a sociological theory of sport and the emotions: A process-sociological perspective. In *Sport and leisure in the civilizing process: Critique and counter-critique*, ed. Dunning, E. and Rojek, C. Toronto: University of Toronto Press.

Maguire, J. and Mansfield, L. (1998). No-body's perfect: Women, aerobics, and the body beautiful. *Sociology of Sport Journal* 15: 109–137.

Markula, P. (1995). Firm but shapely, fit but sexy, strong but thin: The postmodern aerobicizing female bodies. *Sociology of Sport Journal* 12: 424–453.

———. (2001). Beyond the perfect body: Women's body image distortion in fitness magazine discourse. *Journal of Sport and Social Issues* 25 (2): 158–179.

Mrozek, D.J. (1989). Sport in American life: From national health to personal fulfillment, 1890–1940. In *Fitness in American culture: Images of health, sport, and the body, 1830–1940*, ed. Grover, K. Amherst, MA: University of Massachusetts Press.

Penney, A. (1977). Tough is good for you. *The New York Times* (August 14): VI, 50–54.

Real, M. (1999). Aerobics and feminism: Self-determination or patriarchal hegemony? In *SportCult*, ed. Martin, R. and Miller, T. Minneapolis: University of Minnesota Press.

Rose, N. (1996). *Inventing our selves: Psychology, power, and personhood.* Cambridge, UK: Cambridge University Press.

Shilling, C. (1993). *The body and social theory.* London: Sage.

Sporting Goods Manufacturers Association. (2000). *The SGMA report: Tracking the fitness movement.* North Palm Beach, FL: Sporting Goods Manufacturers Association.

White, P., Young, K., and Gillett, J. (1995). Bodywork as a moral imperative: Some critical notes on health and fitness. *Society and Leisure* 18: 159–182.

Wilson, P.S. (1979). Editor's note. *Self* (January): 6.

# CHAPTER 11

# Minimizing the *Maxim* Model? Interpreting the Sexual Body Rhetoric of Teenage Moms through Physical Education

*Treena Orchard, Joannie Halas, and Jennifer Stark*

> *Sara, a high school student, was asked by her guidance counselor if she thought their school for adolescent parents needed to offer physical education classes. Sara's immediate response was "Yes," and then á propos of her latest visit to a strip bar, she expressed, in the vernacular of the local neighborhood discourse: "Who wants to sit and look at a fat chick with stretch marks?"*

This ethnographic story comes from teenage mothers' participation in a high school physical education program designed specifically for adolescent mothers and incorporating the principals of culturally relevant education (Ladson-Billings, 1994) as a means to engage young women in meaningful and relevant physical activities. An articulation of culturally relevant teacher practices, a decision to add physical education to the school curriculum was based, in part, on student feedback regarding the need for physical activity in their lives.

In the above anecdote, Sara's reasoning for why students might benefit from physical education speaks to different aspects of the discursive texts and socioeconomic influences that affect how she, as an unwed, teenage mother, constructs understandings of her body in relation to dominant narratives of female beauty and attractiveness within her local economy. In North America, female bodies are "attractive" if they are thin, and in the reality of this young woman's community life, the bodies of erotic dancers make up part of the vernacular of the local discourse. Sara's response to the guidance counselor's question evokes tensions existing between privileged, mainstream (i.e., white, affluent middle-class, heterosexual, often male-centered and professional) bodily and educational ideologies and the marginalized ideologies held and experienced by young mothers who sometimes succeeded in school, or many times not.

Various aspects of commercialized youth culture (i.e., music, style, romance, consumerism) are common topics in social research; yet, the details of how young people belonging to economically disadvantaged and culturally marginal groups form their identities and make sense of their sexuality are not as well documented nor understood, especially in terms of cross-cultural sexuality.

To demonstrate how local cultural vocabularies are influenced by global discourses of sexuality, the body, and youth culture, this essay discusses the ways adolescent mothers use the highly popular men's lifestyle magazine *Maxim* to inform their sexual expressions and how they manipulate mainstream images for their own purposes, socially and physically. Instead of the (stereo)typical teen magazine that centered around romance, make-up, and fashion trends, with the message that sex is for couples who are in love or married (Carpenter, 1998), the teenage mothers prefer an "unapologetically male" adult magazine with a "frat boy ethos" (Sales, 2002) offering an irreverent blend of soft-porn, cleavage, pop culture, and sexual jokes (e.g., see *Maxim*, October, 2002). It appears that, as young women/mothers, they have gone beyond the adolescent topics featured in *Seventeen* and are more curious about and relate to aspects of social and sexual life as featured in the adult publications.

Launched in Britain in April, 1997 by Dennis Publishing, *Maxim's* target market is the 20 to 30'ish "ordinary guy." It has recorded phenomenal growth, currently with an estimated global readership of 14 million, including global editions in the United States, Holland, Belgium, France, Spain, Portugal, Italy, Poland, Germany, and the Hispanic Americas (see The Press Room, *Maximonline*, 2002). With an impressive guaranteed rate base equaling 2.5 million (newsstand = 1 million, paid subscription = 1.5 million), *Maxim* has become a worldwide circulation powerhouse (Cappell's Circulation Report, 2002). Despite its detractors, who contest the intellectual and cultural value of the magazine, *it* has been described as one of the most commercially successful magazines worldwide (see its web site: Maximonline). As evidence of its popularity, the magazine shows an average paid copy sales of 2,458,150, representing a year to year increase of 47.8 percent, nearly triple its nearest competitors. Despite a declining market for media advertising, *Maxim* topped *Adweek*'s list of Top 10 magazines (Orsini, 2002). From all indications, the *Maxim* brand has become a commercial juggernaut reflecting and informing twenty-first century young adult culture.

Using *Maxim* as a backdrop, this essay discusses some gaps in existing literature reporting on marginalized youth, sexuality, the body, and identity formation. One purpose is showing how ideas surrounding idealized female images in popular magazines like *Maxim* are not unequivocally "bad" but, on the contrary, are sometimes "good to think with." Importantly, "thinking" here is relevant not only for the young mothers, but also for researchers/instructors who ran up against problems when trying to disrupt the "idealized body image" to which the teenage mothers aspire, and the attendant sociosexual behaviors they display. Given that there are multiple and diverse ways whereby people experience their bodies, and that these embodied experiences interact to shape identities that are constructed over time and within specific contexts (Sparkes, 1999), we attempt to explore the sexual body rhetoric of a group of adolescent mothers participating in a culturally relevant physical activity program at their school.

## Culturally Relevant Physical Activity for Marginalized, Adolescent Mothers

The majority of research literature on adolescent pregnancy reports on potentially negative outcomes for both mother and child, with few studies investigating the prospect of positive outcomes and even fewer privileging the perceptions of the adolescent mothers themselves. One notable exception is by Stenberg and Blinn (1993), who encouraged 14 pregnant adolescents to record their feelings toward their selves and their bodies in a journal, finding them using key terms like "fat," "huge" and "ugly" to describe themselves. Concluding that teen pregnancy programs should help young mothers cope with their changing self and body image, they called for research studies that would follow teenage mothers through the raising of their children to gain a more profound understanding of how adolescents view themselves and their pregnancies.

Recognizing this need for more participant-centered research, we used a Participatory Action Research (PAR) methodology to deliver a physical activity intervention for teenage mothers attending a public school designed solely for adolescent parents in Manitoba, Canada.

The school had a student population of approximately 100 pregnant and postnatal young women aged 14 and 20; of these students, 28 took part in the physical activity intervention. Although the student population had a diverse mix of socioeconomic and ethnic backgrounds, as many as 60 percent of the young women were Aboriginal, defined here as "people who self-identify with one or more of the three groups recognized in Canada's constitution: Indians, Metis, and Inuit"; Aboriginal peoples comprise some 11.7 percent of Manitoba's population. These percentages reflect trends toward higher birth rates for Aboriginal women as compared to the non-Aboriginal population in the Province of Manitoba, which has the dubious distinction of having the highest rate of teen pregnancy in the country, it being three times higher than others for young women of Aboriginal descent. Within the population of Aboriginal teen mothers, 90 percent are single.

The supporting rationale for the research study was two-fold. First, with high absentee rates, the vice-principal believed that physical education could be an effective means for motivating students to attend school. Second, the school did not have a physical education teacher, yet students needed physical education credits to graduate from high school. Initially, the vice-principal obtained a small Canadian Association for the Advancement of Women in Sport program grant to provide two consecutive four-month *On the Move* programs, "girl-friendly" physical activity interventions (CAAWS, 2002). The twice-weekly fitness-oriented classes proved to be an immediate success. Yet, despite the program's popularity, project funds soon ran out.

On the advice of a local community worker who was well aware of the school's predicament, the principal investigator (Jennifer Stark) approached the school for permission to expand the physical activity program as a research project. A PAR research proposal was constructed with the research question: What is the meaning of the physical activity experience for adolescent mothers? Once research grant monies were secured (from the University of Manitoba Research Grants Program and the Health Leisure and Human Performance Research Institute), a research team was hired, including a research assistant (the first author of this paper) and two trained Physical Activity instructors, one being the last author.

As a first step, the research team collaborated with students and school officials to expand the school's twice-weekly physical activity program into a meaningful and relevant "*daily*" physical education class. With input from the young mothers, a diverse set of activities were soon offered, including fitness testing, Tae Bo workouts, aerobics, stability ball workouts, step workouts, resistance training, wrestling, belly dancing, funky street dancing, walking in the neighborhood, loosely organized basketball and volleyball at a local community center, soccer-baseball in the field, ultimate Frisbee, low-organized games, Innu games, swimming, roller skating, and visits to the local YMCA.

Data collection methods included fieldwork observations of the physical education classes; focus group and individual interviews with students, physical activity instructors, and teaching staff; hand-written records of planning meetings with staff and students; and analysis of school documents (e.g., assessment tools used in the class) and instructor journals. Interviews were audiotaped, focusing on questions relating to the young women's experiences of the physical education class and their leisure time. For example, they were asked to describe what they liked and disliked about physical activity, what types of physical activities they engaged in after school, and what qualities define a good physical education teacher. In one series of interviews, students took turns interviewing each other about a typical day in the life of a teenage mother. All interviews were transcribed, coded for themes, and analyzed in relation to the research question. To protect confidentiality, all identifying characteristics were changed, and all study participants provided informed consent prior to the start of the research activities.

During the course of the study, the adolescent mothers' sexually playful and sex-focused behavior during gym class prompted Jennifer to question what she interpreted to be their "obsession" with sex. To initiate discussions about various issues related to sex and relationships, she attempted to introduce certain ideas about the body (such as appreciating the one you have, that men should like you for who you are and not your body), sexuality ("appropriate" sexual behavior), and relationships. The mothers often responded with little comment, which was frustrating, if instructive, because their silence forced us to consider its meaning. We wondered if they were still in the "trust-building" phase, and yet the girls were very confident expressing themselves in other ways—suggesting their silence may have had more to do with their interpretations of the instructors' ideas as opposed to a reluctance to share their feelings.

Similar to other research suggesting teenage girls do not passively internalize mass media messages about how they should look, act, and behave (Humphrey, 2001), it seems that a failure to translate certain middle-class "healthy" ideals regarding sexuality, body image, and social behavior into practice among and by teen mothers does not automatically mean that they are defenseless victims of the powerful influence of commercialized images, as modeled in *Maxim*. Instead, as we will show, the girls appeared to adopt a selective process of evaluating and using such media, in some cases, as something to admire, maybe as part of a fitness goal, or as something they acknowledged but knew was unrealistic.

In order to illustrate how the young women expressed thoughts about their bodies, motherhood, and other factors affecting their involvement in the physical education class, the following section presents examples of personally relevant body-self constructions that were identified in the analysis of the research data. This discussion is followed by examples of how Jennifer Stark interrupted the adolescent mothers' performances of sexuality and gender, an interaction that raised more questions than provided answers. The conclusion provides an overview of existing theoretical frameworks employed in the analysis of teen sexuality, the media, and culturally relevant physical activity.

## Body Crossings: Examples of Personally Relevant Body Identities

Using data from interview transcripts, fieldwork observations, instructor journals, and school documents, this section locates examples of how participation in daily physical activities allowed adolescent mothers to construct personally relevant identities that move beyond dominant academic and public policy discourses which relegate teen mothers to being both social and economic burdens on society (Kelly, 1996). In particular, three socially constructed identities are discussed: reclaiming body identity, healthy maternal body identity, and a self-regulated body identity.

### Reclaiming Body *Identity*

In interviews and casual conversations during and after the physical education class, the young women often spoke of wanting to "get their bodies back," referring to their earlier, pre-pregnancy bodies, which were also in the process of maturing to adulthood. Their attempts to reclaim their former bodies were difficult for many because of physical changes that occurred during the reproductive process of being pregnant and having a child (or children). As one mother said: "Cause once you've had kids and you've got like a tummy now and a butt and thighs and stuff, you know, it's just . . . I mean you're not used to it and now it means toning down and getting back into that look and stuff. You have to work harder."

While "losing weight" was voiced as a strong motivation for many in the program, achieving a body that met their expectations of looking good and feeling fit may have been made more difficult because of these mothers' tendency to concentrate on a "dismembered body." That is, most of them targeted certain parts of their bodies that they wanted to work on, like butts, abdomen, or arms, to the exclusion of achieving a holistic sense of well-being through health and physical activity. Nevertheless, many expressed satisfaction with their accomplishments in the program, reported as expecting to lose weight and having done so, or being more active since being on the program.

### Healthy Maternal Body *Identity*

Another theme identified during the research process is the importance that motherhood has played in making these young women concerned about their health. Many said that before they were pregnant they did not care about their bodies or about being healthy, but since becoming pregnant and participating in the physical activity program their attitudes had changed completely. This new consciousness about "health" expands their motivation to achieve a "fit" body beyond a constructed desire for sexual beauty. Rather, achieving a "healthy" body has become a prerequisite that could help them meet the physical demands of being a young mother/student. While establishing caring relationships, the instructors provided the young women with practical skills of how to be physically active so that they could realize their goals within the constraints of their social and economic situations. Using soup cans to build arm muscles, or placing their young children on their legs while doing leg and abdominal exercises, made being fit within reach. The young women appreciated these types of strategies, which bypassed commercial fitness products reserved for paying customers. This effective problem solving may have also made other goals they had formulated for themselves more attainable, including being good role models for their children.

### Self-Regulated Body *Identity*

A number of girls commented on the lack of structure in the school and the related fact that "It is easy to skip [classes] here." Instead of viewing this situation as something they could use to their advantage, most associated it with a lack of concern on behalf of the teachers.

In contrast, they praised the physical activity instructors for what could be termed their "surveillance" techniques (i.e., asking them where they were, what was going on with them, and using class time to discuss their lives). They interpreted these interactions as a sign that someone cared about them.

Most literature on the body, young mothers, and youth identity assumes that the forms of self-surveillance resulting from state or institution-directed regulatory practices and social structures represents a loss of individual agency (Lupton, 1995). However, what emerged from our research is more nuanced. These young women desire some form of surveillance (from trusted instructors) to help them gain control over various aspects of their lives, and such practices also seem to fulfil significant emotional and social needs, of being cared for and of being identified as someone important. Similar to other examples of how physical activity helps marginalized youth (Halas, 2001a, 2001b), participation in the physical education class had a positive impact on the young mothers' desire to be in school.

## Playing Sexuality, Identity Performance: Disrupting Trouble

During the course of our research, we saw how Stark, who shares a similar cultural background (Aboriginal) and youthful experiences with many of the mothers, was frequently puzzled by how much "sex" dominated conversations. In her journals, she reflected upon students' reactions to her efforts to introduce what she perceived to be "healthy" alternatives about the body, commercialized standards of beauty, and relationships. Her frequent advice about being happy with the body you have and the idea that prospective partners should like you for who you are, not just for what you look like, was often met with reluctant nods and displaced by behavior and discussions that seemed to contradict the messages she tried to convey. In particular, she wondered why they were so "sex focused," and why they stayed in abusive relationships.

Examining commonalties and incongruities in cultural vocabularies and sexual discourses, it seemed journal reflections represent good examples of how limiting a middle-class, feminist-based pedagogy can be when delivered in the context of sociocultural and economic realities these moms face on a daily basis. To illustrate, here are some entries from Jennifer's journal:

> ➤ Feb. 25: They asked me if I liked *Maxim* magazine or other magazines like it. I told them that I didn't like them because of the way they portrayed women. The large majority of women pictured in those

magazines are not real women. They've had breast implants, tummy tucks, lipo-suction and in many cases the actual photos have been altered. Every time I look at these women I get depressed about my own body and its imperfections compared to what society considers beautiful.

➤ Feb. 29: I do find that many of the conversations that the girls initiate with me or that they have with each other, sex is often the subject. My question is why are they so sex focused? It seems . . . their lives revolve around sex. They want to be fit so that they will look good, they want to look good so they can have a boyfriend, they want a boyfriend so they can have sex.

In some respects comments made by young women seem to fit the "promiscuous" model of teenagers, a paradigm predicated on the role of various cycles in teenage pregnancy, including poverty, welfare dependency, and child abuse (Kelly, 1996). However, forms of circular reasoning like this only perpetuate negative sociocultural, economic, and racial stereotypes about the young women in question.

## You Go Girl!

Although sex and the body are central to the experience of adolescence, theories of teenage sexuality, physical activity, global youth culture, and the media need to be thoughtfully interpreted and (re)evaluated, particularly for teenage mothers. Monitoring the depiction of young mothers in books, movies, and music videos is useful in understanding how they are represented within and by society.

The playful ways that the young mothers participated in gym activities is another instance where they demonstrated a complex and instructive mix of pragmatic, enjoyable, and sometimes challenging fitness experiences. Our overview of the *reclaiming, healthy maternal,* and *self-regulated* body identities illustrated how the mothers spoke of their bodies and health goals in relation to their daily lives. They conversed and enacted sexually charged behavioral scripts as mothers who care about their children, as youth who want to look sexy, and as young women looking for increased control over important aspects of their future—including their academic potential. Jennifer's willingness to engage in a reflective, cross-cultural dialogue about sex, the body, relationships, and health produced interesting results.

## Conclusions

The literature on physical activity for adolescent mothers is severely limited. As a first point, what this study provides is a glimpse at an effective approach to physical activity instruction for adolescent parents. This program worked because the physical activity instructors used culturally relevant pedagogical practices to develop a curricular program that was meaningful and relevant to the needs and interests of its student clientele. Given the young mothers' desires to develop bodies that would be attractive for current or potential sexual partners, both activity instructors delivered a fitness-oriented program that helped the women achieve their goals while expanding their overall health consciousness.

Second, by participating in culturally relevant physical activities, the young women experienced what we have identified as three personally and socially relevant constructions of self: reclaiming body identity, healthy maternal body identity, and a self-regulated body identity. Contrary to dominant stigma discourses about teenage mothers, this study illustrates how pregnancy can shape personal fitness goals in ways that enable young women to connect physical activity with health and well-being, particularly as they negotiate the intersecting demands of being a mother, student, girlfriend, daughter, worker, and the like. Although the young mothers here liked to focus on segments of their bodies that they perceived needed fixing (e.g., butts, abs, arms), they were also able to articulate how being active could give them energy and help them provide a positive role model for their children. Regarding the impact of daily physical activity intervention on their desires to attend school regularly, they also expressed an understanding of how the physical education provided a needed structure that was lacking in their life. The relationships developed with the physical activity instructors made them feel cared about, and gave them a sense of routine they did not experience in other aspects of their school day.

Third, our research is part of a call for a more sophisticated understanding of on-the-ground realities impacting and confronting youth, specifically teenage mothers, as they form their identities and sexuality, and make sense of their place in the world. Part of this task involves looking at the impact of various forms of media on young women. Our findings highlight the importance of examining how people use media because, as Craik (1994) has rightly said about everyday fashion, it does not merely "trickle down" from dictates of the elite, but changes according to gender, class, and social background.

A final consideration in our discussion of the gaps in the current paradigms of youth culture, sexuality, and physical activity involves the evolution of authentic models of adolescence and the hopeful devolution of dangerous and misrepresentative myths about teenagers and their social roles. Our research findings present differing possible explanations for expressions of sexuality, the use of media, and the role of the gym in identity performance. These explanations and experiences speak, first, to the determining role of culture and its "direct grip" (Bordo, 1993) on our bodies. Related to this comes the need to work toward frameworks addressing the role of macro sociocultural, economic, gender, and sexual forces in the formulation and expression of teenagers' identities. As our data shows, many of the current approaches are simplistic and do not "fit" or tell us anything about the complexity of different kinds of adolescent experiences.

The sexual discourses and communicative strategies of the young women in our study forced us to listen to and decipher their sexual vocabularies. Their seemingly unending store of sexual stories, jokes, and personal experiences provided exciting glimpses into the sexual-body rhetoric of marginal young women, while also opening up further areas for theoretical investigation of the speech, movement, and desires of mothers defying the *Maxim* model. In the lexicon of the *Maxim*-era teenage mom, there is more to "sexercise" than meets the eye.

### References

Bordo, S. (1993). *Unbearable weight. Feminism, western culture, and the body.* Berkeley: University of California Press.

CAAWS. (2002). *On the Move.* Canadian Association for the Advancement of Women in Sport. <http://www.caaws.ca/onthemove/index.htm>

Cappell's Circulation Report. (2002). *Maxim m*agazine named best circulation performer. <http://www.maximonline.com/press_room/20020117_best_circulation_performer.asp>

Carpenter, L. (1998). From girls into women: Scripts for sexuality and romance in *Seventeen* magazine, 1974–1994. *The Journal of Sex Research* 35(2): 158–168.

Craik, J. (1994). *The face of fashion. Cultural studies in fashion.* London: Routledge.

Erikson, E. (1950). *Childhood and society.* New York: W.W. Norton & Company.

———. (1968). *Identity: Youth and Crisis.* New York: W.W. Norton & Company.

Halas, J. (2001a). Playtime at the treatment centre: How physical activity helps troubled youth. *AVANTE 7* (2): 1–13.

———. (2001b). Shooting hoops at the treatment centre: Sport stories. *Quest* 53: 77–96.

Humphrey, A. (2001). Teen magazines: Girls read between the lines. *Voix Feministes/Feminist Voices* 12: 17–28.

Kahan, D. and Barnett, D. (1998). Appropriate physical education practices for pregnant adolescents. *Journal of Physical Education, Recreation and Dance* 69 (3): 34–37.

Kelly, D. (1996). Stigma stories. Four discourses about teen mothers, welfare, and poverty. *Youth and Society* 27 (4): 421–449.

Ladson-Billings, G. (1994). *The dreamkeepers: Successful teachers of African-American children.* San Francisco: Jossey-Bass.

Lupton, D. (1995). *The imperative of health.* London: SAGE Publications.

Orsini, P. (2002). *Adweek* top 10 list. *Adweek eastern edition.* <http://www.maximonline.com/press_room/20020302_adweek_top10.asp>

Sales, N.J. (2002). Girls, interrupted. *Vanity Fair* No. 505 ( September): 250–258.

Sparkes, A. (1999). Exploring body narratives. *Sport, Education and Society* 4 (1): 17–30.

Steele, J.R. (1999). Teenage sexuality and media practice: Factoring in the influences of family, friends, and school. *The Journal of Sex Research* 36 (4): 331–341.

Stenberg, L. and Blinn, L. (1993). Feelings about self and body during adolescent pregnancy. *Families in Society: The Journal of Contemporary Human Services* (May): 282–290.

# PART IV

# Broadcast Media Representations

# CHAPTER 12

# Television and Aerobic Sport: Empowerment and Patriarchy in *Denise Austin's Daily Workouts*

## Melissa Camacho

Traditionally, television coverage of sport has been dominated by coverage of what are considered "male" sporting events. More prevalent, it seems, is women's presence in television sport if their endeavors are less competitive, and/or the focus is on weight loss and "looking good," as opposed to athleticism. In particular, aerobic exercise classes, which use music to guide full-body movements that work the cardiovascular system, are commonly portrayed by the media as innovative means of losing "excess fat" and shedding "unwanted pounds," while promising a new physical appearance that will make one more sexually attractive and ultimately more desirable. While the media focus on sex and sex appeal in aerobics has toned down since the 1980s (Duffy and Rhodes, 1993), sexual rhetoric continues to be embedded in the overall aerobic media discourse.

This analysis critiques the aerobic discourse on Lifetime Television's *Denise's Fit & Lite* and *Denise Austin's Daily Workout*. Specifically, it looks at how this contemporary example of aerobic media text wants to reinforce traditional perceptions suggesting that aerobic exercise ("aerobics") is not an athletic activity, only a part of an overall weight loss regime for women. It discusses how these two texts maintain patriarchal definitions of feminine beauty and sexuality.

## AEROBICS: SPORTS VERSUS HOBBY

In 1968, a former Air Force medical officer, Dr. Kenneth H. Cooper introduced the concept of using exercise to build and maintain a healthy cardiovascular system. His research, conducted for and on young men, demonstrates that one can lose weight while engaging in exercise that improves circulation, increases lung capacity, and helps develop flexible blood vessels (Cooper, 1968, 1977). It led to the popularization of aerobic "dance," a 1970s activity requiring participants to follow strict choreography set to music (Brick, 1996), and "modern aerobics" led to a growth in interest and participation in exercising one's heart to music. But it was women, and not men, as Cooper originally thought, who became the primary participants of the sport.

Classes were full of highly choreographed routines, many incorporating sophisticated dance-like and sometimes unsafe movements (Duffy and Rhodes, 1993). Male participation was often encouraged by marketing aerobics as an alternative (Dean, 1987). Yet, as women are the primary participants of aerobic exercise, it has become less a "serious" athletic activity and more of a hobby (Feder, 1994). While aerobics is considered "dance" by some, it is, in reality, "movement oriented athletic conditioning . . . that coordinates upper body movement and lower body movement" (Brick, 1996, p.3). Like many sports, aerobics focuses on muscle strength, endurance, and flexibility. Unlike most male-driven sports, however, it is mostly non-competitive (Firebaugh, 1989). As a result, both critics and participants have come to usually identify aerobic exercise simply as a weight-loss activity for women.

## AEROBICS AND FEMINISM

The 1970s saw the entrance of more women into competitive and noncompetitive sports. However, the fact that aerobics is a female dominated, noncompetitive sport, as well as an activity used to promote weight-loss, has led some feminists to have multiple and often contradictory views about how feminist ideals may be both reflected and rejected in the sport (Real, 1999). For some, aerobics allows "command, control, and mastery over one's body, and consequently, one's life" (Eskes, Duncan, and Miller, 1998, p.319), while for others, such as MacNeill (1998), it "helps to uphold the feminine values of non-aggressiveness, non-competitiveness, and gracefulness" despite the liberating aspects of women's participation (p.207).

The 1990s unveiled a new look for aerobic exercise, with less dance-oriented choreography, so current routines are generally considered safer because they emulate "real life movements" using muscles the way as they would be in typical daily activities (Duffy and Rhodes, 1993, p.55). The majority of aerobic participants, as well as instructors, continue to be women. Recent studies show that "[d]espite talk of target heart rate and increased endurance, most aerobic [participants] exercised primarily to get slimmer—not healthier" (Duffy and Rhodes, 1993, p.52).

The fitness industry has experienced tremendous economic growth and social acceptance, thanks to marketing experts like Jack Lalanne and celebrities like Jane Fonda, Richard Simmons, Suzanne Sommers, and Cindy Crawford, who were able to use mass media as a means of converting their personal fitness and weight-loss regimes into commercial successes. Women continue to be their primary target. Marketing strategies have led to the mass commercialization of weight loss products, such as informational guides, diet books, audio/video workout tapes, and nutritional supplements (Markula 1995). It has also created a multibillion dollar sports apparel industry, which includes footwear and exercise clothing (Neporent, 1994). While this clothing is theoretically for comfort, much of the sports apparel available today is designed to make a woman appear more sexually appealing while wearing it. Navel-baring sports bras, thongs, and short spandex shorts are designed to accent and highlight a woman's physique while they are participating in a sporting event. Often, the marketing strategies for this apparel emphasize the "new" and more "desirable" woman, one who will achieve weight-loss goals.

Current fitness experts argue that aerobics is changing by focusing more on overall health benefits, as opposed to simply losing weight in order to achieve the "ideal" body type (Duffy and Rhodes, 1993). Still, aerobics continues to be packaged by the media as primarily a weight-loss activity. Media texts suggest doing aerobics will lead to higher self-esteem and social acceptance if one achieves a thinner, more muscular, and more sexually desirable body as the end result of participation.

## FEMINIST MEDIA RHETORICAL CRITICISM

In order to define the ideals with which women must negotiate while engaging aerobic media discourses, one must turn to a rhetorical analysis of the media text. According to Sillar and Groenbeck (2001), "Rhetoric, however defined specifically, always has been concerned with relationships between discourses and their power to influence or control information, identity, beliefs, attitudes, values, and behaviors" (p.31). Rhetoric incorporates humanly created artifacts or symbols, including performances, films, and advertisements, in order to understand "(how) people construct the worlds on which they live and how those worlds make sense to them" (Foss, Foss, and Griffin, 1999, p.7).

Markula (1995) poses that, "Women's relationships with the media image are contradictory: they struggle to obtain the ideal body, but they also find their battles ridiculous" (p.424). Popular magazines, marketing aerobics as an activity that women can engage in not only to be healthy, but to also be sexier, highlight masculinist ideals aerobics can reinforce.

## TELEVISION, RHETORIC, AND AEROBICS

Television brings to the private sphere what are traditionally public events, thus creating a paradox for women. On the one hand, women are invited to become participants in a forum that they may not usually be able to access; on the other, while women may benefit from participating from their homes, they are not being asked to leave this domestic sphere and enter a more public realm. By doing aerobics alone in the private space of her home, the would-be athlete is unable to publicly challenge these contradictory social messages.

Aerobic videos and television programming also highlight the power of visual rhetoric when engaging in aerobic exercise. Based on their research of a popular 1980s Canadian television aerobics program, *The 20 Minute Workout*, Kagan and Morse (1988) pose that many televised exercise routines use production techniques to emphasize and potentially enhance a woman's appearance. For example, camera work such as tilts (up and down) and pans (moving the camera straight across from one location to another) can give a single image multiple meanings dependent on how that image is being shown. Close-ups, and editing techniques can make an aerobic video seem as if it is intended *only for watching* women engaging in aerobic exercise, as opposed to encouraging participation in the exercise itself. The gaze can relate to the instructor's body, inviting looking, as opposed to participating, seeing her as a sexual object and heightening her sex appeal (Andres, 1987).

### Television, Aerobics, and the Promise

Duffy and Rhodes (1993) claim that the fitness industry of the 1990s produced less sexualized media representations of aerobic exercise.

Still, the media continues to confirm the perceived relationship between aerobics, weight-loss, and becoming more sexually desirable, as reflected in contemporary exercise videos that promise the participant-viewer a thinner, better, and more sexually appealing body if she follows the instructor's directions as seen as the videotape. The instructor, who asserts that those who follow her exercise and diet regime will obtain the "ideal" physique, makes this promise in two ways: While her instructions and other taped utterances discuss the physical benefits, the promise is also made *visually* by how she both role-models her looks in front of the camera, as well as how television directors decide to shoot her.

Sampling analyses of the television fitness programs *Denise's Fit & Lite* and *Denise Austin's Daily Workout* demonstrates how this contemporary daily fitness program's rhetorical strategies employed by the show's creators provide contradictory "truths" that women must contend with when engaging these televisual texts. It identifies rhetorical strategies intended to empower women through motivating them to take control of their health and well-being through aerobic exercise, as well as identifying, in the same text, those rhetorical strategies that encourage aerobic activity by reinforcing patriarchal values.

## EMPOWERMENT AND PATRIARCHY: WORKING OUT "WITH" DENISE AUSTIN

Unlike the retail video, which engages the participant-viewer in an unchanging relationship over time, daily television workouts rely on a certain amount of variety in order to engage viewers. Instructors are less likely to rely on their celebrity status, focusing more on their aerobic workouts as being easy and interesting enough for viewers to follow on a daily basis. Routines change, as do clothing and hairstyle of the instructor herself and, in some cases, the space in which the instructor teaches. However, the goal is the same: to provide guidance and advice on how to participate in aerobic activity.

*Denise Austin's Daily Workout* airs on the Lifetime Television for Women Cable Network. Owned by Carole Black, it is a network dedicated to providing advocacy and support as well as entertainment and information to women (McAdams, 1999). The network's official web site (Lifetime.com) states that its mission is to use "the power of the media to make a positive difference in the lives of women"; according to Brady (2001), it enjoys a media penetration rate of approximately 85 million homes. Austin also has her own web site (lifetimetv.com/shows/denise/meet/denise.html).

Most *Daily Workout* episodes follow an earlier Austin show titled *Denise's Fit & Light,* dedicated to teaching less strenuous exercise routines. Austin is both producer and host of both programs. A licensed fitness expert and author, she defines herself as a mother over 40 (Austin, 2001) whose goal has "always been to target women who want to stay in shape" (Anderson-Parrado, 2000, p.24). Each half-hour program airs weekdays back-to-back from 7–8 am, featuring Denise Austin instructing a 20-minute routine that the viewer can exercise along with, thus participating in the exercise "with" her. The routines include low/high impact aerobics, interval aerobics, step aerobics, and more recently, boxing and cardio-kickboxing (a combination of aerobic exercise routines and various forms of martial arts). Stretching, weight training, and/ or abdominal exercises follow the aerobic workouts.

### Methodology

A random time period was chosen for recording the episodes for this study. The episodes selected for this analysis were aired between December 13 to December 20, 2001. Those episodes dedicated to aerobics were included in the following analysis, while those episodes focusing solely on weight training or yoga were not. Interestingly, during the time period that these episodes were recorded, the Lifetime Network promoted Denise Austin's shows as ways to "reduce stress during the holidays" as well as "stay in shape for the New Year." However, the *Fit & Lite* and *Daily Workout* episodes made no reference to the holiday season.

It is important to note that, when applying rhetorical approaches to television, critics must question why the writers/producers of the medium choose the point of view from which they are discussing the subject matter. It is up to the critic to deconstruct what the creators of the text are saying through their choice of dialogue as well as overall production values (Vande Berg and Wenner, 1991). It is within this context that the text is being analyzed. The data is organized into three categories. The first, *rhetoric of empowerment*, includes comments made about women's health, strength, or other elements that appear to support the idea or "truth" that women can be empowered while participating in aerobic exercise. The second, *rhetoric of promise*, includes those rhetorical devices reinforcing the "contract" between the instructor and the participant-viewer that promises physical and/or emotional changes based on patriarchal ideals, which reinforce the idea that women should be thin, toned, and sexy. The third category, *rhetoric of commodification*, consists of rhetoric that links these conflicting values of aerobic exercise to the fitness industry. Within each of these categories, the linguistic and visual rhetorical strategies employed by the creators of the text will be discussed.

### The Rhetoric of Empowerment

Austin begins each televised workout by reminding the participant-viewer that she is their "personal trainer," bringing their workout into their own "bedroom or living room . . . wherever it is that [they] exercise" (12/18). There are no people on camera besides Austin during the aerobic workout. She directly addresses the television audience by directly speaking into the camera, a production technique that serves to establish a seemingly "one-on-one" relationship with the participant-viewer. Participant-viewers can usually see most of Austin's body, if not her whole frame, enabling them to follow her movements as she teaches. Throughout her instruction, she engages in what Delin (2001, p.71) refers to as aerobic "comments" that are made specifically to create "interpersonal relationships between the participant and the instructor." Some of Austin's comments are intended to motivate viewers to participate in the aerobic routine: "As long as you do something for you . . . even if its for a couple of minutes, if you're just starting out, soon you'll be able to do the whole show. That will be great! What an accomplishment!" (12/14).

There are other comments that intend to inspire women to (re)claim a healthy control over their bodies. For example, she reminds viewers that participating in aerobics can improve their quality of life, explaining that it will get oxygen flowing and help their bodies to have energy for the day. Doing aerobics is "doing something healthy" by fighting heart disease. She urges them to get rid of the negativity, to get aggressive. During high-intensity kickboxing she tells participants to "Feel strong, empower your body!" (12/13). Constantly, she encourages participant-viewers to challenge themselves: "YOU are better than you think you are, so do it!"

Austin also seeks to educate participants during the show, telling them that she is educated in kinesiology, nutrition, and aerobic instruction. During each episode, she discusses proper technique, safety precautions, and explains the importance of engaging in specific aerobic patterns.

## The Rhetoric of Promise

In addition to empowering rhetoric in the Denise Austin televisual texts come assertions claiming that viewer-participants can burn fat, lose weight, be sexy, and thus feel better if they do aerobics. It is a contract she strikes up with them, promising that if they follow her directions, they will see these specific results. For example, during one *Fit & Lite* episode (December 13, 2001), Austin announced that doing aerobics would increase energy, elevate moods, and help one look and feel great, adding that looking and feeling great would "improve that self esteem." Throughout her programs, she refers to her aerobic routines as "fat burning," "blasting" fat away.

Reshaping the body is also part of the promise. During a low-impact aerobic routine, Austin tells participant-viewers that they should consistently do aerobics because, "That is when you see that change in your body" (12/14). During interval training, she tells participant-viewers that they are, "Going to see new muscle groups" if they continue that particular routine (12/19). Sometimes she targets specific body parts, such as telling participants that if they lift their knees, they will, "Get rid of that gut . . . no more pot belly!" (12/14). In some cases, she highlights the body's potential for sex appeal, promising that, for example, boxing will make their arms not only "nice and shapely" but also "sexy looking" (12/18). During another episode she refers to "cottage cheese" thighs as one of the biggest problem areas for women; then, during a high-intensity aerobic routine, she discusses reshaping thighs "to the perfect size," claiming that if one did the specific exercises she was doing, she would have "sexy thighs" and nice looking legs (ibid.)

Visually, the contract is further reinforced. Austin instructs each workout in sports apparel that is skin tight, low-cut, and oftentimes extremely revealing. She often wears extremely short spandex or mini 'biker' shorts with a tight-fitting, cleavage revealing halter-top. Her flat abdomen, including her navel, is exposed. Once in a while she will sport a high-cut body suit, revealing the full length of her legs. Not wearing tights or sleeves, only socks and athletic shoes, she is extremely sun-tanned, but has no apparent tan-lines on her body.

While the camera captures her movements in medium or long shots, there are a few brief instances where the camera gazes at her body. For example, during one interval training session, the camera focused for a few seconds on her breasts as she reached over to demonstrate a move. During a *Daily Workout Fat-Burning Rock Aerobics* (12/18), the camera moved in close to her body and slowly panned upward from below her waist to her chest as she talked about how aerobics would transform one's physique. While these instances last no more than a few seconds then that, her body appears fragmented and objectified.

All this takes place within the public sphere not only of television, but also at the location from which her shows are being taped. Austin does not televise her programs from a sound stage or an aerobics studio; instead, she tapes from various vacation spots in North America and the Caribbean, where she exercises on beaches or surrounded by lush vegetation or majestic mountains. In effect, she is creating a three dimensional experience through television. By showing her exercise at locations such as Boca Raton, Disney World Resorts in Florida, the Bahamas, Jamaica, or exclusive health spas of northern California, the camera serves as a point of entry, an entrance into a world of luxury and relaxation. Austin invites them to experience these locations as they exercise from the private sphere of their home. She is offering yet another promise: exercise with her, if viewer-participants too will also share the experience of being at these various resorts, without having to leave home. They appear to be given entry into these public locales, even though Austin promises to bring her exercise programs directly to their private homes.

### The Rhetoric of Commodification

Not only does taping Austin's shows at various resort locations promise the participant-viewer entry into a public, albeit idealistic, place, they also commercialize the aerobic environment. These scenic backdrops make her programs advertisements. In each episode, Austin introduces the location, often sounding like a commercial spokesperson, such as: "Isn't it beautiful behind me? That's the Grand Floridian. It's a great beach and spa . . . it's a perfect place to come and visit and stay and oooh, soothe your body" (12/18). The episodes taped at the Disney Resorts featured Austin wearing athletic apparel with the Disney logo. It was not her body, but the Disney trademark that was being featured visually, as the Disney-brand apparel provided more coverage than Austin's other outfits.

Austin not only advertises the locations from which she is instructing, she also serves as a commercial spokesperson for a variety of products and services related to the fitness industry. These commercials air regularly during each episode, some at the beginning of the program, others dispersed throughout the half-hour spot. She recommends drinking Dannon™ Natural Spring Water as part of a healthy daily routine as she sits on a weight bench surrounded by dumbbells. In another advertisement, she "treats her family to a little fun" by blending healthy shakes for them in an Osterizer™ blender—exposing her domesticity, as her husband and children sit by the fire and play while she blends their snack in their kitchen.

The longest and most sophisticated advertising is a commercial for the LPG™ Cellulite Treatment Center, featuring Denise Austin exercising in what appears to be a home. She is in front of a giant television screen on which we can see her exercising. The ad then shows her lying down on a table while a masseuse appears to break down her cellulite by using a handheld machine on her thighs. Contrary to her promises of obtaining "sexy thighs" by following her aerobics routine, the advertisement suggests that her workout is not effective enough to reshape her own thighs.

Toward the end of each half-hour episode of both *Fit & Lite* and *Daily Workout* a specific video series, titled *Denise Austin's Short Cuts*, is advertised as providing maximum weight loss and body reshaping results "over minimum amounts of time." This ad is followed by the final segment of each episode, dedicated to providing specific advice about exercise and products. Sometimes Austin will answer questions and demonstrate fitness techniques in immediate response to a question posed on camera, but it is unclear if questioners are aerobics participants or spectators. During these segments, she does not advertise products, but is still advertising her expertise as she guides the person through a specific exercise, much as one would expect during a personal training session in a health club or fitness center.

Other episodes feature a final segment titled *Denise's Daily Wisdom*, which are also dedicated to answering what she defines as "Commonly Asked Questions" about health and fitness. While it also packages her as an expert in the field, she will sometimes complement her tips with product promotion. One *Daily Wisdom* segment, for example, features Austin discussing back pain and posture from what appears to be the staircase of her home. She also recommends the use of shoe inserts, and names the specific brand she likes to use. Following the brief monologue, Austin reminds participant-viewers that they deserve to feel good, be healthy, and ends by wishing them a great day.

## CONCLUDING DISCUSSION

While the Denise Austin programs focus considerably on the physical and emotional health benefits of engaging in aerobic activity, the series discourse also contain rhetorical strategies confirming patriarchal values of femininity. These televisual texts, marketed toward women, contain verbal and visual references to what masculinist ideals identify as the beautiful woman: thin, toned, and sexy. Austin herself reinforces this value system with her sporadic use of the term "sexy," as well as her continuous promises of a better looking body, or, at least, some better looking body parts. Her wardrobe, while worn to instruct women, exposes the parts of her body that appear to invite a "gaze" from audiences. Her clothing reveals body parts that are considered beautiful and sexy according to patriarchal values, including long muscle-toned legs, thin thighs, a flat stomach, firm bosom, and thin, graceful arms.

While the camera work occasionally fragments her body, it is Denise Austin's comments about individual and problematic body parts that tend to cause greater objectification. Most of the time the show is produced to allow participant-viewers to see most of Austin's body in its entirety, but much of this visual rhetoric juxtaposes the comments about specific body parts. While attempting to motivate, the fitness celebrity points out body parts that are problematic or that need to be enhanced. This verbal fragmentation of the body also objectifies it.

Clearly, both *Daily Workout* and *Fit & Lite* are marketing tools for the tourism industry. Furthermore, the show's use of these exotic backdrops, combined with Austin's invitations to join her at these locations, tends to reinforce the definition of aerobics as a recreational activity. Other advertisements reflect the role of aerobics in the overall fitness industry. Although most of the product advertising airing throughout her shows does not discuss aerobics specifically, Austin's promised results from the various aerobic sports she teaches are further highlighted. Her visibility in these advertisements reminds audiences of the contract she has with them, even if she is not exercising. She is still telling participant-viewers to follow her example. Participant-viewers are encouraged to buy not only into her ideas and expertise, but also to buy into the overall fitness industry.

Meanwhile, contradictions are evident between what Austin says while teaching aerobics versus what the products she endorses have to offer. While she promises results from her workout, her endorsements perpetuate the idea that additional products and services must also be purchased in order to ensure these results. Thus, participant-viewers must contend with the series' overall mediated messages that selling aerobics as the way to achieve the perfect body, and selling the idea that no matter how much aerobic exercise they do, it will still not be enough to reach the beautiful and sexy physique they should be striving for. They are encouraged to engage in aerobic exercise to improve both physically and emotionally, and are congratulated in their efforts. But they are also being told that what they do will never be enough unless they purchase products and services perfecting the already "positive" results they have achieved through aerobic exercise.

The language used in the Denise Austin television shows indicates that the definition of aerobics endorsed by the media has changed from dance and celebrity enterprise to fitness and health. It also demonstrates that, despite this change, aerobics is still presented by the media primarily as means to look thinner and be more sexually appealing. While the media texts analyzed here provide messages promoting aerobics as a tool for female empowerment, these messages conflict, and as the preceding discussion suggests, are often overshadowed by the fitness industry's attempts to sell ideas, products, and services promising women a body and self-image reflecting patriarchal standards. It is these truths that women must contend with when engaging the mediated discourse of aerobic exercise.

## References

Andersen-Parrado, P. (2000). Denise Austin. *Better nutrition* 62, 2 (February): 24–25.

Andres, K. (1987). Is there too much sex in aerobics? *The starting line: Women and sport = le point de depart: les femmes et le sport* 6 (2): 24.

Austin, D. (2001). *Fit and fabulous after 40.* New York: Broadway Books.

Bialeschki, D.M. (1990). The feminist movement and women's participation in physical recreation. *Journal of Physical Education, Recreation, and Dance* 61 (1): 45.

Brady, D. (2001). "Television for women": No one's laughing now. *Business Week* 1, 3763 (December 24): 56–58.

Brick, L. (1996). *Fitness aerobics.* Champaign, IL: Human Kinetics Publishers.

Cooper, K.H. (1968). *Aerobics.* New York: Simon & Schuster.

———. (1977). *The aerobics way.* New York: M. Evans and Co.

Dean, L.T. (1987). How aerobics scores with men. Is your class a grand slam or a strikeout? *Dance Exercise Today* 5 (8): 46–49.

Delin, J. (2001). Keeping in step: task structure, discourse structure, and utterance interpretation in the step aerobics workout. *Discourse Processes* 31 (1): 61–89.

Duffy, M and Rhodes, M. (1993). Aerobics get real. *Women's Sports & Fitness* 15 (8): 52, 55.

Eskes, T., Duncan, M.C., and Miller, E.M. (1998). The discourse of empowerment: Foucault, Marcuse, and women's fitness texts. *Journal of Sport & Social Issues* 22 (3): 317–344.

Feder, A. (1994). A radiant smile from a lovely lady. *TDR: The Drama Review* 38 (1): 62–79.

Firebaugh, G. (1989). Gender differences in exercise and sports. *Sociology & Social Research* 73 (2): 59–64.

Foss, K.A., Foss, S.K., and Griffin, C.L. (1999). *Feminist rhetorical theories.* Thousand Oaks: Sage.

Hundley, H. (2002). The evolution of gendercasting: The lifetime television network—"Television for women." *Journal of Popular Film and Television* 29 (4): 174–182.

Kagan, E. and Morse, M. (1988). The body electronic: Aerobic exercise on video: Women's search for empowerment and self-transformation. *The Drama Review* 32 (Winter): 164–180.

Loland, N.W. (1998). Body image and physical activity: A survey among Norwegian men and women. *International Journal of Sport Psychology* 29: 339–365.

Mac Neill, M. (1998). Active women, media representations, and ideology. In *Not just a game: Essays in Canadian Sport Sociology,* ed., Harvey, J. and Cantelon, H. 195–211. Ottawa: University of Ottawa Press.

Markula, P. (1995). Firm but shapely, fit but sexy, strong but thin: The postmodern aerobicizing female bodies. *Sociology of Sport Journal* 12: 424–453.

McAdams, D. (1999). Opportunity of a lifetime: Carole Black girds Lifetime for its first direct challenges. *Broadcasting & Cable* (October 18): 22–23, 28–29.

Neporent, L. (1994). Can you remember a time when sports bras and aerobics shoes didn't exist? *Women's Sports and Fitness* 16 (1): 76.

Real, Michael. (1999). Aerobics and feminism: Self-determination or patriarchal hegemony? In *Sportcult,* ed. Martin, R. and Miller, T., 132–150. Minneapolis, MN: University of Minnesota Press.

Sillars, Malcolm O. and Groenbeck, Bruce E. ( 2001). *Communication criticism: Rhetoric, social codes, cultural studies.* Prospect Heights, IL: Waveland Press.

Vande Berg, L. and Wenner, L. (1991). *Television criticism: Approaches and applications.* New York, NY: Longman Press.

# CHAPTER 13

# We Don't Glow, We Sweat: The Ever Changing Commentary about Women's Athletics

## James R. Hallmark

Sexist broadcast commentary has probably been around for as long there have been commentators. The fictional "Newsreel" footage from the 1994 film *A League of Their Own* is typical, with statements such as, "Legging out a triple is no reason to let your nose get shiny. Betty Grable has nothing on these gals!" We wag our heads at statements like this today. That was another time, another era. Modern America would never tolerate such sexist commentary. Right?

Wrong! The more things change, the more they stay the same. To illustrate this point, Penny Hastings (1999) wrote of a male basketball player whose "chest muscles rippled beneath his jersey as he went in for the lay-up. He's 6 foot 4 inches, with dark wavy hair and deep brown eyes; he's drop dead gorgeous . . . a real hunk." Seem absurd? If this fictional description is absurd, Hastings asks, why does *Sports Illustrated* publish this commentary on Olympic figure skating champion Katarina Witt: "So fresh-faced, so blue-eyed, so ruby-lipped, so 12-car pileup gorgeous, 5 feet 5 inches and 114 pounds worth of peacekeeping missile."

Clearly, sexist commentary of female sport continues unabated, seemingly unfazed by larger societal changes. The problem is not limited to media, nor is it sport-specific; indeed, it is pervasive (see Kinnick, 1998), and it bears continued observation and study.

True, women's sports have come a long way since days of almost nonexistent coverage, or depictions of "upgrading a woman's maternal capacity" (Hutchens and Townsend, 1998, p.2). Now, most absurdly sexist talk is gone, and women's sports broadcasting has become prevalent (Bruce, 1998).

Still, an amount of media coverage does not inherently result in equitable coverage. How producers, editors, and announcers comment on women's sports are important determinants. In fact, demeaning or patronizing coverage may be worse than no coverage, keeping women subjugated to men in athletic competition. This study focuses on the preferred reading of broadcast narrative through an analysis of the 2002 NCAA Women's National Basketball Championship using the construct of hegemony and the framework of fantasy theme analysis relative to media depictions of the women athletes and their coaches.

## Literature Review

This is not an under-researched issue (e.g., Duncan and Messner, 2000; Kane, 1996), the former providing a comprehensive examination of the issues and the changing tides, the latter an excellent literature review with a useful classification of the issues such as "hierarchy of naming," "trivialization and sexualization," "asymmetrical gender marking," "ambivalence," and so on. Identifying common barriers to gender equity in media coverage include:

- "Marking" women's broadcasts, such as saying it is the "women's final four" without comparably designating the men's game (e.g., Koivula, 1999). When the National Basketball Association began its "women's" league, officials chose to call it the "Women's National Basketball Association" but made no comparable effort to label the extant league the "Men's National Basketball Association" (Duncan, 1993).
- Demeaning the contribution of women athletes by downplaying their athleticism. Duncan & Hasbrook (1988), for example, have noted more negative announcer comments during women's championship games, concluding such commentary that "trivialized the women's efforts or implied that they were unsuited to sport" (p.18).
- Focusing on women athletes' physically attractive attributes (e.g., beautiful hair, legs, smiles, etc.) and/or their personal lives (e.g., children, husbands, etc). In some cases, women athletes are treated as sex objects (Banet-Weiser, 1999; Bruce, 1998; Duncan and Messner, 2000; Eastman and Billings, 2000; Hastings, 1999; Kane, 1996; Kinnick, 1998; Koivula, 1999, 2001; Silverstein, 1996).

- Devoting less broadcast time to women's sporting events, particularly women's team sports (Duncan and Messner, 2000; Hastings, 1999; Koivula, 1999; Silverstein, 1996; Tuggle 1997; Tuggle and Owen, 1999).
- Using less sophisticated production techniques for women's broadcasts (Duncan and Messner, 2000; Hallmark and Armstrong, 1999).

## Preferred Readings, Hegemony, and Fantasy Themes

Kane (1996) provides an excellent illustration of the potential power of language in sports; focusing on the August 28, 1999 *Sports Illustrated* cover of tennis star Chris Evert where she proclaimed, "I'm going to be a full time mom"; she wrote: "One concern is the suggestion that Evert has completed her career as a professional woman, and thus it is time for her to put all else aside and return to her 'proper' sphere, the home . . ." The editors presented a specific slant to the story, emphasizing "domestic" Chris Evert rather than "athletic."

Stuart Hall (1980) refers to this type of biased "slant" as a "preferred reading." Consumers with reason to doubt the veracity of preferred readings may "argue" the case and oppose them (Bruce, 1998; Kane, 1996), but rarely do so. His theory is consistent with Ernest Bormann's (1972, 1985) fantasy themes and symbolic convergence theories, arguing that people create readings of events to fulfill their own needs. As the group accepts fantasies, they become "rhetorical visions" of events when the fantasy rises to the level of culturally perceived "truth." Media discourse presenting fantasy themes subjugating women athletes is hegemonic; in concert with the actions of women athletes, it acts as a fantasy theme reinforcing a rhetorical vision and giving birth to additional preferred readings subjugating women's athletics. In short, it is a cycle.

## Methodology

The women's National Collegiate Athletic Association (NCAA) Division I basketball championship game, as presented by ESPN, was videotaped on March 31, 2002. The cable sports channel's coverage began approximately 45 minutes before "tip-off" and concluded 10 minutes after the final buzzer, some 2 hours and 55 minutes later.

A professional video service removed the visual portion, leaving only the audio—which was then divided into eleven 15-minute units and one ten-minute unit and distributed to coders for analysis (ten communication graduate students enrolled in a research methodology course, unaware of the specific research focus but knowledgeable of the literature discussing gender differences in sports broadcasts). They were instructed to listen for bias in these categories: marking comments on appearance, personal status, emotional dependence, nicknames, hierarchy of naming, devaluing labels, personality traits, past successes or failures, confidence in victory, humility, attribution of success, and "other," categories based on a comprehensive literature review. Separately, the author reviewed the videotape in an effort to qualitatively identify its themes/preferred readings.

## Preferred Readings

Three primary themes emerged even before play began, as the pre-game show established the preferred readings for the broadcast: "Connecticut's Invincibility," "Women's Basketball is For Real," and "Damsel in Distress." These preferred readings provided the framework through which ESPN expected viewers to interpret and understand the contest. In addition, the preferred readings illustrate hegemony in women's sports broadcasts.

### Connecticut's Invincibility

Before the 2001–2002 basketball season, only three women's teams had completed their seasons undefeated since the NCAA began administering women's basketball (Texas in 1986, Connecticut in 1995, Tennessee in 1998), and only three others had done so prior to NCAA governance (Immaculata in 1973, Delta State in 1975, Louisiana Tech in 1981). The 2002 Connecticut team (aka "U.Conn") would be the fourth NCAA team to finish the season undefeated and the only team to have completed the feat twice.

One preferred reading of the broadcast was, therefore, the perceived invincibility of the 2001–2002 Connecticut Huskies women's basketball team. Indeed, the pregame show began with ESPN veteran and former college basketball player sportscaster Robin Roberts' rhetorical question, "Will we see history tonight?" referring to the rare feat of an undefeated national champion, and producers devoted more than two minutes to a feature on U.Conn's undefeated season.

Roberts questioned her colleagues about the "best team ever." Nell Fortner, coach of the WNBA's Indiana Fever, stressed that if Connecticut won that evening they would become the "measuring stick" by which analysts would assess future teams, how it led the nation in five key categories and had lost only nine times in four years. Vera Jones, color analyst for the New York Liberty of the Women's National Basketball Association, took a different approach, stating that prior to that season, the 1983 and 1984 teams of the University of Southern California had been the best but, after seeing U.Conn, she was convinced they were the greatest. Ann Meyers, perhaps the greatest pioneer in women's basketball, was more cautious, stating that there have been many great teams, and the "best team ever" question is one that may never be answered. And the woman who has probably had more experience on the basketball court than any other, Nancy Lieberman, used an engine metaphor stressing that U.Conn had more "engines," more means by which they could score against Oklahoma; asserting they had the best starting lineup in history and were the best ever passing team; she concluded their record was sufficient evidence.

The theme of Connecticut's invincibility permeated the entire broadcast. Oklahoma was admired for their tenacity and persistence, but the preferred broadcast reading was that it was no match for the superior U.Conn juggernaut. Consider these commentator examples:

- Nancy Lieberman: "Since I arrived in San Antonio, everybody's asked me, 'Nancy, how do you beat U.Conn?' "
- Nell Fortner, before tip-off, that U.Conn was about "kickin' it in and goin'."
- Robin Roberts' final comment before the second half: "Will it be the Huskies finishing with a perfect record?" (Like Fortner, she made no mention of Oklahoma.)
- Mike Patrick, the game's "play-by-play" announcer, made numerous comments throughout the broadcast: "All U.Conn has done is match the best ever allowing only 51.1 points per game over the course of the season"; "U.Conn trying to go 39 and 0 and win a national title, up by 12 at the half over the Sooners of Oklahoma"; "Number 1 and undefeated Connecticut playing the Sooner"; "U.Conn only trailed 15 minutes the entire season"; and, in reference Connecticut player Sue Bird, "She started 117 games for the Huskies and won 113 of them."

Even pregame interviews with the coaches focused on U.Conn's invincibility. Oklahoma's chance, it was argued, was winning only one game, and "Anything can happen." Oklahoma's coach, Sherri Coale, said to ABC/ESPN sportscaster Michelle Tafoya, "You know the great thing is we don't have to beat 'em best out of seven. We just got to beat 'em once."

U.Conn won convincingly. The theme of its invincibility was reinforced in postgame broadcasts, particularly in interviews following the trophy presentation. Michelle Tafoya talked with Connecticut coach Geno Auriemma: "39 and 0. It's only been done once before . . . Can you yet grasp how special this is?" Auriemma responded, "No, I don't think I can." He became overcome with emotion, and Tafoya turned to Connecticut's team leader, Sue Bird, who said "We're the greatest," quickly modified to "*one* of the greatest teams."

### Women's Basketball is "For Real"

Certainly, the theme that women's basketball had come of age and is equal to men's basketball was another preferred reading of this broadcast. During the pregame show, one compelling, carefully choreographed and well-written segment featured various women stars standing alone in front of a microphone, each one providing only a few words of the total narrative, such as: "Play me soft and I'll make you pay . . . My strength is my beauty . . . My scars are my beauty marks of courage on the floor, on the court, on the field and in the back of your mind taken' you off your game . . . I have the power . . . I am the power . . . I got skills . . . This little girl will not be stopped . . . For all the little girls who just wanted to play."

The features, repeated several times during the broadcast, were cleverly produced and interesting to watch. Dozens of prominent women athletes from various sports conveyed the message stated succinctly with one anonymous voice, "I don't glow, I sweat."

In her postgame commentary, Vera Jones stated, "Being here in San Antonio has made me have a greater appreciation for how far this sport has come. To think of sellout crowd of near 30,000. It not only speaks to exactly how far this game has come but exactly where it's going." A theme stressed throughout was that the women's game "has arrived." ESPN actually stressed the theme too hard. The features were clever and cute, but were so heavily produced and so transparently persuasive that their effectiveness was likely limited to reinforcing the convictions of true believers, already fans of women's basketball. In short, the interaction of belief and action can create rhetorical vision, not staged and mediated rhetoric.

### Damsel in Distress

Unquestionably, the most significant example of hegemony in the broadcast comes in the "damsel in distress" theme that was played throughout, especially in the pregame show. The basic theme here is that Oklahoma's coach would not be where she is were it not for the intervention of the male coach in this game, Connecticut's Geno Auriemma, who "helped get her that job." Auriemma was portrayed as the "master," while Coale was relegated to a "cheerleading" role. Commentators consistently portrayed Coale as happy, almost a little puppy dog.

Still, most video shots of Coale was of her crouched on the sideline—cheering and clapping. In perhaps the most telling reinforcement of this rhetorical vision, the announcers tacitly criticized her for poor strategy. Late in the game, trailing by several points, Oklahoma was slow to foul, with this commentary:

> *Patrick*: "Here's my questions, why do you waste the first ten seconds and then commit the obvious foul?"
>
> *Meyers*: "I don't think that they were sure on what to do, letting too much time run off the clock, and Sherri Coale you know, loosing to Geno Auriemma."

Importantly, the camera focused on Coale during this exchange, clearly directing the mistake to her lack of leadership. The end of Meyer's comment may be instructive as well: she did not finish her statement, which is probably just as well, as she appeared to be poised to make a critical comment of Coale's leadership.

This preferred reading of damsel in distress contains two very clear themes. First, the happy little lady is here in the national championship game only because Prince Charming intervened on her behalf and continued to guide, encourage, and advise her through the rebuilding process. Second, he is the master teacher/tactician while she is a cheerleader. It plays well in American society, as it is consistent with the collective rhetorical vision. That Coale played to this theme and openly acknowledged her dependence on Auriemma is classic hegemony.

## But All is Not Bad . . .

Despite what one may conclude from the above narrative, ESPN's production of the 2002 NCAA Division I women's basketball championship game is actually quite good. Sans the "damsel in distress" reading, there is very little of concern here. There were still many advertisements for the men's championship game during the women's game, and broadcasters referred to players as "kids" three times, but no one called the players as "girls."

Patrick and Meyers unnaturally referred to the players by their first and last names almost as though the names were one (Suebird, Staceydales, Catonhill, and such). They appeared to be uncomfortable calling the women solely by their last names, as they would in a men's game. A time or two, Meyers called players by their first names.

A few irrelevant and gender-specific references were made through the broadcast. Meyers chose to inform us that, "Caton Hill for 8 years took dance, jazz and tap and piano," and later that Dales was "going to have a busy next couple of weeks, getting married to her fiancé Chris Shuman who she met in class," but they were the exceptions. Commentators largely stayed focused on the game and avoided most overtly sexist commentary. Frequently, the game was not even "marked" as the "women's national championship game" but simply as The Championship; Robin Roberts saying several times that they were about to crown the national champion. ESPN produced it as a basketball game, not as a women's basketball game. The commentators' language, with exceptions as noted earlier, focused on the game and skills of the players, giving great credibility to the second preferred reading: Women's basketball is for real.

## IMPLICATIONS AND QUESTIONS

While this broadcast represents progress in the media's preferred reading of women's athletics, some troubling issues remain. The "damsel in distress" reading continues to perpetuate a damaging rhetorical vision that women need men's help to succeed. A second component of this theme is equally troubling: Sherri Coale did not take a program from nonexistence to the national title game by being a cheerleader. Accomplishing what she has requires intelligence, skill, determination, hard work, and yes, a little cheerleading. Presenting a theme where the man is wise and the woman is emotional is frighteningly consistent with stereotypical hegemony: the rhetorical vision of the distribution of logic and emotion among genders.

On the theoretical side, it is useful to look at the interplay of the three distinct theories combined for this analysis. While Hall's preferred reading and Bormann's symbolic convergence theories are quite similar, the layering of hegemony on top provides potential ground for fruitful research. For example, is hegemony an inherent part of a dominant paradigm's preferred reading? Can a society-wide rhetorical vision exist that does not suppress, through hegemony, one or more groups? If so, what would this rhetorical vision "look like?" What characteristics would be necessary to achieve such a vision that does not engage in hegemony? What role does the media play in reinforcing this hegemony, particularly as it relates to women's athletics? The interplay of these three theoretical perspectives gives opportunity for future research.

Finally, remember that the media's preferred reading is constantly changing while the rhetorical vision of society shifts more subtly. Is the preferred reading a reflection of the rhetorical vision, or is the rhetorical vision a reflection of the reading? Does the rhetorical vision rely on the preferred reading for its formation? More contemplation is necessary to comment definitively on this question and, much like being the "greatest team ever," it may never be fully answered.

Continuing research on these issues is vital. Monitoring the preferred reading is essential both because of the pervasive influence of the media and the important role sport plays in American society. Kane (1996) has stated, "Perhaps more than any other social institution, sport reflects, constructs, and perpetuates beliefs about male superiority and female inferiority" (p.106). Her comment is both powerful and wise, but I suggest a slightly different interpretation: It is not sport that reflects, constructs, or perpetuates these beliefs, but rather our rhetorical vision of sport. The media, through its presentation of preferred readings, reinforces this rhetorical vision.

Women's games have, indeed, come a long way. Ultimately, however, this must be proclaimed by entities other than current and former women's basketball players and/or those with financial interests in its perceived legitimacy to be taken as anything other than rhetoric. Productions such as ESPN's 2002 NCAA Division I championship game may move women's athletics toward perceived legitimacy by focusing on the talents of the players. The media must do this, however, without simultaneously presenting hegemonic themes that subjugate the participants.

## References

Banet-Weiser, S. (1999). Hoop dreams: Professional basketball and the politics of race and gender. *Journal of Sport and Social Issues* 23 (4): 403–420.

Bormann, E. (1972). Fantasy and rhetorical vision: The rhetorical criticism of social reality. *Quarterly Journal of Speech* 58: 396–407.

———. (1985). *The force of fantasy: Restoring the American dream.* Carbondale: Southern Illinois.

Bruce, T. (1998). Audience frustration and pleasure. *Journal of Sport and Social Issues* 22 (4): 373–398.

Duncan, M.C. (1993). Representation and the gun that points backwards. *Journal of Sport and Social Issues* 17 (1): 42–46.

Duncan, M.C. and Hasbrook, C.A. (1988). Denial of power in televised women's sports. *Sociology of Sport Journal* 5 (1): 1–21.

Duncan, M.C. and Messner, M.A. (2000). *Gender in Televised Sports: 1989, 1993 and 1999.* Los Angeles: Amateur Athletic Foundation.

Eastman, S.T., and Billings, A.C. (2000). Sportscasting and sports reporting. *Journal of Sport and Social Issues* 24 (2): 192–214.

Hall, S. (1980). Encoding/decoding. In *Culture, Media, Language,* ed. Hall, S., Hobson, D., Lowe, A., and Willis P., 128–138. London: Hutchinson.

———. (1985). Signification, representation, ideology: Althusser and the post-structuralist debates. *Critical Studies in Mass Communication* 2 (2): 91–114.

Hallmark, J.R. and Armstrong, R.N. (1999). Gender equity in televised sports: A comparative analysis of men's and women's NCAA Division I basketball championship broadcasts, 1991–1995. *Journal of Broadcasting & Electronic Media* 43 (2): 222–235.

Hastings, P. (1999). Sports language 101: Tracking gender bias in the media. *Knight–Ridder News Service* (April 13). <http://web6.infotrac.galegroup.com>

Hutchens, L.C. and Townsend, B.K. (1998). Gender equity in collegiate sports: The role of athletic associations. *Initiatives* 58 (4): 1–17.

Kane, M.J. (1996). Setting a course for college athletics: Media coverage of the post title IX female athlete: A feminist analysis of sport, gender, and power. *Duke Journal of Gender Law & Policy* 3 (1): 105–117.

Kinnick, K.N. (1998). Gender bias in newspaper profiles of 1996 Olympic athletes: A content analysis of five major dailies. *Women's Studies in Communication.* <http://www.cios.org>

Koivula, N. (1999). Gender stereotyping in televised media sport coverage. *Sex Roles* 41 (7/8): 589–604.

———. (2001). Perceives characteristics of sports categorized as gender-neutral, feminine and masculine. *Journal of Sport Behavior* 24 (4): 377–394.

Silverstein, S. (1996). *Full-court press? The New York Times' coverage of the 1995 women's NCAA basketball tournament.* Paper presented to the Commission on the Status of Women at the annual meeting of the Association for Education in Journalism and Mass Communication, Anaheim, CA. (ERIC Document Reproduction Service No. 400 551.)

Tuggle, C.A. (1997). Differences in television sports reporting of men's and women's athletics: ESPN SportsCenter and CNN Sports Tonight. *Journal of Broadcasting and Electronic Media* 41 (1): 14–24.

Tuggle, C.A. and Owen, A. (1999). A descriptive analysis of NBC's coverage of the centennial Olympics. *Journal of Sport & Social Issues* 23 (2): 171–182.

# PART V

# Visual Media Representations

# CHAPTER 14

# Game Face: Sports Reporters' Use of Sexualized Language in Coverage of Women's Professional Tennis

## Kimberly L. Bissell

*If you went into a supermarket today in . . . Omaha, and walked up to a mother balancing three children on a grocery cart and asked her to name a top female tennis player, my guess is that she wouldn't give you just one name, she'd probably give you three, four or even five: Venus, Serena, Jennifer, Anna (of course), not necessarily in that order, with a Monica, Martina or Lindsay sprinkled in. Ask this same woman to name a top male player, and she probably would struggle after she got past the requisite André and Pete. It's getting to the point where much of the nation is on a first-name basis with the women who play tennis.*

—Christine Brennan, *USA Today*

Tennis, female athletes in general, and the news media particularly have all evolved dramatically since the 1970s. Despite an equal number of players on the professional circuit and an equal number of tournaments on the professional circuit, female tennis players still have not received news media coverage comparable to male players. Furthermore, coverage of female players seems to focus more on demeanor, dress, and personal lifestyles and focus less on the on-court activities. This essay focuses on the type of coverage top female tennis players have received in newspapers throughout the country over the last 25 years.

In addition to becoming household names over the years, professional female tennis players have made great strides in breaking down the gender barrier on the court. Gender inequities within the frame of tennis parallel coverage of other men's and women's sports. While audiences have witnessed changes in the news coverage of female players, much of this coverage still seems to reinforce notions of traditional gender roles and male hierarchy. Photographs of André Agassi, Pete Sampras, and Andy Roddick have far exceeded the number of photographs of Jennifer Capriati, Venus Williams, or Justine Henin. Furthermore, many newspaper and magazine articles about male players are longer and have more prominent placement within the sports sections. On the flip side, take the case of Anna Kournikova, who has received media attention not for her play on the court but rather her sexuality. Coverage of Kournikova aside, female athletes and athletics, in general, still remain largely invisible in the media. Studies of broadcast coverage of women's sports have found that fewer than five percent of televised sports news covered women's sports, and approximately five percent of newspaper stories are devoted to female athletics or athletes (Tuggle, 1997).

Because of tennis' social acceptability in the ranks of female athletics, we have subsequently witnessed great increases in female participation in the sport. The number of women participating professionally in tennis has tripled between 1978 and 1998, while attendance, prize money, and media coverage of women's tennis have also increased over the last two decades. General media coverage of female players has also contributed to interest in the sport; for example, recent coverage of the Williams sisters, Venus and Serena, and their involvement with various advertising campaigns has arguably helped generate interest in the game.

## LITERATURE REVIEW

### Inequities in Coverage of Male and Female Athletics

We have witnessed steady progress over the last quarter century toward equity in the participation and funding of female athletics (Hallmark and Armstrong, 1999); however, general media coverage of female athletics has not witnessed such a turn-around. The inequity in coverage of male and female sports is manifested in column inches of stories, the placement of articles within the newspaper, the use of art on the page, and the range of sports and athletes depicted (Tuggle, 1997).

The trends in newspaper coverage of male and female athletes appear to be fairly consistent in studies conducted over the last decade. For example, Calia (1993) analyzed coverage of women's sports in college newspapers before and after Title IX, finding that men's sports were covered in a "superior manner in these news outlets" (p.52). In their analysis of female sports coverage in NCAA news, Shifflett and Revelle (1994) found that male athletes received more than twice the coverage of female athletes in text and just under two times the coverage of female athletes in visuals. Wann and Schrader (1998) found in their analysis of men's and women's sports coverage in University-sponsored newspapers that coverage of female athletes and athletics paled in comparison to coverage of male athletes and athletics and that coverage inequities were most prominent at larger universities. Overall, the coverage itself tends to reinforce hegemonic beliefs that sport is a male domain.

### Types of Portrayals—Sexualized Sports Rhetoric in News Media

The resounding finding with regard to the type of media portrayal female athletes receive is that media coverage overemphasizes femininity and sexuality (Sage, 1998). Some studies have revealed the language commentators and reporters use when referring to male and female athletes in a sports media presentation emphasizes gender inequalities. Duncan (1992) reports, "This presentation of women's games as derivative of a male standard signaled a consistent presentation of female athletics as inferior" (p.1). By way example, Duncan et al. (1990) reported that female athletes were referred to in broadcast as "girls," "young ladies," and "women," whereas men were referred to as "men" instead of "boys," "young fellas," or "young men."

Furthermore, female players were much more likely to be referred to by their first names as compared to men (304 references to women's first names versus 44 references to men's first names). The authors had similar findings when they examined the adjectives used to describe the male and female athletes. Duncan et al. (1990) report that words such as "big," "strong," "gutsy," and "brilliant" were used to describe male tennis players during coverage of the 1989 U.S. Open finals, whereas words such as "fatigued," "frustrated," "panicked," "choking," and "vulnerable" were used to describe female players. The authors report, "When women were described as strong, it was often done in ambivalent language: 'big girl,' 'she's tiny but so effective,' and 'her little jump hook.' There was little ambivalence in the descriptions of men: these were 'big' guys with 'big' forehands who played 'big games' " (p.1).

## News Coverage of Tennis

Media coverage of women's tennis has not really deviated from the ideological patterns of male dominance in sport. Studies conducted over the last two decades have found gender inequities with regard to the amount of coverage as well as the type of coverage. Hilliard's (1984) analysis of magazine articles about professional female tennis players found that a great deal of attention was devoted to off-court aspects of the players' lives. He further found mention of players being "emotionally troubled, unfulfilled, and torn by role conflict" (p.252). A follow-up study showed that, "Some comments rather pointedly evaluated the women in terms of traditional standards of feminine beauty" (p.253). The suggestion from past research is that emphasis on physical appearance and physical beauty is one way to undermine or detract from emphasis on athletic accomplishment.

## Methodology for Studying Newspaper Coverage of Women's Tennis

The data consists of 1,109 newspaper articles from some two dozen mainstream media sources written about professional female tennis players since the 1970s. Since analyzing coverage of every professional player in the last 30 years was not a manageable task, the focus was limited to players who were considered the "top" players of their time, as determined by rankings. Six top-ranked players from the last 25 years were selected based on each players' overall ranking and participation in major tournaments throughout the year: Chris Evert, Tracy Austin, Martina Navratilova, Steffi Graf, Jennifer Capriati, Venus Williams. Furthermore, the analysis was narrowed to include articles written about each player's performance in one of four Grand Slam events—The U.S. Open, The French Open, The Australian Open, and Wimbledon. On two occasions, news articles about players in non-Grand Slam tournaments are included as a precursor to analysis of Grand Slam play.

In many cases, the articles were chosen because they were about a player's winning of a tournament. Some players, such as Jennifer Capriati or Venus Williams, may have received intense media coverage throughout the years for non-tennis related activity and behavior.

Analysis was limited to newspaper articles found on section fronts and inside pages, columns, and editorials.

### *Procedures*

Articles used in this analysis were found in newspapers published in the United States and from around the world, most selected from Lexis/Nexis Academic Universe and a few (38) copied and viewed from newspaper archives on microfilm. Each player's name was entered as a search term, and then all articles published between January 1 to December 31 of each year (1976–2002) were retrieved. From retrieved articles, only articles relating to one of the four major tournaments were selected. Finally, based on the number for each year of coverage, 25 percent of the stories published were read and analyzed. The 25 percent were systematically sampled using every fifth story. News articles retrieved from microfilm date between January 1, 1973 to December 31, 1976. A census of all stories published in *The Washington Post* and *The New York Times* about women players in one of the four major tournaments was conducted, and from that sample, every other article was read and analyzed.

The articles were scrutinized in an attempt to identify themes and patterns found in the content related to players' athletic skill, their physical appearance, and their character and behavior on and (sometimes) off court. This approach is similar to the one Hilliard (1984) followed, making for a critical means to determine what patterns have continued and what may be different in media coverage of women's players today.

## FINDINGS FROM THE 1970S: SPORTS REPORTAGE ON CHRIS EVERT AND TRACY AUSTIN

The 1970s proved to be a tumultuous yet exciting decade for women's tennis. Many rivalries began, and women finally began to get press coverage that at least appeared to match coverage of men's tennis in space and prominence on the page. A review of 213 articles between 1973 and 1979 indicate a few trends that were common in coverage of the game; mainly, they were very different from what we see today. The articles were longer, often running between 1000 and 1700 words compared to 500 and 1000 words now, but more importantly, they allowed for depth and analysis of the game. Many column inches were devoted to highlighting cross-court winners, drop volleys, and backhand down-the-line shots. The reporters in the late 1970s and early 1980s who covered women's tennis seemed to rely more heavily on quotations from players and coaches, as the bottom half of many stories went from quote-to-quote with little transition. Analysis was handled in the top half of the story, and quotes were placed at the bottom half. Not surprisingly, the articles used for this study were all written by male reporters.

Descriptions of emotions and emotional reactions to play were one of the many ways sportswriters differentiated women from men in news analyses. In many of the stories written about the two players in the 1970s, reports about displays of emotion were common.

Female players during the late 1970s and early 1980s also tended to make news on the sports pages after childbirth, after marriage, or after recurring illnesses that seemed to distract from play. Sportswriters, in some cases, may have reported on male players' marriages or relationships, but neither appeared to interfere with the player's game as it did for women. While the sports reporters were indeed descriptive and had an equally masterful hand on the language, the sexualized rhetoric did not seem to make its way into news articles as much as it does now. It is possible reporters now are more brazen, but it is equally possible that today's reporters now are just more comfortable using sexualized language to describe women.

### Tracy Austin

Despite skill and strength on the court, Tracy Austin was rarely written about without descriptions of "a sweet teen in pigtails," or having a Little Red Riding Hood image. Age and cuteness were emphasized before skill.

References, both direct and indirect, to age were common throughout the analysis of the women players. In some cases, youth was attributed to faltered play; in other cases, old age was blamed for a mishandled game. Chris Evert was on the receiving end of both types of references, as she was a top player in the game for more than a decade.

### Chris Evert

Sportswriters often compared Austin to Evert, both debuting on the professional circuit at early ages and both with "all American girl" characteristics that made each likeable and crowd favorites. Chris Evert won her first Wimbledon and French Open in 1974, and her first U.S. Open in 1975. By 1978, at the "tottering" age of 23, she

had been elevated to Queen status, but she had also earned the reputation of the "Ice Maiden" for her diligent, focused play on court. In
the mid-to-late 1970s, women's tennis saw many changes with the
development of the Women's Tennis Association (WTA) and the
separation of the women's tour from the men's. During this time, one of
the greatest rivalries in women's tennis was beginning: Evert's ongoing
and long-lasting rivalry with Martina Navratilova. While Evert was
called the "old lady" in the press, reporters still gave the nod in style,
grace, and strength to Evert in story after story.

The emphasis on and descriptions of emotions throughout news
stories of female tennis players is an immediate strike against mental
toughness and physical strength. Most importantly, the clearly biased
language can create an even larger gap between the equitable coverage of men and women's tennis. The women players were "sweet"
and "gracious" even though most of the adjectives used to describe
Bjorn Borg, Jimmy Connors, or John McEnroe were descriptors of
strength, power, and aggression—"tough" and "hard-nosed." The
gendered language makes each woman appear even more feminine,
although success on the court requires the strength, agility, and fitness
level of an elite athlete.

News coverage of Evert was fairly consistent for more than a
decade though. Readers were reminded of her cuteness even 15 years
after she played her first Grand Slam match. Her strength was delegit-
imized consistently via references to "Little Chrissie." Most importantly, sports writers felt the need to remind readers of a woman's real
role in life: marriage, childrearing, and housekeeping.

## The 1980s and 1990s: Martina Navratilova and Steffi Graf

While the mean age of nationally ranked players was higher in the
1980s than it had ever been, the mean age of top 10 and top 20
women was at its lowest in more than 20 years. Between 1980 and
1984, 136 women players under 18 were nationally ranked, compared
to 55 from a decade earlier. Furthermore, there were 128 nationally
ranked female players in both the 16 and under and 14 and under
categories. The youth phenoms of the decade were starting a ruckus,
causing analysts to wonder "at what age it will end?" (Galenson,
1995, p.2). Youth phenoms were not new to the 1980s and 1990s, but
these two decades had their share of young stars.

The 1980s represented rivalries, in some cases youth versus "old"
age, and the 1990s represented the donning of a new era for women's

tennis. One rivalry receiving a great deal of newspaper attention was the one between Chris Evert and Martina Navratilova that spanned more than a decade. This rivalry is undoubtedly one of the best known in the history of the game. Yet, during the years of competition between the two, Navratilova's coverage in the press was markedly different.

### Martina Navratilova

Navratilova was considered a foreigner, and despite her defection to the United States from Czechoslovakia, she struggled to gain acceptance by fans and by the press. When she first started playing on the professional tour, reporters and the public speculated about her sexual orientation, and when it became fairly clear to fans that she was a lesbian, her star power seemingly decreased even more. Even though Navratilova found success on the court much of the time, she often fought a larger battle in the press room and on the newspaper pages the next day. As an individual, she was detached because she was a foreigner and a homosexual to boot. She was rarely a crowd favorite, especially when she was playing against Evert.

Some sportswriters attributed Navratilova's emotional instability to family problems and frustration with the Czech press. Much was written about how she had tried for months to get her mother and father permission to visit the United States, and, as many sportswriters reported, the attention she devoted to family issues "undoubtedly interfered with her ability to focus on her game."

### Steffi Graf

Like many other top-ranking professional tennis players, Steffi Graf exploded onto the tennis scene as a teenager and quickly earned respect for her calculating game, explosive serves, and powerful ground strokes. She was fairly stoic during press interviews and gave reporters very little to report on beyond her on-court activities. Graf quickly demonstrated to the press and the public that she wasn't as hands-on as some of her predecessors: It was a rare moment to catch her laughing or smiling; she didn't take liberties with her answers during press interviews; her persona was her game and nothing else. Graf was referred to as "West Germany's teen-age tennis machine" (Dwyre, 1988), and later descriptions of her activities scream of her power: "unparalleled success," "unsurpassing athletic talent," or "choke-hold on the game."

Graf, though, seemed to give reporters little else to report on outside of her game, and subsequently, most news articles about her detail her ability to rip apart opponents in remarkably short periods of time. Because it appears to be Graf's nature to be stoic and somewhat aloof in meetings with the press, it seems as if reporters had very little to grasp onto except her game. Furthermore, it was easy for reporters to comment on her game and style of play because she crushed just about every player she came in contact with on her way to the top of the rankings. Much of the published rhetoric used to describe Graf's game emphasized her toughness, her resilience, and her power. Graf, it seems, didn't get raked over the coals much for her on-court demeanor.

She seemed to avoid much of the press reportage on teen stars falling victim to youth. Several writers between 1987 and 1989 reported that Graf managed to avoid succumbing to the "late-adolescent crises" that had truncated the careers of her predecessors such as Tracy Austin and Andrea Jaeger and certainly a few who followed, such as Jennifer Capriati and Monica Seles. On occasion, however, she is reduced to a "girlish 19 (year-old)" phenom and she is attributed in ways that highlight her youth, as in "she said with an embarrassed giggle."

While it is certainly somewhat refreshing to find a player who has not been crucified by the press because of her age, Steffi Graf seems to represent an exception to the rule.

## The Twenty-First Century: Jennifer Capriati and Venus Williams

Joel Stein and colleagues (2001) wrote that the players of the new century have a "potent combination of talent, glamour and tennis-kid brattiness," (p.55), reporting that it is this display of arrogance and attitude on the court that has bumped women's tennis into primetime programming in the last few years. The players from the new century have a mix of power, finesse, and drama that have enabled the women's game to morph from its previous place of white tennis skirts, pigtails, and polite interactions across the net. But, one of the biggest changes in the face of women's tennis has been the admission of and acceptance of Blacks into the country club. Fans and players liked Zina Garrison, but it is questionable whether she helped open the door to other women of color on the tennis circuit. She was accepted but the acceptance seemed to be more of an anomalie than a reality. With the dawning of this new decade has come a nod to a broader circle of players. Venus and Serena Williams have added color to the mix, but their acceptance into the club hasn't been altogether smooth. Martina Navratilova, who fought her own battles against discrimination of homosexuals, says the Williams sisters are being treated with kid gloves.

While the 1990s witnessed changes in attitude and attire in the women players, players of the new decade have had to confront being sexualized by the media and being given media time that emphasizes gender and sexuality rather than play. Denham (2001) reports that female tennis players are frequently photographed between games and sets, with greater attention given to appearance and shape rather than a "diving drop shot or leaping overhead slam" (p.38), arguing that physical appearance is worth as much to commentators and advertisers as ability, and, in some cases, it is worth more. Arguably, the twenty-first century has witnessed a change from pigtails and ponytails to Lolita-like stars.

### Jennifer Capriati

In the little more than a decade that Jennifer Capriati has played on the professional circuit, her game, her personal triumphs and defeats, and her personal characteristics and traits have received coverage in the tabloid circuits as well as the traditional sports news outlets. Early coverage of Capriati as she hit the professional tour at 13 emphasized her age, which seems to have lead reporters into discussions of "girlish activities."

Many of the examples of gendered language come in the analysis of a player's triumph over another. As one player is praised, the other is often touted as having succumbed to youth, to personal struggles, or even mental unpreparedness. Sally Jenkins (1990) wrote about Graf's dominating play against Capriati in the 1990 U.S. Open, praising Graf but describing Capriati as childish and immature:

> Steffi Graf drove Jennifer Capriati to a sugar binge, the 14-year-old wolfing brownies, swigging ginger ale, sucking on a lollipop and chewing gum at the same time . . . There is something irresistible about a match between Graf, the former child star, and Capriati, the current Shirley Temple of tennis . . . Graf dismissed Capriati, 6–1, 6–2, in the fourth round at the National Tennis Center to wipe the grin off the Florida teenager's face. Capriati sprayed errors around the court in a disappointing exhibit of nerves, and then did what 14-year-olds do: she stuffed a wad of gum in her mouth.

Comments like this are fairly representative of the type of early coverage Capriati received in the press and is also representative of coverage of her predecessors. She was a teen phenom when she won, while her losses were chalked up to adolescent youth and inexperience. Capriati was reported to engage in girlish activities off the court, and it was rare when her physical attributes were *not* commented on in early press coverage of her game. The words "Comeback Kid" certainly seem to follow her around in the headlines. And as reporters and news writers describe her triumphant return to a top world ranking, her body shape and size become a common topic for discussion.

Coverage of Capriati has certainly changed over the years, and she may be at a point in her career where she has earned enough respect to have her game critiqued with her personal triumphs and tragedies getting buried deeper in news stories.

### *Venus Williams*

The language used to describe Venus Williams, and her sister, Serena, could be easily summarized in a few words: volatile, aggressive, and raw. In many cases, it seems as if the language used to describe Venus was similar to language used to describe African American men decades before. Headlines in papers around the world describe the "power of the sisterhood." Just as each player has been characterized or framed in a particular way, Venus Williams was and is no different. The rhetoric used to describe her is surrounded by terms of power, domination, and strength.

In the months prior to the U.S. Open in 1997, Venus' name was barely mentioned in the press around the world, but some sports analysts were predicting big things following her appearance in the final game of the U.S. Open in 1997 when she lost to Hingis. Like many players before her, Venus Williams made a name for herself first by appearance and demeanor and then by style of play. Sportswriters described her hair, her attire, her attitude on the court, and her ability to " 'blow Hingis away one day, blow themselves (Venus and Serena) the next.' It was only later that journalists saw fit to mentioning her game. In the later years, her powerhouse hitting was used in the lead of news stories, but it took Venus a while to earn as much respect for her game as her "volatile temper on and off the court."

## DISCUSSION

In the earlier decades, Tracy Austin, Chris Evert, and Evonne Goolagong were the "sweethearts" of the circuit, as popular for their game as for their demeanor on and off the court. The last decade has taken tennis fans into an era of the "babes"—where the supermodel-like players are sexualized and immortalized like none before them. Many sportswriters have taken great pleasure in capitalizing on the looks of Anna Kournikova and Maria Sharapova, and it seems as if female players today are either lumped into the "cute," "hot," or "babe" categories or the "dominating," "powerful," or a "force to be reckoned with" categories.

In recent years, much more has been made of the players' physical appearance, level of fitness, and exposed skin. Much more could be written about the presentation of women in sporting news, and arguably, the mention of height, weight, dress size, and hairstyle could be eliminated from the text altogether. But, it is these descriptions that help separate the women from the men. The rhetoric is laden with language associated with feminine traits, and, most importantly, the presentation of women's tennis news consistently portrays women as inferior to men.

Although the distribution of power and success may appear to be more equally distributed, sportswriters still find ways to undermine and delegitimize the women's game. Sports commentators speak of the three sets women play versus the five for men, even though during many non-Grand Slam events, men and women play the same number of sets. They compare the speed of the serve between the game's heaviest hitters, and continue to knock each female player off the pedestal every time mention is made of "emotional breakdowns" or "emotional immaturity." From the attributions to the adjectives, the language used by sportswriters connotes weakness instead of strength, inferiority rather than dominance. Even though some articles highlighted the strength of various women's games, the underlying message found in the descriptions of physical attributes and emotional mind frames signal that the presentation of women's tennis is decidedly different from that of men.

The dominant themes in tennis coverage can be categorized in several ways: discussions of age, descriptions of physical characteristics, descriptions of hair and attire, descriptions of demeanor with the press, and, most importantly, the use of language that clearly places the female athlete in a figurative slot behind her male counterparts. Sage (1998) says that male sports superiority is just one of the unresolved issues of gender inequity in sport; his idea of gender inequality based on physical traits was evident in most of the news articles written about women players. Sportswriters might have used descriptions of height and weight in one paragraph, then mentioned serve speed and powerful overheads, and then a few paragraphs later they emphasized breaks in concentration or attributed losses to not having a handle on emotional issues.

The sportswriters of these articles may have had the greatest intent, but the use of informal language, the use of more feature-style news articles, and the use of gendered language have reduced women's tennis to just another thing men can do better. It is difficult to imagine that in the dawning of the new century, female players are still struggling for equitable coverage in space and prominence on the sports pages and for reportage that summarizes the highlights of a match without reducing each player to a status of inferiority via gendered and sexualized rhetoric.

## REFERENCES

Brennan, C. (2001). Women serve up more interest. *USA Today* (August 30): C3.

Cahn, S.K. (1993). From the "muscle moll" to the "butch" ballplayer: Mannishness, lesbianism, and homophobia in U.S. women's sport. *Feminist Studies* 19: 343–365.

Calia, G.N. (1993). An historical analysis of the impact of Title IX on student media presentation of women as athletes. *ProQuest Digital Dissertations* (online). <http://wwwlib.umi.com/dissertations.html>

Denham, B.E. (2001). The sexualized female athlete: Ethics issues in mediated communication. *Media Ethics* 13: 38–41.

Duncan, M.C. (1992). Gender bias in televised sports. *FAIR website.* <http://www.fair.org/extra/9200/sports-bias.html>

Duncan, M.C. and Hasbrook, C.A. (1988). Denial of power in televised women's sports. *Sociology of Sport Journal* 5: 1–21.

Duncan, M.C., Messner, M., and Williams, L. (1992). *Coverage of Women's Sports in Four Daily Newspapers.* AAF. {Online}. <www.aafla.org/9aar/ResearchReports/ResearchReports1.htm>

Duncan, M.C., Messner, M.A., Williams, L., and Jensen, K. (1990). *Gender stereotyping in televised sports.* Los Angeles: Amateur Athletic Foundation.

Dwyre, B. (1988). A hard sell: Chris Evert charms, but tennis, Olympics remain an uncertain love match. *The Los Angeles Times* (September 24): 13.

Finn, R. (1990). Sabatini stuns Graf. *The New York Times* (September 18): 1.

Galenson, D.W. (1995). Does youth rule? Trends in the ages of American women tennis players, 1960–1992. *Journal of Sport History* 22: 1–14.

Hallmark, J.R. and Armstrong, R.N. (1999). Gender equity in televised sports: A comparative analysis of men's and women's NCAA Division I basketball championship broadcasts, 1991–1995. *Journal of Broadcasting & Electronic Media* 43 (2): 222–235.

Hilliard, D.C. (1984). Media images of male and female professional athletes: An interpretive analysis of magazine articles. *Sociology of Sport Journal:* 251–262.

Jenkins, S. (1990). No. 1 Graf leaves it to others to place her in history—so far. *The Washington Post* (September 4): B1.

Sage, G.H. (1998). *Power and ideology in American sport: A critical perspective.* Champaign, Ill: Human Kinetics.

Shifflett, B. and Revelle, R. (1994). Gender equity in sports media coverage: A review of the *NCAA News. Journal of Sport & Social Issues* 18: 144–150.

Stein, J., James, J., Bower, A., Hingis, M., and Davenport, L. (2001). The power game. *Time* (September 3): 54–62.

Tuggle, C.A. (1996). Television sports reporting of female athletics: Quantitative and qualitative content analysis of ESPN Sportscenter and CNN Sports Tonight. *Pro-Quest Digital Dissertations* (online). <http://wwwlib.umi.com/dissertations.html>

———. (1997). Differences in television sports reporting of men's and women's athletics: ESPN Sportscenter and CNN Sports Tonight. *Journal of Broadcasting and Electronic Media*, 41: 14–24.

Wann, D.L. and Schrader, M.P. (1998). The inequitable newspaper coverage of men's and women's athletics at small, medium and large universities. *Journal of Sport and Social Issues* 22 (1): 79–88.

Women's Sports Foundation (1997). Women's Sports Facts. <www.womenssportsfoundation.org>

# CHAPTER 15

# The Vamp, the Homebody, and the Upstart: Women and the Language of Baseball Films*

*Linda K. Fuller*

If the notion of "baseball moves" seems like an oxymoron (Fuller, 1990), adding dimensions of gender and language might make them seem all the more so—especially if one considers that, in the more than 100 baseball films produced in the United States since Thomas Edison's Ball Game of 1896, women have been stereotypically portrayed. According to sports historians Zucker and Babich (1987, p.23), they "Generally fit into one of three categories: The Vamp, who causes the hero's downfall; The Homebody, who suffers with the athlete and wants him to quit; and The Upstart, who dares to enter the world of sports and is ridiculed for her efforts."

Comparable to the 1950s breaking of the ethnic barrier with *The Jackie Robinson Story*, this chapter aims to look at the baseball film genre in terms of its gender barrier, considering the visual and verbal evolution of women as stereotypes and also as players. Put into a context of women as stereotypes in baseball films, as opposed to women as players in baseball films, it considers "the gaze" in reverse, women as audience, women as object, women actually playing the game, and three women's baseball films in particular: *Girls Can Play* (1937), *Squeeze Play* (1979), and Penny Marshall's *A League of Their Own* (1992). Throughout, critical media reaction is considered from a feminist perspective.

* A chronological filmography, including producer(s), director(s) and/or writer(s) is available from the author.

## WOMEN AND MEN, BASEBALL,
### AND LANGUAGE

Sexism is rampant in our cultures and, in the United States, in our national pastime (Berlage, 1994; Dickerson, 1991; Erickson, 1992; Ryan, 1995; Wood and Pincus, 2003), nowhere more evident than in its unique vocabulary. Replete with innuendoes about sex, violence, and the ultimate goal of scoring more than the other guy, baseball is, in essence, a game of bats and balls.

Those balls might be lively, juiced, doctored, blistered, blocked, blasted, bled, blown, bombed, booted, hammered, crushed, flipped, pumped, tumbled, donged, or dead spitballs, scorched, and a really hard-hit ball means that a batter is "on the screws." Screwballs derive from a pitch invented by Carl Hubell. And, how about the expression made famous in a television commercial by Greg Maddox and Tom Glavine that, "Chicks dig the long ball."

Bats might be bottle bats, fat bats, fungo bats, gavels, or sawed-off bats, that part of the bat giving a maximum transmission of force being known as the "sweet spot." The slang term for a baseball bat is an "ax." Substitute hitters or runners are pinchers. We "bat around" ideas, brainstorming just like ballplayers practice before a game. According to Ryan Gray (2002, p.10), an "A" lick refers to the batter hitting a ball as far as *he* can hit it (emphasis mine), or why the batter might want to "grip it and rip it." Or hitting a home run is said to be "going deep." Why else do men brag about sexual exploits in terms of getting to first, second, or third base, the goal being to go *all the way home*?

The business of the sport concerns itself with acquisitions and agents, trades and releases, options, castoffs, waivers, and ongoing negotiations. It eschews interference or obstructions. Players need the manager's approval to swing or steal, known in the game as the "red light," and instructions to batters might be "short and sweet." The power plays and producers are known as the "big guns," and the slang term for power is a punch.

Equipment might include batting cages, radar guns (like the Jugs, which measures velocity of a pitch), foul poles, gloves, or Iron Mike, a one-armed pitching machine. The infield is called a dance floor, the baseball field a diamond, the dugout is a "hole," and home plate is called a "dish." The team that scores first is said to have drawn first blood. To protect themselves, baseball players might use face masks, jock straps, chest protectors, gloves, pads, cleats, batting helmet, and guards. To prepare their upper bodies to swing, they might make a movement called "cock." The best players are called tough cookies, tough customers, tough homres, or studs; the bad ones are termed "stiff." All are "sluggers," and, needless to say, there are lots of positions.

When a team needs to win to stay in contention, the players are said to have their "backs against the wall." When it is scoring especially well, it is said to "blow it wide open." Easy teams to beat, after all, are known as "cupcakes." When there are loaded bases, they might be called chucked, drunk, or juiced; or, the "sacks are jammed," and yet another notion was used in the British film *The Full Monty*. Of course there are also fakes and fantasies.

As audiences, we encourage our favorite pitchers to "bring the nasty" or "bring the pain" for hard throws. We don't want them to have weak tosses that might ricochet, as in the "chuck and duck," or to have soft throws known as rubbers or a "cunny thumper." When he throws weak stuff he might be accused of "serving up meat." The pitcher who aims for corners is known as a "nibbler," and we award ones successfully reaching the "nice spot." "Suck it up," or "Gotta have ya," we yell in encouragement. When we're unhappy with the umpire we might holler, "Kick yer dog blue," meaning that they are blind and need a seeing-eye dog.

Is it really all play? It might be a "bang-bang play," when a base runner hits the bag just before the ball gets there, or vice versa. It might be a banger, a blooper, a choke, a closer, a fly ball, a force play, a curve, a cut, a foul, a force play, a hit, a hurl, a pinch, a rubber, a sacrifice, a safety, a pit, a steal, a strike, a suicide squeeze, even a clutch—when one comes from behind. A "basher," like a "mauler," consistently belts a really hard ball. Amateur play is "bush." When it has been a hard-fought game it is determined to have been a "tussle," and when there is a two-game series in the major leagues it is known as a sleepover. Throughout, the ultimate goal for these baseball players is to "find a hole." Going "all out" and "winning at all costs" is the mindset in the battle; the alternative, after all, is getting spanked.

Baseball, according to film historian Ronald Bergan (1982, p.9), is a man's world: "Women are invariably seen in reaction shots to men's actions . . . Good women inspire men to physical triumph, floozies destroy them." Denise Heinze (1995, p.28) has noted that, "Films about baseball greats centered in the heroics of the men on and off the field; women's heroism in these films was a function of their dedication to their men." Barbara Grizzuti Harrison (1992, p.50) admits to watching baseball movies because she likes watching men: "To feel safe—and pretty—I need a man to cover the bases. For me, women and sports just aren't the wild thing."

But perhaps the bottom line in this issue is consideration of women as audience. With the box office successes of *Bull Durham* in 1988 and *Field of Dreams* in 1989, everyone became a baseball fan—especially women, it was noted. Still, "More than half the old baseball films were, in fact, what used to be called women's pictures" (Sheed, 1989, p.H14)—special targets for weepies like *Pride of the Yankees* (1942) and other stories based on real-life baseball players.

## WOMEN IN BASEBALL FILMS

*According to most baseball films, a woman's place is on the sidelines. Her role is to worship and support her ballplayer boyfriend, husband, or son. She cheers him when he is streaking; consoles him when he slumps; nurses him when he is injured; forgives him when he does wrong.*

—Howard Good, *Diamonds in the Dark*

"Discussions of the representation of women in film have centered on the image of the woman as it is visually and narratively constructed," Elizabeth Cowie (1997, p.3) has observed. Those images emerge from sociopolitical definitions and discourses, from notions of image as identity, and also from societal desires for those images. Almost from the start of baseball films, for example, the idea has been that ball players would win "the girl," and/or that she would want a winner. It began as early as 1911's 1,000-foot silent *Hal Chase's Home Run*, which has real-life major leaguer Chase winning for the home team so that his girlfriend would marry him. There was the melodrama of saving the pretty maiden in *Right Off the Bat* (1915), Buster Keaton vying for a girl who had called him a "sissy" in *College* (1927), and "comic sports hero" Joe E. Brown played a Chicago Cubs ballplayer in *Alibi Ike* (1935) showing off to win the girl (Olivia DeHavilland). *One Run Elmer* (1935) has Buster Keaton playing baseball against a rival to win the fickle girl, and William Bendix joins the game in the 1950s comedy *Kill the Umpire* to keep his wife. Even *It's My Turn* (1980), the first baseball film directed by a woman (Claudia Weill), features Michael Douglas as a major league baseball star who woos Jill Clayburgh away from her live-in boyfriend. *The Slugger's Wife* (1985) breaks the "man-using-baseball-to-get-girl" syndrome with Michael O'Keefe as a self-centered ballplayer going after aspiring rock star Rebecca DeMornay; Garrett (1990, p.36) has called it "baseball abuse."

Most of the desirable women in baseball films are wealthy, well-connected by birth. *Play Ball* (1925) tells of a senator's son who is a rookie in the big leagues involved with a millionaire's daughter, just as *Warming Up* (1928) features the daughter of the team's owner. Other times, desire can get in the way. Alice Day as the vamp in 1930's *In Hot Curves* turns the head of the baseball star (Rex Lease), but his buddy helps him come to his senses in time to win the big game. Another vamp and her virtuous friend momentarily break up two baseball players' friendship, but they reunite for the World Series in *They Learned About Women* (1930). In 1956's *Great American Pastime*, the wife (Anne Francis) hates baseball, but the husband wants to coach to be closer to his son; soon, he meets widow Ann Miller, who flirts with him to get him to play her son. A smash hit on Broadway, *Damn Yankees* (1958) was about an avid Washington Senators' fan who sells his soul to win; the devil sends temptress Gwen Verdon to lure the slugger (Tab Hunter), and complications begin when he tries to back out of the deal. *Long Gone* (1987) can only be described as sexist baseball: William L. Petersen is "Stud," Virginia Madsen a former Miss Strawberry Blossom, and the theme is that women are evil, men's undoing, but you can't resist them. Class is an underlying theme in *Summer Catch* (2001), Freddie Prinze, Jr. as a major league hopeful vying for the attention of a beautiful young woman (Jessica Biel) who summers in Cape Cod.

Other times, the game uses romance as a subplot, as in the 1914 *Love and Baseball*, an excuse for Hall-of-Famer Christy Matthewson to perform pitching and batting heroics. *Fast Company*'s (1929) small-town baseball hero now with the Yankees is hopelessly in love with a vaudevillian (Evelyn Brent) who doesn't know he's alive. Lloyd Nolan plays a World Series pitching hero who becomes romantically involved with Irene Hervey as a British spy caught up in a case with murder and sabotage information of a munitions plant in *Mr. Dynamite* (1941). In *It Happened in Flatbush* (1942), Nolan is the manager of the Brooklyn Dodgers; trying to hide a mistake from his past, he builds up a romance with Carole Landis, the top stockholder, who becomes an inspiration for him. *Take Me Out to the Ball Game* (1949) stars Esther Williams as a team owner who is involved with Frank Sinatra and Gene Kelly. Martha Coolidge's *Three Wishes* (1995), set in 1950s California, has Mary Elizabeth Mastrantino as the doting widowed mother of a young boy befriended by Patrick Swayze as a drifter who helps the youth league ballclub, just as Barbra Streisand uses baseball as a bridge between her and Jeff Bridges in *The Mirror Has Two Faces* (1996) albeit in reverse in terms of her being the one telling him about how the game is played. In *BASEketball* (1998), so named for being a combination of baseball, basketball, and volleyball, a wife wants to take over the team, Jenny McCarthy playing Ernest Borgnine's mistress with the statement, "I gave him the best three months of my life." Kristin Davis (of *Sex and the City* fame) has her relationship with Matthew Modine strengthened by a 12-year old boy who discovers a mint Honus Wagner card in *The Winning Season* (2004, on TNT). And we all were rooting for Drew Barrymore to become a Red Sox fan in *Fever Pitch* (2005).

Sometimes, if rarely, we even got women who could play the game. 1936 saw *Slide, Nelly, Slide!*, a 20-minute comedy about the rivalry between two women's softball teams—one sponsored by a hot dog firm and the other by a mustard factory. *Gracie at Bat* (1937) was another slapstick film, with Andy Clyde taking over the helm of a girl's softball team; in 1941, a group of showgirls took him on as their coach in *Lovable Trouble*. 1976's *Bad News Bears* has an ace pitcher who just happens to be a 12-year-old girl: Tatum O'Neal speeds the team's transformation under Walter Matthau. *Blue Skies Again* (1983) saw a woman as a new candidate for the Devils' second base position. Robyn Barto: a softball player who tries to crack the big leagues, including chewing tobacco and certainly hitting an impressive ball; yet, it was an unqualified box office bust. JoBeth Williams' *Frankie & Hazel* (2000) profiles two young girls, one of whom is a ballet dancer who really wants to play on the boy's baseball team, the other who wants to run for mayor.

Most typically, women in baseball films are found on the sidelines. They serve as secondary characters, as family members, or as zany personalities to compliment their men. Consider the many baseball biopics, with stars like Teresa Wright as Eleanor Gehrig, the stand-by wife in *Pride of the Yankees* (1942). June Allyson is the wife of real-life White Sox pitcher Monty Stratton (*The Stratton Story*, 1949), who continued after his leg was amputated following a hunting accident. Joanne Dru played in *Pride of St. Louis* (1952), the story of Dizzy Dean, and Doris Day was the wife of baseball pitcher Grover Cleveland Alexander in *The Winning Team* (1952). In *Fear Strikes Out* (1957), the wife waits it out on the sidelines while her husband (Karl Malden) pressures Anthony Perkins as real-life outfielder Jimmy Piersall. *Ladies Day* (1943) features "Mexican Spitfire" Lupe Velez starring with Eddie Albert as a wacky flirt who single-handedly manages to mess up a major league team's pennant drive; other wives kidnap her to keep her away from Albert during the World Series, as he can't play when she is around. The wife in 1989's *Field of Dreams* combines both the supportive and silly qualities in the Capra-esque story (Fuller, 1991), while in *For Love of the Game* (1999) Kevin Costner's love interest remains just an adoring girlfriend (Kelly Preston). Rachel Griffith is there as a multi-tasking mother/wife for Dennis Quaid starring as the real-life older baseball coach Jim Morris in Disney's *The Rookie* (2002): "Now is the time to really dig deep!" is a notable refrain.

At most, women serve as inspirations. *It Happens Every Spring* (1949) features Jean Peters helping college professor Ray Milland, who discovers a wood repellent and becomes a pitching star for the St. Louis Cardinals. The prayers of a little girl (Donna Corcoran) are answered by the Angel Gabriel, who sends the spirits of former baseball greats onto the field to help the Pittsburgh Pirates in *Angels in the Outfield* (1951, remade in 1994). Glenn Close as Robert Redford's "girl back home" in *The Natural* (1984) sacrifices herself in what baseball writer Roger Angell (1989, p.49) describes as Bernard Malamud's "magical-mystical story" to her man's world of baseball. Woman as a different kind of inspiration appears in 1988's *Bull Durham*, where smart and sexy Susan Sarandon is at last a women who understands baseball, and likes looking at its players. And *Major League* (1989) has a woman team-owner inspired to make money off baseball, if in a screwy scenario whereby she wants to get out of her franchise and so deliberately wants to lose both games and fans. "Foregrounding the irreconcilable aspects of cultural difference," Vivian Sobchack (1997, p.187) states, "one of the film's running gags involves the ongoing conflict between a blonde Anglo players, identified as a fundamentalist Christian, who insists the team pray before every game, and a player from the Dominican Republic who maintains a voodoo shrine in his locker and insists on sacrificing live animals in hopes of winning. Suffice it to say that the film ends with the team winners and the Dominican culturally triumphant."

## WOMEN'S BASEBALL FILMS

There are even some motion pictures that can be labeled (sort of) as making up a genre of women's baseball films. *Girls Can Play* (1937) was the first sound era feature film dealing primarily with women in sports. Interestingly, it was a mystery (Rita Hayworth poisoned the team's catcher) and not a comedy—which virtually all films about women athletes would be from then on. Although the sporting event is employed as a pretext, it is nevertheless the first feature-length movie about softball. The next such film with women baseball players was nearly a half-century in the coming, and then *Squeeze Play* (1979) was nothing more than a screwball sex comedy. The boys from the Beavers team in the Mattress Companies Softball League are more interested in baseball and beer than in them, so the "girls" decide to form their own team, taking on an alcoholic coach to show them the ropes; the Game: Beavers versus Beaverettes. Then, in 1992, the gender barrier in baseball films was truly broken (Fuller, 1993).

## A LEAGUE OF ITS OWN (1992)

### *Background*

From 1943 to 1954, when World War II threatened to drain the Major Leagues' "manpower," the All-American Girls Professional Baseball League (AAGPBL) was founded, including teams from five mid-western states. Started for $250,000 by chewing-gum magnate Philip Wrigley, owner of the Chicago Cubs, it began as a modified version of softball. Early on, underhanded pitching was required, then sidearm pitching began in 1945, and by 1947 over-handed pitching took over. "The players ranged in age from 16 to 23. Many were students or young schoolteachers who had grown up playing a ball with the boys in the neighborhood" (Walters, 1992, p.10).

"Prior to their first season," Ron Edelman (1994, p.121) has pointed out, "the players are sent to charm and beauty school to learn how to act like 'ladies.' Their uniforms, abbreviated dresses that reveal lots of leg, are unfit for sliding into bases or pivoting for the double play. Primarily, the women are expected to be sex objects." One of their posters boasted, "Beautiful Girls Plus Appealing Costumes Plus Grade A Baseball." Although they drew some 7,000 people to Chicago's Wrigley field, averaging some 110–130 games per season, the 450 women players languished in obscurity until recently. In 1988, a permanent exhibit about the league was unveiled at the Baseball Hall of Fame in Cooperstown, New York, and luckily Penny Marshall decided to make a movie about it.

"These players were expected to be terrors on the field while remaining models of femininity," according to Lori Moody (1992, p.34). That meant "wearing makeup and following strict codes of conduct that prohibited drinking or smoking in public, required social engagement to be approved by their chaperone and forbade uniforms from being shorter than six inches above the knee." They also had to go to charm school, learning how to walk in high heels, enunciate properly, and perfect their posture by walking with books on their heads. Wrigley insisted on "ladylike behavior": they could not smoke, and could not wear slacks.

*Media Reviews*

In 1987 the 28-minute documentary *A League of Their Own* was released. Centering on a then-recent reunion of the AAGPBL players in Fort Wayne, Indiana, writer/director Mary Wallace "outlines a tumultuous sports saga and celebrates a fit and spirited group of Americans now in their sixties and seventies" (Sragow, 1991, p.66). Their reminiscences are wonderful, ranging from pranks to pride.

Penny Marshall decided to bring this little-known slice of Americana to the big screen in the summer of 1992. Using nearly the same title but bringing in box office big names like Geena Davis, Tom Hanks, Madonna (!), and Lori Petty, there was quite a bit of pre-release ink about the Columbia movie's debut. *The New York Times Magazine* (Orenstein, 1992), for example, featured Penny Marshall on its prestigious cover and included a seven-page spread. Against blockbuster sequels *Alien 3*, *Batman Returns*, and *Lethal Weapon 3*, the film opened quietly in July, drawing some $82.8 million each weekend as word about it spread. Press responses differed.

*Entertainment Weekly* (Gleiberman, 1992, p.39) originally gave the film a "C+" rating: "From its jokey, one-note characters to its endless baseball montages, *A League of Its Own* is all flash, all surface: It's a great big trailer for itself." Later, when it was released on video, another *EW* reviewer (Rachlin, 1993, p.58) gave it a "B+," saying it represented "a breakthrough in women's sports movies: It's a celebration of sport for sport's sake." Pointing out how most movies mixing women and sports have emphasized romance, it was refreshing to see women wanting to play the game.

"In *A League of Its Own*, director Penny Marshall makes the cardinal mistake all mediocre baseball-movie makers do: She encourages the audience to believe that the act of hitting the ball over the fence is the major achievement of a player . . . whereas baseball truths are far more stately, elegant, subtle, and measured," critiqued Barbara Grizzuti Harrison (1992, p.50). Although applauding the film as "a sparkling example of women directing, starring in, and dominating the action of a major motion picture," the Christian Science *Monitor* (Sterritt, 1992, p.12) said it missed a feminist pitch: "It's not a deep-thinking film, and I wish it probed more thoroughly into the feminist issues it raises, instead of finessing them in a goopy finale."

*Newsweek* (Ansen, 1992, p.54) called *A League of Its Own* "a mixture of shtik, schmaltz and feminism. Marshall's amiable entertainment . . . (a) very likable pop historical comedy." Film critic Janet Maslin (1992, H11) of *The New York Times* concentrated on the notion of character in *A League of Its Own*, complimenting Penny Marshall for casting "the principal roles entirely against type, and the results are wonderfully unexpected. Audience is the focus taken by *The New Yorker* (Sragow, 1991, p.66): "Marshall directed it with both eyes on the audience . . . What's actually being programmed these days is the audience: Marshall and company want people to come out saying that they laughed and they cried." Claiming that the film "aims for the tear ducts and the funny bone as ruthlessly as the big-action fantasy hits go after the viscera," Sragow says that it, "begs the viewer's kindness, then abuses it." *Rolling Stone* (Travers, 1992, p.109) took a Nineties perspective: "The story has the makings of a stinging feminist manifesto. That, however, is not what director Penny Marshall delivers. Marshall's take is uniquely her own—lots of laughs, lots of heart and very little sermonizing."

Mainstream sports media also kept aware of *A League of Its Own*. Anticipating it, *Sport* (Lewis, 1990, p.14) wrote, "In Hollywood, imitation is the sincerest form of flattery—and the surest route to a hit." On the heels of the spate of baseball films that appeared in the 1980s (Fuller, 1990), this movie probably was inevitable; what adds is that the women featured played what sportscaster Dizzy Dean called "good old country hardball." And finally, here is *Sports Illustrated*'s (Wulf, 1992, p.4) review: "*A League of Its Own* singles through a drawn-in infield, moves to second on a sacrifice, steals third after avoiding a pickle, runs through the third base coach's stop sign and scores when the catcher drops the ball in a home plate collision. In other words, (it) . . . succeeds beyond expectations and despite some mawkish moments."

## IMPLICATIONS FOR SEXUAL SPORTS RHETORIC

*The body has historically been much more integral to the formation of identity for women than for men. If women had defined for themselves the ideals of their bodily shape or decoration, this would not be problematic. It is the denial of this right in the history of western cultural representation, in medical practice, and in the multi-billion dollar pornography, fashion and cosmetic industries, that has granted women only squatters' rights to their own bodies.*

—Myra Macdonald, *Representing Women*

Besides bodies, besides box office demands (both in ballparks and movie houses), and besides sociocultural visual representations, we can easily see from the simple example of how women are treated in baseball films that textual language analysis opens wide worlds of insight. Examining both verbal and nonverbal scripts and scenarios allows us to begin to understand how engrained sexism is in sport(s); appropriately, action should be the next step to get beyond the "good girls"/"good bad girls"/"bad bad girls" associated with their cinematic representations.

An article in the 1991 issue of *Women's Sports & Fitness* (Tilin, p.11) pointed out: "Some of baseball's best players . . . haven't yet been inducted into the Baseball Hall of Fame yet, even though it's been 40 years since they quit playing." Unquestionably, sports equity still evades women. Yet, maybe one good result of *A League of Its Own* was that the Colorado-based National Fastpitch Association (NFA), a women's professional fast-pitch softball league, was encouraged to become a reality. In 1995, the Women's Pro Fastpitch (WPF) tour was launched, its original teams known as the Carolina Diamonds, Durham Dragons, Georgia Pride, Orlando Wahoos, Tampa Bay FireStix, and Virginia Roadsters. Renamed the Women's Professional Softball League (WPSL) four years later, it was forced to disband due to financial problems, but hopes to regroup for the Olympic Games or general leagues (Neft, Cohen, and Neft, 2001). Just as underdog teams triumphed recently in the majors, we can hope that grit for all minorities will pay off sometime soon.

Are "Diamonds are a girl's best friend"? Reviewing women and the language of baseball films historically and socioculturally offers a unique opportunity for us to consider that focusing on thematic spectatorship suggests news ways to situate and develop feminist film theory's interest in gendering the gaze. As to the future for women and sports films—chances are it will only be "fantasy baseball."

### REFERENCES

Angell, R. (1989). No, but I saw the game. *The New Yorker* (July 31): 41–56.
Ansen, D. (1992). Big laughs and cheap thrills. *Newsweek* (July 6): 54.
Bergan, R. (1982). *Sports in the movies.* New York: Proteus Books.
Berlage, G.I. (1994). *Women in baseball: The forgotten history.* Westport, CT: Praeger.
Cowie, E. (1997). *Representing the woman: Cinema and psychoanalysis.* Minneapolis, MN: University of Minnesota Press.
Dickerson, G.E. (1991). *The cinema of baseball: Images of America, 1929–1989.* Westport, CT: Meckler.
Edelman, R. (1994). *Great baseball films.* New York: Citadel Press.
Erickson, H. (1992). *Baseball in the movies: A comprehensive reference, 1915–1991.* Jefferson, NC: McFarland.

Fuller, L.K. (1990). The baseball movie genre: At bat, or struck out? *Play & Culture* 3: 64–74.

———. (1991). "Triumph of the underdog" in Baseball Films. In *Beyond the stars 11: Plot conventions in American popular films*, ed. Loukides, Paul, and Fuller, Linda K., 53–60. Bowling Green, OH: Popular Press.

———. (1993). *In a league of its own: Penny Marshall breaks the baseball film genre for women*. Paper delivered to the Popular Culture Association conference, New Orleans, Louisiana.

Garrett, K. (1990). Baseball goes to the movies. *Sport* (March): 35–37.

Gleiberman, O. (1992). Comedy of errors. *Entertainment Weekly* (July 10): 39.

Good, H. (1997). *Diamonds in the dark: America, baseball, and the movies.* Lanham, MD: The Scarecrow Press.

Gray, R. (2002). *The language of baseball: A complete dictionary of slang terms, cliches, and expressions from the grand ole game.* Monterey, CA: Coaches Choice.

Harrison, B.G. (1992). Sex and the World Series. *Mademoiselle* (November): 49–50.

Heinze, D. (1995). Angel in the ballpark: Women in baseball films. In *Gender in popular culture: Images of men and women in literature, visual media, and material culture*, ed. Rollins, Peter C. and Rollins, Susan W., 25–46. Cleveland, OK: Ridgemont Press.

Lewis, J.D. (1990). The girls of summer. *Sport* (August): 14.

Macdonald, M. (1995). *Representing women: Myths of femininity in the popular media*. London: Edward Arnold.

Maslin, J. 1992. A "league" where Eddie can't play. *The New York Times* (July 12): H11.

Moody, L. (1992). The girls of summer get their ups. *Union-News* (July 12): 34.

Neft, D.S., Cohen, R.M. and Neft, M.L. (2001). *The sports encyclopedia: Baseball.* New York: St. Martin's Griffin.

Orenstein, P. (1992). Penny Marshall: Making it in the majors. *The New York Times Magazine* (May 24): 18.

Rachlin, J. (1993). Fair play. *Entertainment Weekly* (February 12): 58–59.

Ryan, J. (1995). *Little girls in pretty boxes: The making and breaking of elite gymnasts and figure skaters.* NY: Doubleday.

Sheed, W. (1989). Why can't the movies play ball? *The New York Times* (May 14): H14.

Sobchack, V. (1997). Baseball in the post-American cinema, or life in the minor leagues. In *Out of bounds: Sports, media, and the politics of identity*, ed. Baker, Aaron and Boyd, Todd, 175–197. Bloomington, IN: Indiana University Press.

Sragow, M. (1991). Three strikes. *The New Yorker* (July 13): 66–67.

Sterritt, D. 1992. Close, but no home run. *The Christian Science Monitor* (July 3): 12.

Tilin, A. (1991). Baseball: A league of their own. *Women's Sports & Fitness* (November/December): 11.

Travers, P. (1992). Bat girls on the line. *Rolling Stone* (July 9–23): 109.

Walters, L.S. (1992). The real days when women went to bat. *The Christian Science Monitor* (June 16): 10–11.

Wood, S.C. and Pincus, J.D. (2003). *Reel baseball: Essays and interviews on the national pastime, Hollywood and American culture.* Jefferson, NC: McFarland.

Wulf, S. (1992). Field of dames. *Sports Illustrated* (July 6): 4.

Zucker, Harvey Marc and Lawrence J. Babich. (1987). *Sports films: A complete reference.* Jefferson, NC: McFarland & Company, Inc.

# CHAPTER 16

# Britney, the Body and the Blurring of Popular Cultures: A Case Study of Music Videos, Gender, a Transcendent Celebrity, and Health Issues

*Catherine Sabiston and Brian Wilson*

It is well documented that mediated images of the "ideal" female body—the tall, thin, attractive body and the more toned, athletic body increasingly in vogue—are linked to body image disturbances and feelings of dissatisfaction with physical appearance for many (young) women (e.g., Bordo, 1993; Cusumano and Thompson, 1997; Dionne et al., 1995; Hesse-Biber, 1996; Lavine, Sweeney, and Wagner, 1999). Among the many concerns expressed by those critical of these portrayals is that very few females are genetically able to achieve the body shapes, sizes, and traits depicted in the media, yet many continue to internalize and make efforts to attain these bodies (Markula, 1995). In the same way, these depictions have been critiqued because they implicitly support the deceiving and problematic belief in a relationship between having the "ideal body" and being healthy, successful, and productive (Bordo, 1993).

Common to these studies has been an emphasis on the potential influences of celebrity icons. Sociologists of sport and leisure, who in many cases are part of critical media studies, are among the leaders in studying links between media, celebrity, gender, and the body. As a recent review by Cole (2000) reveals, a wealth of research has focused on topics in such areas as media, deviance, and sport celebrities (e.g., describing how "acceptable" and "transgressive" bodies are defined through sport media), and on celebrity bodies, consumer culture, and the fitness industry (e.g., describing intended and unintended consequences of the promotion of certain body types). Underlying most work on these topics is an acknowledgement that messages about the body come from various sources (e.g., advertising, movies, fitness videos), are promoted by various celebrities (i.e., Michael Jordan, Magic Johnson, Jane Fonda, Anna Kournikova), and are in many cases ambiguous.

It is especially relevant to note in this context that perhaps the most pronounced example of a celebrity whose active body has been marketed and consumed in diverse and ambiguous ways is singer/actress Madonna, not an "athlete" per se. There are instances in the sociology of sport literature where bodies like Madonna's that transcend various popular culture genres (i.e., music and sport) are referred to (e.g., MacNeill, 1998). However, there is little work considering the relevance of, for example, music videos and lyrics as a way of understanding celebrity bodies' impacts on adolescents.

David Rowe, one of the few to focus on connections between sport, leisure, and music, has argued that these two cultural forms require joint attention, "Not only because of their raw popularity and economic significance, but also because each is devoted to the body and its pleasures by means of both participation and spectatorship" (p.9). He considers sport and music are each "key cultural industries of the body, constantly replenishing the stock of corporeal images which also function as metaphors of social and cultural change" (ibid).

The goal of this essay is to speak on these various issues about the body, gender, health, media, celebrity, and intertextuality through an analysis of music videos and accompanying lyrics by one of the most well-known and well-publicized of today's female celebrities: Britney Spears, a rock phenom who, according to *Forbes* (2002), is among the most influential females in the last decade. That influence, unfortunately, also has been blamed for increases in body image disturbances among young girls. On the most obvious level, this study is pertinent because it allows for a discussion and evaluation of some claims about media impacts relevant to sexual rhetoric surrounding the body. In the same way, it allows us to address some of the shortcomings in the literature, such as the disparity of work describing relationships between music culture, transcendent celebrities, the body, and sport.

Attempting to address issues dealing with the language about celebrity bodies, leisure, and popular culture through a case study of Spears, we have organized this chapter as follows: First, a theoretical framework is developed for examining those areas that are sensitive to both political, economic, and feminist concerns. This is followed by the presentation of a case study of the lyrics and images in three Britney Spears videos/songs, with particular attention to various emergent messages about and expressed through the body. We conclude with a discussion of the ways these findings pertain to and inform existing literature, and with recommendations for future work in the area.

## THEORETICAL CONSIDERATIONS

This essay is guided by a political economy view of popular culture that is sensitive to relationships between bodies and consumer spectacles, and a feminist perspective on mass media acknowledging the ways existing power relations are reinforced through portrayals of gender implicitly supporting dominant/problematic ideologies about the body. Both these positions are underscored by a more psychological-based understanding of the impacts of celebrity and "ideal body" portrayals on young people's perceptions of themselves.

Approaching our analysis of music images and lyrics and music celebrities as they pertain to various body and sport related culture industries, we were guided by David Whitson and Rick Gruneau's (1997) essay "The (Real) Integrated Circus: Political Economy, Popular Culture and Major League Sport," which powerfully describes the processes by which leisure and entertainment industries have become increasingly integrated as they attempt to attain economic advantages—advantages most often gained through the cross-marketing of products, merchandise, and brands, and David Rowe's (1995) *Popular Cultures: Rock Music, Sport and the Politics of Pleasure*, a useful extension of this economic argument, as he focuses on and describes specific ways music and sport cultures have become increasingly blurred in recent times—what some have called "postmodern" times (cf., Rail, 1998). These cultural features are crucial for understanding not only how big business might benefit from music-sport relationships, but also the ways celebrity bodies promoting these integrated industries have become increasingly indistinct/aligned. These works are especially pertinent to the case of Britney Spears, who has been associated with products ranging from Pepsi products and Skechers sneakers to appearing in a NASCAR-related film and on an episode of the syndicated animated television series *The Simpsons*, whereby her physique was emphasized.

Marg MacNeill's (1988, 1998) essays on gender portrayals and fitness-related videos/shows likewise extend Rowe's (1995) and

Whitson and Gruneau's (1997) work by linking political economic concerns with feminist-based media analyses of (non-sport) celebrities' active bodies. MacNeill remains sensitive to both the ways that power differentials between males and females are reinforced through mass media depictions of women and ideal bodies, and to the ways that young females' (perceptions of their) bodies can be disciplined and controlled through these portrayals.

Linking these theoretical arguments of prominent critical media scholars and sociologists with existing research examining body image and media, our hope is to provide a more comprehensive basis from which to consider the potential impacts of Britney Spears portrayals as an expression of sexual rhetoric that is often revealed through sport.

## METHODOLOGY

With the goal of developing a better understanding of the types of messages that young females are exposed to, and discussing potential implications, in-depth analyses of three Britney Spears' songs and videos were conducted: *Baby one more time* (release date: January 1999), *Oops . . . I did it again* (release date: May 2000), and *I'm a slave for you* (release date: October 2001). All three songs are title tracks, and the corresponding albums have debuted at the number one spot on *The Billboard 200* (mtv.com), a music distribution and ranking index based on popularity and demand.

Textual analysis techniques were used to conduct the study, the intent being to detect possible ideological contexts and messages embedded within Britney Spears' videos. The research was partially guided by Duncan's (1990) interpretive/semiotic analysis of sports photographs and Bradby's (1992) discourse analysis of musical lyrics in some of Madonna's songs. We propose that this analysis is suggestive of possible interpretations of music videos and lyrics and illustrates the use of body discourses in this form of media similar to sexual sport media rhetoric.

## RESULTS AND ANALYSIS

Although a variety of themes emerged from the analysis, three stood out. These related to: 1. Power and control; 2. Identity development; and 3. Gender stereotypes and sexuality. In the most general sense, the video images and language were contradictory in that they could be read as both articulations of female power and as expressions of submissiveness—although throughout, the "ideal" female body was promoted. Also pertinent was the development and evolution of Spears' mediated persona over the videos (e.g., "from schoolgirl to Diva"). These various themes were reinforced through a combination of visual portrayals and lyrical messages.

### Visions of Empowerment, Words of Submission

A range of contradictory messages about power and control in the lives of females are entrenched in Britney Spears' videos and songs. In some cases, as the lead female character in the videos and the lead vocalist for the songs, she is seen as dependant on and submissive to male characters. This is especially evident in *Baby one more time*, which features images and lyrics supporting dominant notions of masculine strength and knowledge. For example, the main chorus line in the song is, "Hit me baby one more time," a line suggesting in this instance that she wants "another chance" with the absent and now-dominant, seemingly rough/strong male character. Spears' submissiveness is also reinforced through the video's camera angles and lighting, emphasizing her loneliness and inferiority. This is especially evident in scenes where her head is bowed or resting in her arms with solemn, saddened eyes gazing at the audience—poses accompanied by lyrics such as:

> My loneliness is killing me,
> I must confess, I still believe
> When I'm not with you I lose my mind
> Give me a sign

Having said this, when Spears sings that she, "Shouldn't have let you [i.e., the male character] go," it seems that an ambiguous power relationship is being described, and that her character, while emotional and angst-ridden, was an active decision-maker in the relationship (i.e., not necessarily "out of control").

Spears' video and song *Oops . . . I did it again*, while including implicit allusions to submissiveness, embodies many themes that support notions of female empowerment and control. For example, at the beginning of the video, she descends from a spaceship to join a cast of dancers/actors/others. She appears to be the leader, not only from her dramatic entry "from above," but also from her attire: a red suit that contrasts with others' less prominent attire. Her positioning as the dominant figure is reinforced when she restrains a male dancer with chains, and when she is shown to be "yearned for" by a male astronaut to whom Spears appears disinterested. Spears' aggressive actions and intense facial expressions similarly support this portrayal of a dominant female figure. However these messages are to a certain extent mitigated by her lyrical admission to being out of control:

> Can't you see I'm a fool in so many ways,
> But to lose all my senses,
> That is just so typically me.

The portrayal of Spears as an empowered female is less conditional in her most recent video for the song *I'm a slave for you*. Her more assertive positioning is most evident from the predominantly eye-level angles that are used throughout the video, angles that, according to Duncan (1990), are indicative of an individual's superiority and dominance. Once again though, the lyrics, articulating Spears' dependence on the male character, contradict the video's images of female power. The following repeated and emphasized sequence is most relevant in this context:

> I'm a slave for you.
> I cannot hold it; I cannot control it.
> I'm a slave for you.
> I won't deny it; I'm not trying to hide it.

In offering these interpretations, we acknowledge Bradby's (1992) suggestion that lyrical messages in pop songs like these are less important (i.e., less spectacular, less noticeable) conveyors of meaning than the corresponding visuals. In this sense, the predominant images of Britney Spears in control could be interpreted as "more relevant" than the often lyrically based messages of disempowerment.

This aside, it is important to consider the independent existence of songs and the corresponding rhetoric. According to Bradby (1992), the freeing of music as language, as opposed to music as image, is paradoxical because songs have, and continue to endure, in commodity form as soundtracks and albums; only recently have music videos been sold as commodities, albeit as music image and language combined. Music language has its own meaning, with images dependent on the rhetoric that supports them.

### *From Innocence to Independence,*
### *from Schoolgirl to Diva*

We next explore Britney Spears' mediated identity development. According to Synnott (1993), the body is the prime symbol and determinant of identity. It is evident from the evolution of Spears' songs and videos that her body and physical characteristics are the principal mechanisms through which her identity and development are inferred, displayed, and celebrated—just as athletes' relationships with and understanding of their bodies tend to shape their identity (Hargreaves, 1994). More specifically, Spears' songs and videos provide evidence of her mediated identity crisis, or her apparent struggle between and development from adolescence and adulthood—a struggle evident from changes in her physical appearance, the construction and maintenance of her body, and related/supportive rhetoric.

The inexperienced and innocent mediated identity of Spears is conveyed in the lyrics and poses of her first video, *Baby one more time*. The lyrical reference to "baby" appears to have largely romantic connotations (e.g., "Oh baby, baby I shouldn't have let you go"); yet, the video contexts—school-related areas, such as a classroom, courtyard, and gymnasium—suggest a youthfulness and innocence. In contrast, the song from her subsequent album, *Oops . . . I did it again*, shows her to be both an agent and a product of change. There is more emphasis on her robust body and physical characteristics that imply an older female adolescent. The suggestion that the Spears character in the video is more romantically experienced than before (or than the audience thinks she is) is especially evident from the lyrics in the chorus:

> Oops! . . . I did it again
> I played with your heart, got lost in the game
> Oh baby, baby
> Oops! . . . You think I'm in love
> That I'm sent from above
> I'm not that innocent.

The final line is emphasized through a combination of higher volume lyrics and a close-up of Spears' face. Prominent images of a powerful and seductive Spears dressed in red overshadow less remarkable images of Britney in youthful and (deceivingly) innocent-looking white clothing. This is a somewhat unstable mediated identity, although the dominant reading of a powerful, more "grown-up" Spears seems clear.

## THE MILLENNIUM'S MADONNA?

Although existing research has demonstrated females in popular culture are usually displayed in stereotypical, feminine-appropriate roles and poses (Bordo, 1993; Davis, 1997; Duncan, 1990), Kellner's (1995) study of Madonna highlights the contradictory character of some contemporary portrayals and, more pertinently, emphasizes the idea that any interpretation of dominant and sexualized images and rhetoric of women need to be understood in relation to the values and beliefs of the media analyst.

Kellner's argument is relevant to Britney Spears' videos—images and language that could be viewed, on one hand, as challenging to traditional female roles and, on the other hand, as contributing to a media environment that is dominated by "ideal" young female bodies. Evidence for the more conservative interpretation could be found in video portrayals of a sexualized Spears' body emphasized through her form-fitting attire such as spandex sports bras, faux leather suits, mini skirts, and tight jeans. Lyrics like the following complement these images: "There's nothing that I wouldn't do" from *Baby one more time*; "I played with your heart, got lost in the game" from *Oops . . . I did it again*; or "Baby, don't you wanna dance upon me" and "I really wanna do what you want me to" expressed in *I'm a slave for you*.

## DISCUSSION

The most striking findings that emerged from this study were that messages embedded in the Britney Spears videos (i.e., through visual images and lyrics) were often contradictory, that portrayals of Spears evolved over the three videos (from the earliest video to the latest), and most pertinently, that images of the "ideal body" were in all cases present and emphasized—although gender stereotypes continually were mildly subverted.

Relating these findings to previous work on celebrity icons and political economy (e.g., Rowe, 1995; Wernick, 1991; Whitson and Gruneau, 1997), it is important to reiterate that images and language studied here exist within a much broader context of Spears' portrayals. At the same time, by creating links with her image and, at least inadvertently, with the language she presents and the music industry of which she is a part (and, in turn, with the publicity she receives through other sponsors), the "vortex of publicity" that Wernick (1991) referred to is created and fuelled.

Extending these arguments in ways that inform the more feminist-oriented analyses of MacNeill (1988, 1998) and Kellner (1995), we suggest our findings provide a basis from which to suggest that Spears' positioning as a feminist figure who holds power and is often "in control" is questionable. While she was often shown to be a figure who could be adulated and respected for her accomplishments (e.g., as a charismatic presence within the video and as a successful female performing artist and businessperson more generally), because her identity was so much defined by her ideal and often sexualized physique and through her romantic relationships with males, her pro-feminist positioning was diminished.

Perhaps most notable in this context is how Spears compares to the mediated Madonna against whom she is so often measured. Like Madonna, Spears' videos and musical lyrics embody various, often conflicting symbols and meanings—with an inconsistent interplay between music images and lyrics. Unlike Spears, though, Madonna's transgression is far more consistent and radical (and original) than anything Spears has approached. It would be a stretch to call Spears' shift from the semi-innocent schoolgirl to diva-temptress noncon-formist or experimental when it does not seem to challenge conven-tional understandings of femininity beyond showing a sometimes powerful, sometimes submissive young woman in a variety of seduc-tive poses. In the end, Madonna and Spears are similar in being con-tradictory figures within feminist discourses who are, above all, defined by their marketing prowess, with their music videos being, "at bottom, advertisements for songs" (Kellner, 1995, p.292).

Our findings also speak to existing claims by some researchers that health-related behaviors and attitudes portrayed in music videos are possible conveyors of meaning for young people (American Academy of Pediatrics, 1996). Finally, we assert that constructions/portrayals of Britney Spears are contributors to a media environment that privi-leges and promotes the ideal female body. That is to say, even if Spears' videos are "read" as pro-feminist texts, where her portrayals are powerful, athletic, and in-control, are revered for their potential to empower and inspire young female viewers, *it is still unquestionable that Spears remains defined by her body and its presentation.* Although we certainly cannot claim from these focused findings that mediated images of Spears and interpretations of her lyrics "lead to" body image disturbances, we unhesitatingly assert that the images and language reflect societal preoccupations with the female body, as has been argued in work on media, gender, the body, and sport (Cole, 2000). In this way, our case study of Spears could be viewed as a departure point for research like Wertheim, Mee, and Paxton's (1999), inter-ested in the relationship between an environment where there are high numbers of images and agents promoting and reflecting preoc-cupations with the feminine body, and the tendency for adolescents to view these depictions as "normal" or "ideal."

## RECOMMENDATIONS AND CONCLUSIONS

From the above findings and commentaries emerge a variety of departure points for future research and practical action. On the broadest level, this study highlights the need to focus more research attention on the diverse and vast media environment within which young people maneuver. This means not only identifying key sites where messages about the body and gender are distributed, but also relationships between the popular cultures that may work together to promote these messages—especially the music/sport relationship. At the same time, it is essential to remain sensitive to underlying political economic interests that inspire these same messages and (strategic) linkages.

Acknowledging that textual analysis is limited as a method for understanding the potential impacts of media on audiences, we strongly suggest that future research be conducted focusing on the meanings young females give to "ideal body" portrayals like those studied here. Through audience studies providing a more detailed and nuanced sense of young peoples' experiences within the type of media environment we have outlined here, a better understanding of media impacts can be discerned. The hope is that this enhanced sensitivity to relationships between media consumption and everyday life will be helpful for health educators encouraging adolescent females to recognize themselves in ways that have less to do with physical appearance. In the same way, we suggest that by identifying the various gendered messages that exist about the body, especially those emerging in the languages of popular cultures like sport and music, that these relationships can be better understood.

### REFERENCES

American Academy of Pediatrics. (1996). Impact of music lyrics and music videos on children and youth. *Pediatrics* 98 (December):1219–1221.

Bordo, S. (1993). *Unbearable weight: Feminism, western culture, and the body.* Berkeley, CA: University of California.

Bradby, B. (1992). Like a virgin-mother? Materialism and maternalism in the songs of Madonna. *Cultural Studies* 6: 72–96.

Brown, J. and Schulze, L. (1990). The effects of race, gender, and fandom on audience interpretations of Madonna's music videos. *Journal of Communication* 40: 88–102.

Cobley, P. (1994). Throwing out the baby: Populism and active audience theory. *Media, Culture and Society* 16: 677–687.

Cole (2000). Body studies in the sociology of sport: A review of the field. In *Handbook of Sport Studies*, ed. Coakley, J. and Dunning, E., 439–460. London: Sage.

Cusumano, D. and Thompson, K. (1997). Body image and body shape ideals in magazines: Exposure, awareness, and internalization. *Sex Roles* 37: 701–720.

Davis, L. (1997). *The swimsuit issue and sport: Hegemonic masculinity in* Sports Illustrated. Albany, NY: SUNY Press.

Dionne, M., Davis, C., Fox, J., and Gurevich, M. (1995). Feminist ideology as a predictor of body dissatisfaction in women. *Sex Roles* 33: 277–285.

Duncan, M. (1990). Sport photographs and sexual difference: Images of women and men in the 1984 and 1988 Olympic Games. *Sociology of Sport Journal* 7: 22–43.

———. (1994). The politics of women's body images and practices: Foucault, the panopticon and Shape magazine. *Journal of Sport and Social Issues* 18: 48–65.

Forbes Magazine. (2002). The celebrity 100. <http://www.forbes.com/static_html/celebs/2002.html>

Hargreaves, J.A. (1994). *Sporting females: Critical issues in the history and sociology of women's sports.* London: Routledge.

Hesse-Biber, S. (1996). *Am I thin enough yet? The cult of thinness and the commercialization of identity.* New York: Oxford University Press.

Kalof, L. (1999). The effects of gender and music video imagery on sexual attitudes. *Journal of Social Psychology* 139: 378–385.

Kellner, D. (1995). Madonna, fashion, and image. In *Media culture, culture studies, identity and politics between the modern and the postmodern,* ed. Kellner, D., 263–296. London: Routledge.

King, B. (2002). It's a date: Britney's taking NASCAR to the movies. *Sports Business Journal* (June 17): 3, 49.

Lavine, H., Sweeney, D., and Wagner, S.H. (1999). Depicting women as sex objects in television advertising: Effects on body dissatisfaction. *Personality and Social Psychology Bulletin* 25: 1049–1058.

Lewis, J. (1991). *The ideological octopus.* New York: Routledge.

MacNeill, M. (1988). Active women, media representations, and ideology. In *Not just a game: Essays in Canadian sport sociology,* ed. Harvey, J. and Cantelon, H., 195–211. Ottawa, ON: University of Ottawa Press.

———. (1998). Sex, lies, and videotape: The political and cultural economies of celebrity fitness videos. In *Sport and postmodern times,* ed. Rail, G., 163–184. Albany, NY: SUNY Press.

Markula, P. (1995). Firm but shapely, fit but sexy, strong but thin. The postmodern aerobicizing female bodies. *Sociology of Sport Journal* 12: 424–453.

Rail, G. (Ed.) (1998). *Sport and postmodern times.* Albany, NY: SUNY Press.

Rowe, D. (1995). *Popular cultures: Rock music, sport and the politics of pleasure.* London: Sage.

Stern, L. (2002). Body image: The idealization of thinness. *The Vancouver Sun* (July 27): A22–A23.

Synnott, A. (1993). *The body social: Symbolism, self, and society.* London: Routledge and Kegan Paul.

Wernick, Andrew. (1991). *Promotional culture: Advertising, ideology and symbolic expression.* New bury Park, CA: Sage.

Wertheim, E., Mee, V., and Paxton, S. (1999). Relationships among adolescent girls' eating behaviours and their parents' weight-related attitudes and behaviours. *Sex Roles* 41: 169–187.

Whitson, D. and Gruneau, R. (1997). The (real) integrated circus: Political economy, popular culture, and "major league" sport. In *Understanding Canada: Building on the new Canadian political economy,* ed. Clement, W., 359–385. Montreal: McGill-Queen's University Press.

Wilson, B. and Sparks, R. (1996). "It's gotta be the shoes": Youth, race, and sneaker commercials. *Sociology of Sport Journal* 13: 398–427.

———. (1999). Impacts of black athlete media portrayals on Canadian youth. *Canadian Journal of Communication* 24 (4): 589–627.

# PART VI

## Classic Case Studies

# CHAPTER 17

# NASCAR's Boy Wonder: Jeff Gordon as Ambivalent Sex Symbol in a Macho Subculture

*Scott A.G.M. Crawford*

A good case can be made here that the National Association for Stock Car Racing (hereafter known as NASCAR) is modern America's new national pastime. One of its founding fathers was the late "Bill" France Sr. who, in every aspect, fitted in with the "good ol boy" ethos. At six feet, five inches tall and 230 pounds, France was of imposing stature and a dominating presence. In 1938, as an inexperienced garage and service station operator, he joined a friend and took over the promotion, organization, and publicity of the many Daytona Beach stock-car races, and in a matter of weeks, the two-some amassed more than $4000. Brad Herzog (1995) points out France's visionary qualities: "[he] saw a need to regulate promoters and assure collection of prize money, to form a standard set of rules and specifications for all drivers and automobiles, to inaugurate a national championship and then a point system, to provide insurance for the drivers, and to create a central head-quarters" (p.188). France died in 1992 but had he been alive today he might have rubbed his eyes in disbelief. As Crawford (2002) has written: "A backwoods, regional, noisy 'bump and grind' chase had metamorphosed into—via the Winston Cup—thirty-some races in nineteen states with four million spectators and prize money of $25 million . . . In 1999 seventeen of the top twenty attended sporting events in the United States were NASCAR races, and NASCAR was worth $2.8 billion in television rights" (p.300).

The evolution of NASCAR in the post World War II is dramatic, and the picture that emerges is a unique cultural canvas shaped by an intriguing mix of fact and fiction, self-image, mythology, stereotype, caricature, character, hyperbole, and all manner of oral traditions— from true stories to tall tales, with the embrace of out-and-out lies— that have colored the sport and crafted a mosaic that, to this day, defines what NASCAR is all about. Richard Pillsbury's (1995, p.270) seminal essay explores the sport and its interaction with complex landscape ensembles. An ode to Richard Petty opens his narrative. The occasion was a fall race in 1992, Petty's retirement race after competing in 1,185 races. A crowd of 115,000 was on hand to cheer the grandfather of stock car racing and the sport's most stellar performer. The race sponsor was "Hooters," a popular chain of American restaurants where the beer is nicely chilled, there is an abundance of traditional home-style and Southern cooking, and the waitresses wear skimpy, revealing costumes. "Hooters" sells itself as a place where hot-blooded males ogle (leer?) at pretty young women, soak up ale, and fill their bellies with good grub. Pillsbury frames the rubric of how stock car racing came into being, listing the forces that then and now (seem) to sustain it: "White Lightning, Rednecks, and Blue Ribbon." "White Lightning" refers to the early roots of NASCAR, when it is claimed that illicit booze was driven from illegal stills and sold all across the old South by salesmen who shipped their alcohol in "souped up," stripped down streetcars that could outrace and out-duel any chasing arms of law enforcement. "Rednecks" refers to the view that early fan support came from a blue-collar working class, almost exclusively white, primarily male, who left school and went straight into the laboring world without any college education. And "Blue Ribbon" refers to a cheap beer, brewed that is seen to be part and parcel of the rituals and ceremonies associated with stock car racing.

## Sex and Stock Car Racing and Racers

Sex and sexuality have always been an integral aspect of stock car racing. Pillsbury (1995) describes the "shows us your bits" posing, posturing and, it has to be stressed sexist, exploitative and— sometimes— offensive relationship between younger female spectators and male race fans:

> As race time nears, fans make their ways to the stands to drink more beer and ogle the passing "parade" of scantily clad young women roaming back and forth across the front of the stands ostensibly looking for their

seats. Crowd response to these young women becomes increasingly pointed as the heat rises and the beer flows. First, wolf calls erupt as the more attractive, less dressed parade down the platform, then rebel yells follow, and finally more explicit comments are shooted out. The drama culminates sometime after the beginning of the race when a young woman accommodates the crowd and parades topless down the front walkway of the stands until the security guards arrive. (pp.284–285)

Stock car racing without question was energized by a collection of daring, skilled, and highly competitive drivers who performed in the spotlight and were adeptly marketed and promoted by NASCAR. Drivers such as David Pearson and Bobby Allison were seem to be gritty, "no holds barred" drivers who willingly would go fender to fender and transform their flying racing machines into combative missiles. They were tough, mean, and laconic.

"The King" was Richard Petty, whose lean frame made him look like a Gary Cooper figure in that classic Western movie *High Noon*, about courage, character, and taciturn toughness. Yet, despite his regal nomenclature, Petty's greatest asset was his "common man" persona: He was approachable, easily identified, collegial, and yet his sterling racing successes marked him as an extra-ordinary man. Herzog (1995) has written of 1967 as Petty's breakthrough year, likening his NASCAR record of 55 career wins as epoch-making, as significant as Wilt Chamberlain's 50-points-per game season, Mickey Mantle's triple crown performance, and O.J. Simpson's 2000-yard running total in football. He comments about Petty's charisma and the unique manner in which he attracted a charging legion of supporters who followed him as if he were equal parts messiah, muse, and icon. He clearly fit in well with a spectator subculture that liked its heroes to be uncomplicated, aggressive, and macho.

Following Petty's retirement, a number of other drivers jockeyed for supremacy on the NASCAR circuit, including Dale Earnhardt and Jeff Gordon. Earnhardt was cut from Petty cloth. He was middle aged, without a college education, and divorced. And he had an uneasy relationship with his rebellious son Dale Earnhardt, Jr., who eventually came to be a winner in Winston Cup races. Earnhardt played up his mean reputation of being tough, profane, and prone to anger, and enjoyed creating a legendary machismo image that favored black colors and raced under the soubriquet of "The Intimidator." His untimely death, at the 2001 Daytona 500, saw him no longer as the country's premier racer, but the outpouring following his death revealed that the "No. 3" was revered, adored, and beloved.

This essay sets out to examine the life and celebrity status of Earnhardt's most famous adversary: Jeff Gordon. It analyses the ambivalent appeal of "the Kid," an angelic-looking and still boyish figure who, in his early 30s at 5 foot 7 inches and 150 pounds, hardly fits the Petty/Earnhardt image. The mystery and magic of Gordon's emergence as a stellar driver is that the language used to describe, classify, and categorize him—either by journalists or by fans—has been located within a landscape where elements of sex appeal, sexuality, and sexual preference are highlighted in a manner that never came to the fore in the rhetoric used to describe his predecessors.

## JEFF GORDON AS MATINEE IDOL

In almost every respect, Gordon's upbringing, training, education, and apprenticeship has made him seem different from other NASCAR drivers. As a four-year-old Californian, Gordon was a fiercely competitive BMX (mountain bike) rider. He graduated from Pittsboro High School in 1989 as prom king and a year later won the U.S. Automobile Club (USAC) full midget championship. During the decade of the 1990s, his performances were outstanding, winning in 1994 the inaugural Brickyard 400 at the Indianapolis Motor Speedway. Then in 1995, 1997, and 1998 he won the Winston Cup championship. "By the end of 2000 Gordon's racing credentials were, by any yardstick, astonishing. In 257 starts he secured 52 wins, 122 top five finishes, and 159 top ten finishes, and his prize money totaled $29,570,670," writes Crawford (2002b, p.339).

### Developing a Persona

Right from the outset, Gordon's youthful profile created a division within NASCAR fans—a polarization or literal schism among NASCAR's devoted following. Stock car fans either took to, and embraced, a driver who had the clean looks of a matinee idol, or roundly rejected him and made him the focal point of their displeasure, antipathy, discontent, and disfavor. His arrival on the NASCAR scene marked the first time that sections of a stock car crowd repeatedly took it upon themselves to target him with intense barrages of jeers, catcalls, heckling, and verbal abuse.

Sport, especially American sport, has always had strongly homophobic elements. A 2002 *Sports Illustrated* piece (Lemon) analyzed the American fixation with homosexuality in sports, posing the question of why Americans remain so fascinated with the presence of gay athletes in team sports: "The glib answer is that the issue lies at the nexus of three powerful cultural forces: sex, sports and celebrity . . . From the fan's perspective the idea of gay athletes forces heterosexuals to confront stereotypes of gay men as lightweight or less than masculine. There are also issues of privacy and of how much we should know of our athletes' personal lives" (p.12).

For reasons that are still difficult to understand, Jeff Gordon raised the ire of some fans because there was the perception that he was gay. The fact that there was not any evidence to support such speculations did not alter what went on. The intensity of this communicated "language" of dislike has been summarized by Poole (2002) who mentions an Internet site that allows an anti-Gordon clique to purchase a video of him self destructing and hitting the wall of a race track. At the Charlotte Motor Speedway there are booths that sellout T-shirts inscribed with the words "Fans Against Gordon," each word capitalized to clearly convey the message.

During his rookie season, Grodon met and then married Brooke Sealey, an attractive model; yet, the marriage did nothing to change the vehemence of Gordon's fan base, who continued to either love or loathe him. He was still seen as straight or gay. Sealey was a born-again Christian who was devoted to daily Bible readings, church attendance, and a commitment to the temperance movement, all supported by her husband. While passionate about racing and winning, Gordon's top three priorities have been God, faith, and church. Next comes his wife and marriage.

Gordon's 1990s victories increased his fan "reactions," both positive and negative. George Tiedemann (2001) points to some elements of the Gordon persona that have played a role in marginalizing him as a NASCAR celebrity: "Handsome and articulate, clean cut and savvy" (p.8) he won races and Winston Cup series rather too easily, and, "The explosion of brilliant colors that makes his car [and his outfit] gives him an unthreatening, sunny aura" (p.6). Poole (2002) artfully suggests that NASCAR fans find it difficult to see Gordon as a "helluvafella," and that his "evangelical" version of masculinity in a contemporary culture (p.8) engenders in fans a heated irrational response that transforms their splentic rage into a focused war cry of "spear the Queer." The key element is manhood.

## METHODOLOGY ON GORDON'S IMAGE

A summer, 2002 graduate class of 20 physical education students at a midwestern university were an asked to react to a Gordon advertisement.

The group, equal numbers of men and women, were aged from 23 to 25. They respond to a nine-foot Pepsi dispenser with Gordon smiling widely, his dark hair stylishly cut and paradoxically, as he celebrates victory by shaking a Pepsi bottle and then holding it up to spray— perhaps—rival competitors, his pit crew, or spectators. The symbolism of this gesture is especially meaningful, assuredly neither cosmetic nor incidental, manifestly demonstrating support for the sponsored product (Pepsi) and reaffirming the conflicting perceptions (misperceptions?) of who is the "real" Jeff Gordon. Once again the issue is more than just image, it is about the perception of maleness. Gordon is posed as if a young peacock but the cues of the "true male" are absent. He appears more model than race car driver.

The students used words such as "cute," "handsome," "All American," "dark hair," "clean cut," and "attractive." Only two male students reported negatively on Gordon. One thought he was cocky and arrogant and that his jumpsuit looked "incredibly stupid." Another reckoned him to be a "geek" and "boring." One female student spoke of Gordon as "sexy/hot," and the second oldest female used these adjectival labels with him: "sparkle," "fresh," "youthful," "firm," "shapely," "nice," "well put together," "sweet," "coiffed," and "perfect." Note the interesting traces of ambiguity.

In 1996 and 2001, Gordon was recipient of the True Values Man of the Year Award in recognition of his concern for the well-being of children, and in 1999 he and his wife established the Jeff Gordon Foundation. It is all too easy to play down such charitable good works as attention gathering, ego-driven opportunities for self-aggrandizement.

## Changing Times

Then, as the 2002 Winston Cup series moved from winter to spring, Gordon's persona and his fans underwent a radical overhaul as what had looked like an idyllic marriage was torn by a bitter divorce. The accusation was "marital misconduct." As they didn't have a prenuptial agreement, at stake is a $10.5 million beachfront mansion at Highland Beach, Florida and portions of Gordon's personal fortune, valued at $45,000,000, of which his wife is demanding half.

There is a palpable sense that Gordon will forever be seen as an ambivalent sex symbol in a macho world of snarling engines and flying machines. Confederate flags, long-neck beer, and the music of Jonny Cash, Waylon Jennings, or Willie Nelson seem the antithesis of his style.

## Conclusion

While "Gordon bashing" has already been discussed here, it is important to spell out the splenetic nature of this hostility. A ceremonial prerace circuit of the track by Gordon can make sections of the crowd boo, and if he wrecks during a race, these individuals will mount an ovation. Such fans have a legion of anti-Gordon gripes. One can wonder if the antipathy is about chemistry, rapport, and/or contact. Certainly, large numbers of fans throughout Gordon's career have felt distanced from a man who simultaneously embraced God and *Seinfeld*, played videogames, water-skied and scuba-dived, and read *People* instead of *Playboy* or *Penthouse* magazine.

This writer has conceived of Jeff Gordon as being a modern J.M. Barrie's ethereal, forever-a-boy protagonist Peter Pan. Questions continue to be raised about the image and resilience of Gordon's boy wonder character. In an extensive piece in *Sports Illustrated* (MacGregor, 2002), the conclusion was that, despite NASCAR's employing "square-jawed All-American hotshot(s) like Jeff Gordon" (p.61), the future of the sport seemed to lie with younger drivers like Earnhardt, Jr.

A final postscript serves as a reminder about Gordon's most enduring impact, the very ambivalence of fan feelings about his character, personality, and presence. In mid-July, 2002 at the Chicagoland Speedway, NASCAR drivers raced to win the Tropicana 500. The *Associated Press* (2002) wrote of Dale Jarrett and Bobby Labonte drawing thunderous roars from the sell–out crowd; as for Gordon, "The ovation . . . [was] mixed liberally with boos" (B3). Varda Burstyn (1999) has made a compelling observation that people who are identified as threatening (and Gordon's racing persona does threaten and challenge the traditional stereotype of the manly athlete) can be isolated , stigmatized, and cast in the role of cultural scapegoat. While Gordon has escaped the political vitriol of being labeled as "pinko faggot" and "commie queer," he continues to be the victim of an unrelenting barrage of homophobia.

### References

Associated Press. (2002). Younger Waltrip reaching iconic status among fans. *Charleston Times Courier* (July 18): B3.

The Beat. (2002). *Sports Illustrated* 96, 18 (April 28): 29.

Bechtel, M. (2002). Here he comes. *Sports Illustrated* 97, 3 (July 15–22): 139.

Burstyn, V. (1999). *The rites of men: Manhood, politics and the culture of sport.* Toronto: University of Toronto Press.

Crawford, S.A.G.M. (2000). Dan Gurney. In *The Scribner encyclopedia of American lives—sports figures*, ed. Markoe, A., 369. New York: Charles Scribner.

———. (2002a). Bill France Sr. In Markoe, *The Scribner encyclopedia*, 300.

———. (2002b). Jeff Gordon. In Markoe, *The Scribner encyclopedia*, 339.

Herzog, B. (1995). *The sports 100: The one hundred most important people in American sports history.* New York: Macmillan.

Lemon, B. (2002). Not out at the plate. *Sports Illustrated* 96, 23 (June 3): 18.

MacGregor, J. (2002). Dale Earnhardt Jr. and NASCAR nation. *Sports Illustrated* 97, 1 (July 1): 61.

Milbourn, J. (2002). Drivers keep grip on wheel, faith. *Associated Press* (October 3). Source material at <www.nascar.com/2001/NEWS>

Pillsbury, R. (1995). Stock car racing. In *The theater of sport*, ed. Raitz, K.B., 270. Baltimore: Johns Hopkins University Press.

Poole, David. (2002). *Race with destroy: The year that changed NASCAR forever.* Tampa, FL: Albian Press.

Tiedemann, G. (2001). *Trading Paint.* New York: Total Sports Illustrated. 8. www.nascar.com/2001/FANS-//communities.msn.com/ FansAgainst Gordon. www.peoplejustlikeus.org

# "Hey, I'm the Coach's Wife, not the Team Mom": The Rhetoric of Little League Mothers' Role Performances

*Kim Golombisky*

## PROLOGUE

March 15, 1996: After writing about Little League mothers all week, I opened my local newspaper to a feature on the Northeast Little League (NLL) and its founder, Kathy Eber. The photo cutline read: "Kathy Eber and her son, Richie, have received many awards for their involvement in Little League—he for playing, she for organizing" (Ridge, 1996, p.9). Not mentioned was Kathy's husband, who coached their son's team to an undefeated season last year. Also missing from the story were the two Eber daughters, except for a clause about how the parents "carted their daughters to dance lessons." There was no recognition of the elder daughter's softball participation. The article quoted Kathy saying, "I've always been around sports, but I've never been much good them. I was always the cheerleader. That's why it's so fun for me to watch my kids do well at sports" (ibid). Voila, my exemplar: the Little League family.

## INTRODUCTION

This chapter makes four points: First, social performance is inherently suasory. Second, in the case at hand, enacting the Little League family comprises a sexual rhetoric instantiating hetero-normative gender. Third, mothers' role in this rhetorical performance represents both complicity and resistance, what HopKins (1995) might call the "toss" of communication's "performance turn" and Conquergood (1992, citing Scott, 1990), a "counterperformance" or "hidden transcript." Last, the ceremonial performance of Little League does not cast daughters in its production of what is framed as "family."

The literature is full of descriptions of sport as male ritual, male identity socialization, male peer group bonding. More recently a maturing feminist literature critiques sport's historical male exclusivity, encouraging an appreciation of female athletes as well as their history. Few scholars, though, have explored the role of *family* participation in organized sport. By exclusively highlighting the official sporting drama unfolding on the playing field, one can miss an equally riveting unofficial performance around the sidelines, where mothers and wives enact another set of scripts.

On the other side of the backstop, women may learn to enjoy and pass on knowledge about knitting together a community to support and contain sport designed for male children. Mothers may grouse from time to time about overt sexism, but they betray their consent to this form of male socialization by also cheering for it. Whatever gender scripts they have for home, work, community soccer, dance lessons, and more, at the baseball field, mothers may help enforce the stereotypical patriarchal, white, middle-class, able-bodied, heterosexual nuclear family's pre-eminence.

I know because in 1996 I had been an NLL mother for six years. During that sixth season, what for me began as an exploration of the work of publicly performing the family in Little League quickly became a reflective discovery about how mothers contribute to their own as well as their daughters' marginalization for the sake of their sons. Over the years, during informal conversations at the ball field, I collected unselfconscious but telling quotes and stories, some of which appear here. Then, however, as I openly acknowledged that I was writing a "gender critique of Little League," I began to get a more self-conscious kind of feedback. Some mothers laughed out loud at the idea. Others nodded knowingly: "You bet." Still others grew defensive, even hostile.

Approaching Little League baseball as a ceremonial performance of the gendered nuclear family in an effort to examine mothers' role, my observations come from participation in a mostly white, upper-middle-class community organization that began in 1990 to serve a rapidly growing suburban area. My partner, our two sons, and I participated in Northeast's development from its formation. Mothers' Little League script, I contend, is constitutive of Little League baseball as we know it; taking on this role, mothers implicitly consent to gender role boundaries. While some mothers may have felt uncomfortable with the parts they played, they were more ambivalent about rejecting parallel male scripts for their sons. Most mothers viewed Little League as a wholesome family activity, and valued their own function keeping competitive aggression within emotionally and socially safe limits as baseball inculcated their sons into male culture. Nevertheless, these mothers embodied a rhetoric of rigid gender roles.

This essay first introduces performance as a theoretical frame for approaching mothers' Little League participation as sexual rhetoric. Second, although baseball is a community ritual designed to socialize boys into male culture, a review of the literature shows that scholars do not account for the function of women in this process. Third, an examination of NLL family performances reveals not only that mothers' roles are integral to Little League but also that daughters' roles are absent. Fourth, highlighting mothers' presence raises questions regarding traditional interpretations of community rituals such as Little League. The liminal frame of boys' baseball may be playful "what if," but the broader ceremonial functions of the Little League organization communicate "what is" regarding heterosexual binary sex/gender and the female's subordinate status. Mothers, then, as Little League's supporting characters, are complicit in this socializing rhetoric. Finally, when reconsidered, some mothers' performances may be read as expressions of resistance.

## THEORETICAL FRAMEWORK: CATCHING THE PERFORMANCE TOSS

Defining rhetoric to include nonlinguistic human action, Burke (1935, 1941, 1945, 1950) understood rhetoric as dramatistic: "The broad scope Burke sees for rhetoric is summarized in his statement, 'Wherever there is persuasion, there is rhetoric. And wherever there is *meaning*, there is *persuasion*,' " (Foss, Foss, and Trapp, 2002, p.194, citing Burke, 1950, p.172). In short, Burke's approach to rhetoric includes socialization.

Decades later, McKerrow (1989) and Ivie (1994, 1995) appropriated the performance studies metaphor to redefine critical rhetoric, even though Sells (1997) points out that McKerrow's moral critic and Ivie's artful critic as activists both retain their power to *perform* what McKerrow (1989, p.172) called "a sensible reading of the discourse of power." However, HopKins (1995) and Conquergood (1992) made the crucial, seemingly commonsense yet under-theorized, connection between rhetoric and everyday social performance.

The significance of the performance turn, according to both Conquergood and HopKins, is opening a space to accommodate the subaltern. Conquergood (1992, p.90, quoting Scott, 1990, p.183) points out that "resistance is not limited to insurrections and uprisings": "Foot-dragging, pilfering, grumbling, 'conning,' and gossiping about one's overlords are the strategic 'infrapolitics' of the powerless that prepare for and underpin rebellion when it does break out."

## ACCOUNTING FOR WOMEN IN LITTLE LEAGUE'S RITUAL SOCIALIZATION

At Mort Field, before every NLL game, the home team reluctantly yields the diamond to regroup in the dugout as the visiting team, followed by its coaches, swarms onto the field to warm up. Meanwhile, mothers stroll, grouped in twos and threes, wave to other groups, connect with running packs of younger children to dole out dollar bills for concession candy, and move on to regroup again. Long before the umpire barks, "Play Ball," the game already has begun.

The parallels between Mort Field's choreography and scenes from Richard Schechner's (1988) *Performance Theory* are unmistakable. It is easy to get caught up in Schechner's exotic ethnographic examples of tribal dramas (like baseball games) embedded in community rituals (like Little League) as stylized ways of maintaining the social fabric, as safe structures where aggression and conflict become benign competition. His "efficacy-entertainment" braid becomes real when applied to youth sports—play interwoven with instrumental and moral learning. Little League serves as a kind of rite of passage, albeit a liminoid one (Turner, 1986), for little boys developing masculinity.

Similarly, Fine (1987) describes Little League baseball as a process of pre-adolescent boys' socialization into adult male sex roles. He compares the game to a dramatic performance, the boys performing and the coaches directing. The diamond is a set. Parents as fans become the audience. Yet, he doesn't address the larger function of Little League as a family ritual in which this baseball drama unfolds. He hardly mentions families at all, except to say that Little League as an organization respects the family's integrity—the schedule never interferes with other family institutions like school or church. Regarding roles, Fine writes that coaches as role models teach skills and moral philosophy, while parents (code for fathers) sometimes struggle to confine themselves within their appropriates roles, performing neither over-involvement nor under-involvement. He also observes that within the structure of Little League, fathers and sons find an environment facilitating mutual bonding.

This literature, however, begs some questions: What are the women doing during Schechner's (1988) fabulous rituals at liminally mysterious ceremonial centers? Where are the mothers of Fine's (1987) Little League players? Where am *I* as a Little League mother? While Schechner (1988) offers insight on Little League as a ritual performance, his perspective is androcentric. He seems drawn to the anthropology of those tribal "men's house institutions" that Kate Millet (1970) likened to Western male sport culture. Sabo and Runfola (1980, p.201), exploring "Jock" culture, elaborate her thesis:

> In preliterate societies, the men's houses serve as a social nexus of patriarchal association and emotion. These cultural centers of male ritual and values are experimental theaters in which youngsters make their tenuous passage from boyhood to manhood. . . . In order to insure male solidarity and the overall segregation of the sexes within the tribal group, any breach of house norms is met with severe censure and even social ostracism.

How about the realization that mothers may not notice what they are doing by performing their Little League roles: consenting to and perpetuating—performing—not only their own invisibility through segregation but also their own gendered status *as* women. They are, in essence, contributing to their own sidelining. Mariah Burton Nelson (1991, 1994) makes a compelling connection between male sports culture, *the weaker sex*, and violence against women. She shows how sports socialization, beginning with little boys, valorizes male strength and virility, glorifies violence, disparages women and women's bodies, and sets competition as the standard for social relations. Reminding readers that coaches, in order to make *men* of their players, punish *unmanly* performances with taunts of girlishness, she observes that women don't want "sissy" sons, at the same time wisely cautioning they should not want the other extreme: "brutal sons who grow inured to their own pain or to the pain of others" (p.4). Bell (2002), however, ultimately calls this play: "Women's place in these rites, at the sidelines, obviates other performances—backstage, private, and oriented to maintenance, not transformation—as outside the purview (and view) of what 'counts as an actual.' "

## NLL Family Roles and the Gendered Division of Labor

With boys ages 7 and 11 playing and a father coaching, baseball for our family was all-consuming work from late January tryouts through the June-July All-Star team season—nearly half the year not counting the second fall instructional Little League season that the Florida climate affords. Although at first I resisted my part, I soon got pretty good at *doing* middle-class baseball mother, and in fact rather enjoyed my increasing proficiency. As a family, we all accommodated the rigor of the season's weekly schedule of four or five practices and three or four games, and to a significant degree, this transformed regular family life into a community cause. Everyone had a specific part to play. My script had been there all along: Mothers functioned as the glue keeping everyone working together, despite the schedule's and the league's political and competitive centrifugal forces constantly threatening to fling the organization and its individual families apart. They crossed borders as if they did not exist, chatting with mothers on opposing teams, cheering others' children whenever they wanted to, and, just as quickly, ending any child's mischief off the field. Northeast mothers talked—behind the scenes, at the games, and on the phone. Their function was, in a word, communication.

Given the rigid segregation of our roles and the gendered complementarity of our role relationships, NLL was very much about publicly performing an ideal of that elusive social construction called the nuclear family, even when the players' families represented single-parent and other nontraditional models. Boys signed up to play and learn. Fathers signed up to coach and authorize public ceremony. Mothers signed up to be Team Mom, bring snacks, or work the concession stand. Daughters and sisters, however, mostly amused themselves under the bleachers.

Every year we all got a little better at performing our NLL family roles. When we did it well, it was an efficient system covering all the proverbial bases of family function. We were a team. American baseball—supported by sports media—continues to affirm "gender-based divisions of labor in the traditional American family," according to Trujillo (1994, p.102); as he summarizes it, baseball mythologizes the strong, skilled, aggressive male hero triumphing in the spotlight and the weak, unskilled, subordinate female cheering from the sidelines.

## THE RITUAL AND CEREMONY OF LITTLE LEAGUE AS GENDER AS-IFNESS

Having expanded Little League's performance frame to include what happens off the baseball field, acknowledged the presence of women, and explored family roles, we question the function of Little League. As a seasonal, public, community-sponsored institution designed to teach little boys physical fitness and citizenship through sportsmanship and team spirit, it qualifies as ritual, formal, and repetitive interaction guided by rules to communicate social purpose and organization. But, more than that, it is about ceremonial performance of formal family roles and rules that communicate gender status. The *ritual* of youth baseball may function as liminal space for adolescent male socialization, but the *ceremonial* structure of the Little League organization, in which baseball safely nests, functions as an indicative rhetoric about gender difference.

Gender rules of family and Little League communicate that men are athletic and women are not. Men are the focus of attention while women are marginal. Masculinity is competitive; femininity, supportive. Boys play; girls don't. Fathers direct as mothers support fathers' authority on, and their sons' performances in, baseball.

If the Little League family is a ceremonial performance of gender status, its structure is designed to support the ritual transformation of sons into men. Ritual performances represent a subjunctive frame distinguishing "play" from "reality." Little League as ceremony "counts." It communicates not subjunctive "what if" but indicative "what is." While playing baseball may afford boys the opportunity to *pretend* they are men, performing Little League roles requires families to "pretend they are not pretending," as HopKins (1995) noted of the duplicity required for such performances. The Little League baseball family meta-communicates indicative gender as-ifness, laying out unspoken gender rules. "As-ifness, as a stable reaction, is the expression, *in action*, of illusion," Henry (1971, p.xvii) observed about families. "The illusion must be maintained in order for people to carry on" (ibid). Little League families act *as if* gender makes a difference. Parents act *as if* boys were more important than girls.

## Little League Mothers' Resistance

Initially, playing a Little League mother put me on the defensive. The whole set-up was at odds with my identity, and I had no intention of identifying with those other mothers gossiping in lawn chairs. I resented their coaching my responsibilities—bring snacks, scrub the concession stand, collect walk-a-thon sponsors. Gradually, though, I developed lasting female friendships. I enjoyed watching the boys develop from season to season. I didn't mind my enhanced status as a coach's wife. I forgot what made me uneasy at the field. Later, a friend's subtle resistance reminded me: While she was trying to watch her son bat, a parent interrupted her with yet another schedule question. Irritated, my friend snapped, "Hey, I'm the coach's wife, not the team mom."

Self-awareness sometimes does require a nudge. When another Northeast friend discovered that I was looking at Little League in terms of gender, she responded less than supportively: "So we're invisible?" she demanded. "It's not about us. It's about the guys—you know—fathers and sons. I mean it's when we let go, hand them over . . . Isn't it?" Nevertheless, her pause and question—"Isn't it?"—became the loosened knot that unraveled the entire charade. Thereafter she took any opportunity to ask questions about feminism, which meant many hours on the phone that spring.

Other mothers tacitly communicated that they were in on the "the pretense." Another mother friend, one who enjoyed her position on the board of directors, was unaware of my research project when she shared the following comment: "He (the league president) told me I was biting off more than I could chew by wanting to be the game-day field manager this year. He's worried I can't handle it because I have to be out here all day dealing with the coaches, umpires, and parents." She paused to roll her eyes, "Like that's not what we (moms) all do anyway." Her ironic attitude supports my understanding of the Little League mother's role as a communication function.

All this suggests at some level that the mothers understood asymmetrical gender scripts and did signal their resistance. Furthermore, such speeches from Little League mothers position woman within the system, not outside it, simultaneously revealing some cracks in its structure. Still, one theme remained unvoiced: recognition of daughters/sisters' standpoint in the Little League family.

## CONCLUSIONS

To summarize, enacting the NLL family comprised a rhetoric adopting myths about the patriarchal family, male physical superiority, stereotypes of motherhood and fatherhood, sons' greater worth than daughters, and women's lower status in the social hierarchy with its gendered division of public and private labor. Significantly, this case provides evidence of women's centrality in the Little League ritual as well as their "hidden transcript" (Scott, 1990) of resistance. Most significant, however, this analysis suggests that playful spaces of subjunctive "what if" in male sports are circumscribed by and may depend upon ceremonial performances of indicative gender as-ifness. If young male athletes are encouraged to rehearse manhood on the playing field, then they must know the rules of gender before they can pull off manly performances.

While it is dangerous to generalize about Little League based on participation in one league, particularly one serving an affluent white community, it is safe to say that it continues to be a male socializing ritual designed for male children. This ritual recognizes neither the women's work required to produce it, nor the ways in which its celebration of the heterosexual nuclear family does not include daughters, not to mention nontraditional forms of family.

Sport as ideology (sports*man*ship), sport as institution (Little League), sport as ritual (baseball), and sport as practice (Little League family role performances) all contribute to a cultural rhetoric that renders sport a celebration of the male sex. Although women and the feminine are not valued in this symbolic discourse, both are required to produce it. Here lies the paradox for feminist theory: Despite the many physical, social, and psychological benefits girls accrue from playing team sports, simply encouraging daughters to play ball does not critique sports as a masculine enterprise developed by men for men as a means to define manhood and males as physically superior. Nor do the lessons girls learn in sports critique competitive relations in other social arenas. Yet girls and women who don't accrue these benefits or learn these lessons are at a distinct disadvantage in a culture already persuaded, first, that men remain *the* authority on sports and, second, that sports prepare one for adult (code for male) success.

Beyond asking how performance can do more work for communication, this study raises three questions. First, what processes already have persuaded diminutive male tee-ball players to shun female teammates? Considering the scope of U.S. youth athletics, sports scholars may need to focus on younger female and male athletes and earlier sports practices than in the past. Second, given the instance of Little League mothers, what other backstage and otherwise obscured performances not only contribute to sports' sexual rhetoric but also represent opportunities for intervention? Third, and finally, how might academics create "static" as activists or public intellectuals? HopKins (1995, p.236) enjoins us, "Especially as theorists, we need to perform our roles with as much noise as possible."

## Epilogue

In the three and a half years since I drafted this essay, the drama of NLL turned to girls' softball. In spring 1998, with 500 children registered to play, the league abandoned Mort Field for a brand new complex it had already outgrown. And the local newspaper published an editorial I wrote questioning the league's commitment to girls

(Golombisky, 1998). Over the next year, girls' softball at Northeast enjoyed a relative surge in popularity. At its peak, the girls fielded four teams, drew large enthusiastic crowds, and played on the same lighted fields as the boys. During the season, though, a group of softball parents created some static of their own by complaining to the newspaper about the league's "second class" treatment of their daughters. When the paper broke the story, I was encouraged that Little League mothers and fathers recognized classic disparities between female and male athletes. The girls' parents charged that the league refused to pay for softball umpires as it does for baseball, provided softball with inferior equipment compared to baseball, and forced the girls' teams to play by less competitive rules than the boys. Softball parents said the message was clear: softball does not get the same priority as baseball, and the league has lower expectations for the girls' abilities.

## References

Bell, E. (2002). When half the world's a stage: A feminist excavation of Richard Schechner's theory of "Actuals." *Theatre Annual* 55: 112–131.

Birrell, S. (1992). *The woman athlete: Fact or fiction?* Paper presented at the National Girls and Women in Sport Symposium, Slippery Rock State University, Slippery Rock, PA. February 6–9.

Burke, K. (1935). *Permanence and change: An anatomy of purpose.* New York: New Republic.

———. (1941). *The philosophy of literary form: Studies in symbolic action.* Baton Rouge: Louisiana State University Press.

———. (1945). *A grammar of motives.* New York: Prentice-Hall.

———. (1950). *A rhetoric of motives.* New York: Prentice-Hall.

Conquergood, D. (1992). Ethnography, rhetoric, and performance. *Quarterly Journal of Speech* 78 (1): 80–97.

Fine, G.A. (1987). *With the boys: Little League baseball and preadolescent culture.* Chicago: University of Chicago Press.

Foss, S.K., Foss, K.A., and Trapp, R. (2002). *Contemporary perspectives on rhetoric,* 3rd ed. Prospect Heights, IL: Waveland.

Gazella, K. (1999). Uneven playing field?: Parents of daughters who play Northeast Little League softball say when it comes to rules and equipment, boys baseball teams fare better. *St. Petersburg Times* (April 30): North of Tampa, 1.

Goffman, E. (1959). *The presentation of self in everyday life.* Garden City, NY: Doubleday.

Golombisky, K. (1998). Teach girls to be strong, confident. *St. Petersburg Times* (October 11): North of Tampa, 1.

Henry, J. (1971). *Pathways to madness.* New York: Random House.

HopKins, M.F. (1995). The performance turn—and toss. *Quarterly Journal of Speech* 81(2): 228–236.

Ivie, R.L. (1994). Scrutinizing performances of rhetorical criticism. *Quarterly Journal of Speech* 80 (3): 1.

———. (1995). Productive criticism. *Quarterly Journal of Speech* 81(1): 1.

McKerrow, R.E. (1989). Critical rhetoric: Theory and praxis. *Communication Monographs* 56 (2): 91–111.

Millet, K. (1970). *Sexual Politics.* Garden City, NY: Doubleday.

Moore, A. (1999). Girls softball makes tentative comeback with teams. *St. Petersburg Times* (December 10): North of Tampa, 7.

Nelson, M.B. (1991). *Are we winning yet?: How women are changing sports and sports are changing women.* New York: Random House.

———. (1994). *The stronger women get, the more men love football: Sexism and the American culture of sports.* New York: Harcourt Brace & Company.

Rappaport, R. (1968). *Pigs for the ancestors.* New Haven: Yale University Press.

Ridge, K. (1996). Little League was big job for mom. *St. Petersburg Times* (March 15): North of Tampa, 9.

Sabo, D.F., Jr. and Runfola, R. (1980). *Jock: Sports and male identity.* Englewood Cliffs, NJ: Prentice-Hall.

Schechner, R. (1988). *Performance theory,* revised ed. New York: Routledge.

Scott, J.C. (1990). *Domination and the arts of resistance: Hidden transcripts.* New Haven, CT: Yale University Press.

Sells, L. (1997). *Toward a feminist critical rhetoric: Subjectivity, performance, and the body in feminist public address.* (Unpublished doctoral dissertation, University of South Florida, Tampa).

Trujillo, N. (1994). *The meaning of Nolan Ryan.* College Station, TX: Texas A&M University Press.

Turner, V. (1986). *The anthropology of performance.* New York: PAJ Publications.

CHAPTER 19

# "Man-On": The Culture of Girls' Soccer

*Sally Cole Mooney*

At a recent State Championship soccer match between two New Orleans private school teams, the girl who scored the winning and only goal bought herself a yellow card for an action that would have been perfectly in keeping with the way boys play, and are expected to play, soccer. She pulled off her jersey and ran ecstatically around the field. No, she was not cited for displaying flesh, for copying Brandi Chastain's muscle-y revelation of her sports bra, never mind the fact that the sports bra has been outerwear for years at any road race in an American city. She was wearing a T-shirt under her jersey on which, in an amazing act of foresight, she had penned a message to her boyfriend: "This goal's for you." So what foul did she commit? Excessive celebration. That yellow card underscores the feeling I have had for years now: Girls' soccer is a radically different game from boys' soccer, despite the Women's World Cup victory and Title IX rules. In their hairstyles, their dress, and their style of play, soccer girls represent a "dunning-down" of male flamboyance, with coaches and referees reinforcing this unwritten rule. Only in their language, borrowed intact from male coaches, do these female players approximate the males.

## HAIR

Part of the reason I have always liked soccer is that it differs so radically from the buzz-cut militarism of football, a game that celebrates brute power, ganging up, physical size, and mindless motion. Soccer, by contrast, is individualistic, based on skill instead of size, and on quick decision-making by the player instead of set plays. This difference manifests itself most obviously in hairstyles. Male soccer celebrates hair. It rejects male norms for over-the-top, gender-bending styles: the pony tail, the dreadlock, the long, greasy freestyle of the Italian national team players, the shaggy goateed look of Alexi Lalas, the Mohawk of Curtis Mathis. Locally, our boy players mimic the pros. Recently, at a regional tournament in Oklahoma City, a New Orleans Under-15 club team bleached their hair platinum. The dreads became even more outrageous; the redhead looked bizarre; the black striker approximated Dennis Rodman. But the same club's Under-13 girls' team, who had won the State tournament in the Under-14 age group, and had more cause for celebration, looked like female players everywhere: plain. They slicked their hair back into ponytails, just like the Women's World Cup players did, exposing bare, healthy, sun-tanned faces. Female players are marked by their lack of adornment, in direct opposition to the males. Our girls wear only sunscreen on their faces, vaseline for chapped lips, plain elastics around their pony tails— no makeup, no face paint, no dyed hair or flashy styles. They look like "girls next door." Some girls' high school teams wear matching hair ties in their ponytails, but when they do they call up images of dance teams and pep squads—conventional outlets for female athleticism—not of soccer teams, famous for their flash.

## Dress

In their dress, it's the "tame game" all over again. While the boys strut around between matches, shirtless, with shaved legs and even sometimes arms—earrings and neck chains commonplace—the girls keep covered and demure. They'll switch from cleats to soccer sandals, remove socks or switch jersey for tee shirt, but an unwritten rule bans female flesh. In soccer, sports bras remain undergarments. And on the field, girls may roll their shorts one waistband up. But a self-imposed rule forbids more than that. One hot spring tournament in Baton Rouge I saw the unthinkable: A girls' team, in response to the heat, was playing with shorts up at least two rolls, jerseys tucked up under sports bras, leaving midriffs wonderfully bare. The girls stopped to gawk. "I can't believe it. What team is that?" one of them asked. "The Soccer Sluts," another answered. In this freest of games, the girls still follow a pre-Madonna dress code. The boys bend gender rules; the girls embrace them.

## CELEBRATION

Yet in hotel parking lots at tournament time, these same girls' teams will flaunt their arrival, with car windows advertising player names and numbers, boasting of victories and titles held: "Ashley, #15," "Allison, #10," "The Rage," "The Fury," "The Sting." The boys' cars, by contrast remain unadorned. It is as if, denied excess in dress and celebration, the girls displace their longing for it onto some safe symbol of self, whose power they may freely claim. Once again, their method of display follows pre-established female grooves—those well worn by cheerleaders and pompon girls—sign-making, locker-decorating, ribbon-tying, banner-trailing. Driving their flamboyant cars, these female players almost match the strut and swagger of their boys' team peers. But when the car doors open, the drama fades as identical, dunned-down forms pile out: fresh faced, pony-tailed, sleek, and tanned.

This same displacement struck me as I watched the 1999 Women's World Cup games. The television cameras zeroed in again and again on the faces in the crowd: invariably those of preteen girls, covered in face paint, ecstatic in expression. And yet that excess once again emerged from a female in the role of fan, not from a female athlete. Looking at a photo of the Women's National Team, one would never guess their stature in the soccer world—champions twice over in a global contest, the premier kickers of soccer butt. They look like young women anywhere, toned by Jazzercise. David Letterman was dead-on in christening them the "Babe Team"—Mia Hamm, Ivory-girl pretty; Brandi Chastain, Heather Locklear in shin guards (see Longman, 2000). Who would guess they could play so well? And why don't they flaunt it? We know what happens when they do, when borrowing from the male game one rips off a shirt to celebrate the self, one's own clutch goal with the whole world watching. Brandi had to backtrack the whole of the next day on national television, with Julie Foudy to give her support. The cameras replayed the crime as often as the Challenger explosion. And just what was the crime, the bra or the gloating, the reveling in one's own sweet moment of power and nerve? My daughter's reaction suggests the latter. When the shirt came off, she said in awe, "Wow! She's got a six-pack." And, it might be added, the gall to strut it (see also Bamberger, 1999).

## STYLE OF PLAY

The boast, the swagger, the strut in any form, tends to males on the soccer field, as in the world. The female defers, covers up, remains unmarked and understated, even when she plays the game. Although women play as well as men, they play a different style of ball. They move with precision, first to the ball, control it in a few deft steps, then pass or feed it to an open mate. Our girls' team has mastered cooperative play. As state champs, they routinely dominate their matches. But they've been known to lose for their failure to score, to break from the pack, and take the shot—the assertive blast—conferring glory on its agent. It is that very glory girls find hard to take, teach each other not to want, and learn to hide their craving for. In the last few minutes of that New Orleans high school championship match, the losing team gave up its chance to tie when a striker paused, the goal within her grasp, then dished the ball off to a teammate. I have seen this happen time and again—the player move out of her comfort zone—then find her way back by passing the ball.

Girls' soccer seems to be an athletic version of a corporate truth: women govern by consensus. The top-down, executive-decision style belongs to the office run by males with the soccer equivalent the shot-on-goal, all power focused in the foot of one, who acts for all to win the game. To take the shot asserts the self in that flamboyant way the female shuns. She is more at home with the assist, which lets her shine in a supporting role, still a player, but also a fan. Our coach himself reinforces this "rule," often taking out the player who scores, almost certainly one who scores more than once, the hat-trick—three goals, that ultimate soccer plum—the emblem of excess, and therefore forbidden. "If there's to be glory, let's spread it around," he seems to say, so that watching girls' soccer calls up the image of an oiled machine, a product of composite parts, with boys' games all bells and whistles: a series of daring solo flights—long spells of dribbling, diving headers, fancy footwork, and bicycle kicks. In clinics, our girls have all the same moves—but to-a-girl they underuse these spotlight-grabbing talents, opting instead for the crisp pass, the hallmark of teamwork (see also: Akers, 2000; Carlson, 1999; Festle, 1996; Hamm, 1999; Littman, 1999; Stokell, 2002).

## FOULING

That different attitude toward transgressing, so apparent in the players' dress and hairstyles, emerges too on the field of play. Our girls, for the most part, play by the rules, the foul unintentional and frowned upon: an elbow, a trip, a high kick, a bump. The boys, by contrast, have made the foul an integral part of the way they play, a strategy by which they gain the advantage, a risk they deliberately choose to take. I don't think I have ever watched a game where male players didn't pull on jerseys to slow down opponents who were beating them. A player on my younger son's team was famous for his dramatic dives. He invariably garnered a free kick for his talent, often shifting the game's momentum and always earning his teammate's respect. Even the coaches reinforce this feeling that fouling belongs in soccer games. I learned this quite dramatically when a fullback on my older son's team committed a flagrant foul in the box. He was carded and removed from the field as the enemy set up for their penalty kick. I watched the sinner approach the bench, expecting to hear an outburst from the coach, but instead saw him shake this player's hand. Both my sons have confirmed that as sweepers their job was to preclude the shot-on-goal, with fouling the option when all else failed. My daughter, a sweeper too, has never pulled a player's shirt or fouled a player in the box. And if she had, neither coach nor teammate would shake her hand. The girls consider the intentional foul a sign of failure, of loss of control, while the boys see this break as a mark *of* control, establishing their dominance (see Bredermeier and Stephens, 1996; Mummendey and Mummendey, 1983). In this way, the soccer pitch reflects the rules of the culture-at-large, with boys the Huck Finns, lovable transgressors; girls are the Aunt Sallys, civilizing forces.

## LANGUAGE

In light of these many gender distinctions, hearing girls' soccer makes me smile. In their speech, the girls have lifted intact the words their all-male coaches say. While seeing distinctly female play, the spectator hears a unisex script, "man-on" called out to warn a girl of another girl's approach, the "man" often slender, pony-tailed, and blonde. By the time they were U-10s, our girls had adopted this useful term—as defenders mourning the other team's goal, "But it was my man"; as goalies pointing out an open player, "Whose man is that?"; as any player warning "Katie, MAN-ON!" or even the shorter version, "MAN!" In many ways the game itself determines the language its players use, with soccer intuitive, fast and unscripted, thus demanding a clipped, unambiguous code. What better phrase than "man-on" for speed? What need to tailor it to fit a girl? Only in Mississippi have I heard it altered, a coach admonishing a sweet Southern thing for failing to stay on her "mark." Everywhere else, the players "mark up" at critical junctures by getting on their "man."

The running dialogue of soccer games is less obviously, but still consistently male: a string of bald imperatives, with the volume on high, the kind of language none of our girls would use in any other context: "drop," "time," "through," "wide," "one-two," "switch," "push up," "clear," and that almost-sentence, "got ya back." My daughter's translation points up the beauty of this masculine mono-syllabic talk in dispersing information across a field and especially to the one with the ball, intent on the action at her feet, and thus in need of her teammates' eyes:

- "Drop": You've run into a wall of opponents, but here in the backfield we're wide open, so pass the ball back.
- "Time": There's no one coming on you, so don't panic and screw it up.
- "Through": Pass it upfield to an open space, and I'll make a run.
- "Switch": All the bodies are bunched up on your side of the field, but the other side has lots of space, so send it over there.
- "Wide": Kick the ball to the wing, who will cross it back in front of the goal.
- "Push up": Defenders, move up to pull the opposing forwards off-side.
- "One-two": I'm giving you the ball, but I'm making a run and expect it back.
- "Clear": We're in trouble back here; just boot it the hell upfield.
- "Got You Back": Should you get in trouble I'm right behind you and can help out.

On the soccer field, indirection and subtlety—all the habits of female speech (tag endings, disclaimers, commands phrased as questions)— would never work. The ball and the game would be lost in translation. But the terse command, this unisex shorthand, ensures the success of an improvised game-plan. So important is the players' talk that I once heard a coach explain to a player that he was benched for being "mute." Our girls have learned to talk the talk unfettered by the rules of sex—until, that is, they cross the line, committing the equivalent of flashing their bras, by swearing within the range of the ref. This slip stops the referee in his tracks, and usually draws a yellow card, whereas boys enjoy a wider range. "Fuck" inevitably rates a card, but our girls have been carded for saying "damn." One of their coaches banned their chant—"NOSA, KA all the way"—when he learned what KA stood for: "Kick Ass." And once, in Gulfport, Mississippi, our smallest girl got a yellow card for "My God."

All in all, our most talented club team plays like girls, as do world champs Mia Hamm, Brandi Chastain, Christine Lilly, Julie Foudy.

Behind the aggression, the talent, the speed and the heart, lie all the markings of the female sex: modesty, deference, self-monitoring, rule-following, flesh-covering, spotlight-shunning and, oh yes, winning. In many ways the game of soccer selects for a female style of play, the winners those who best adapt to the cooperative venture that it is, as long as someone takes a shot. I just wish our girls would have more fun: dye their hair blue, play in their sports bras, show off their foot skills, shoot from midfield, be less controlled and more exuberant, like Brandi Chastain and her New Orleans apprentice, like every boy's team I've ever watched; in short, be as bold in their play as they are in their talk.

## References

Akers, M. (2000). *The game and the glory: An autobiography*. Grand Rapids, MI: Zondervan Publishing House.

Bamberger, M. (1999). Dream come true: Michelle Akers and the nineteen other members of the World Cup winning US soccer team gave America a summer to savor forever. *Sports Illustrated* (December 20): 46.

Bredemeier, B.J. and Stephens, D.E. (1996). Moral atmosphere and judgments about aggression in girls' soccer: Relationships among moral and motivational variables. *Journal of Sport and Exercise Psychology* (June):158–173.

Carlson, M. (1999). Why it was more than a game. *Time* (July 19): 64.

Festle, M.J. (1996). *Playing nice: Politics and apologies in women's sports*. New York: Columbia University Press.

Hamm, M. (1999). *Go for the goal: A champion's guide to winning in soccer and life*. New York: HarperCollins.

It went down to the wire. (1999). *Newsweek* (July 17): 46.

Littman, J. (1999). *The beautiful game: Sixteen girls and the soccer season that changed everything*. New York: Avon.

Longman, J. (2000). *The girls of summer*. New York: HarperCollins.

Mummendey, A. and Mummendey, H.D. (1983). Aggressive behavior of soccer players as social interaction. In *Sports violence*, ed. Goldstein, J.H., 111–128. New York: Springer-Verlag.

Stokell, I. (2002). *Coaching women's soccer: A revolutionary approach to putting play back into practice*. Chicago: Contemporary Books.

# CHAPTER 20

# The Making of the Perfect Sacrifice: A Rhetorical Analysis of Football Coaches' Descriptions of their Wives

*Diana L. Tucker*

Fans often view coaches as leaders as they might view politicians as leaders, seeing them as leaders of their teams but also as civic leaders. Sometimes they are even revered as national leaders, even "god-like." When it comes to the sports world, fans may believe that not only are coaches ever present, they may even be all-knowing, all-powerful. Some football coaches' wives have told me that when they got married they were told to read a certain book by a certain football coach, basically told to go to some "all-knowing" source to find out what their lives would be (should be) like. This suggested to me that football culture actually has an informal handbook for "how to be a coach's wife," coming in the form of football coaches' publications— some autobiographies, others "how to coach" texts.

When coaches talk or write about their job, it is serious to them, so when they write about their wives, it should be taken seriously, as it functions rhetorically as a type of coaching. Mention of one's wife (and how the wife is mentioned) is in part coaching other wives how to properly enact their gender role. For instance, the infamous West Point coach Earl Blaik (1960) wrote that his wife, Merle, "Has been the perfect football wife. She always accepted the ceaseless demands of coaching on my time, and took as much interest in my players as if they were her own sons . . . She aged through the games even more rapidly than I did, and, if it is possible, suffered even more anguish from and was even more intolerant of defeat. She paid the price" (69).

## Methodology

This analysis began by searching publications for mention of football coaches' wives. Perusing publications by them found that the wives (either theirs or another coach's wife) were mentioned over 125 times, a count that included the entire chapter on football coaches' wives from Ralph Sabock's book, *The Coach* (1973). Other publications analyzed include autobiographies and "how to coach" texts by Earl Blaik (1960), Mike Holovak and McSweeney (1967), Paul F. Dietzel (1971), Pepper Rodgers and Thomy (1976), Chuck Knox and Plaschke (1988), Joe Paterno with Asbell (1989), Bo Schembechler and Albom (1989), Jerry Glanville and Miller (1990), and Bill Reid (1994). Two themes about coaches' wives emerged from the analysis of these texts: Family Caregivers and General Caregivers.

Using a Burkean analysis (1941, 1973), trying to understand a rhetor's worldview, seemed most appropriate here—especially the notion of "cluster analysis" for the keywords. Of particular help came fleshing out an umbrella term for the whole analysis: "Issues of Surrogacy."

### *Surrogacy*

In contemporary usage, the word "surrogate" is usually associated with infertility and surrogate motherhood, the latter being one who carries a baby to term for another person. The traditional definition specifically means to substitute for another person in *any* way. According to *The American Heritage Dictionary* (2000), it comes from the Latin *surrogatus*, meaning to elect in place of another, a derivative of the Latin words *sub* (under, below, inferior) and *rogare* (to ask). It would seem that the rhetoric of football coaches' public communication asks football coaches' wives to be surrogates in numerous ways. Particularly as "scapegoats." When a football coach describes his wife's activities, behavior, and reactions, he is often making her a scapegoat by making her "too good for this world." Burke (1941) explains that there are three ways a scapegoat becomes "worthy" of sacrifice: First, the scapegoat can be an offender against legal or moral justice; second, s/he can be sacrificed fatalistically; or third, s/he can become the scapegoat and be sacrificed because of his or her high value, because s/he is the "most perfect sacrifice."

It is this last type of sacrifice that operates in football coaches' publications. Because she is "too good for this world," the coach's wife becomes the perfect vessel as sacrificer. She sacrifices for her family and for others in the extended football family. While she does not become the "fall guy/gal" who others blame for things that go wrong, nevertheless she becomes the scapegoat because she is the one upon whom others heap their burdens and she is expected to take these burdens willingly. These burdens often put her in the surrogate role as a father for her children, a mother for players.

The themes of "Family Caregiver" and "General Caregiver" show how the football coach describes his wife as a private sacrificial scapegoat, and then as a public scapegoat, rhetorics that function to relieve his guilt of not being at home, of not being able to be completely personal with the public, by showing that his wife is the more perfect person to do these things. She becomes the sacrifice because she does it well. This is illustrated in the following paragraphs, which focuses on the private realm of caregiving, of the family.

## The Private Sphere: Family Caregiver

The theme of "Family Caregiver" emerged the first time I read through the football coaches' publications, sensing that being feminine, and making motherhood, wifehood, and family priorities was key to the proper gender role for a football coach's wife. Examining the publications, searching for the terms, "wife," "mother," and "woman," I charted the associational terms that surrounded these three words. Most of the associational terms the authors used were descriptive in nature, and in three different ways: The first group of descriptors included those words that the authors use to describe their wives' physical features. Second, the most prevalent descriptors are ones pertaining to a wife's character. Third, many of the coaches referred to the jobs their wives were expected to perform.

These three categories of descriptors for "Family Caregiver" invite readers to perceive a coach's wife in a particular way: Specifically, from descriptors for physical attributes and character to believe that the proper football coach's wife would never have a bad day. It seems that she is always beautiful and cheerful. Coaches Chuck Knox (1988), Bill Reid (1994), and Joe Paterno (1989) used such terms as "cute," "little," "fair," "lovely," and "womanly" referencing their wives, Jerry Glanville (1990) being the only author to put a definite *focus* on his wife's physical features—we are introduced to the notion of the "perfect coach's wife."

Most coaches emphasized their wife's character over physical features. Character terms included being "unselfish," "warm," "concerned," "patient," "devout," "faithful," "sweet," "cheerful," "courageous," "smart," "committed," "busy," "devoted," "accepting," and "humorous." For example, Joe Paterno (1989) dedicated his book to his wife: "*To my wife and friend, Sue*. I hope your goodness, talents, and unselfish commitment to your family, to people, and to Penn State glow as brightly on every page of this book as your warmth and concern have touched all who know you." While this dedication is touching, it also functions rhetorically as foreshadowing her as heroine, even martyr.

Because so many of the coaches' autobiographies mention their own irritability and their wives' cheerfulness, readers may not be encouraged to look for discrepancies, but will more likely look for those who confirm the status quo. Even more revealing is that the "successful" coach's wife only acknowledges the hardships of sticking with her coach by displaying "patient humor." In order to be a good football coach's wife, it would seem to be imperative that one has humor—the wife is supposed to laugh at her situation instead of getting angry about it or trying to change it. The football community rewards those with the best "patient humor" by asking them to take their humor to the public arena.

### Victorian Foremothers

While football is a relatively modern game, the coach's wife (or as coach Mike Holovak refers to her: "Mrs. Coach") is expected not only to have patient humor, but also to act as if she exists in an earlier era. When likening her behavior, as explained by the coach, to the behavior of women in Victorian times, the good football coach's wife is the epitome of the "true woman," when the "separate spheres" doctrine dominated. This concept pertains to the idea that men and women have different places or roles in society, and that those roles are perpetuated and sanctioned through generations of adherence to and practice of mundane rituals. In short, women were relegated to the home, while men began to venture out into other worldly pursuits.

As was true of women in the Victorian era (Campbell, 1989), women who are married to football coaches find that their efforts are geared for others. It is easy to see how, if a coach's wife has a career of her own but feels compelled also to adhere to such constraints of "true womanhood," her time and well-being could be stretched thin. This is especially true when some factors of her "job" come into play, such as making clothes, saving money, cleaning, guiding the family, raising the family, moving the family, and comforting the coach. These are the most obvious burdens heaped upon the coach's wife. Specific associational clusters in this category include "role," "business," "work," "clean," "money," "pregnant," "kids," or "children," "house," or "home," "family," "kitchen . . ." and "alone."

### Caregivers

Ralph Sabock (1973) explains the difficulty the wife's job as a family caregiver often entails: "Most of the unhappiness that occurs with coaches' wives arises because they never really understood what is involved in coaching and what kind of demands this profession makes on the coach and the family. It takes a special kind of wife to cope with this . . ." (p.78). Statements such as this, in fact books such as this, help to verify the status of the coach and what he says about the wife's role in football. Bill Reid (1994) was even more blunt about her job: "It was her business to fall in with whatever you wanted to do and make the best of it even if it should happen to be something that she did not wholly like" (p.322). These kinds of statements also reify the importance of having a wife to do certain jobs for the coach. Joe Paterno (1989) explains how he never thought about how his only pair of good pants just happened to be clean for every game; when he got them muddy and Sue said, "You did it again. Every week the same thing . . . Got your pants muddy . . . I just cleaned them," he says it never even occurred to him. All he knew was that, "I owned one good pair of pants, and every Saturday morning they were clean" (p.107).

Understood: it is the wife's job NOT to say anything about coaching, but just to be supportive of her husband's coaching career. The wife's success at this job is relayed in two ways: Sometimes a coach writes about how his wife made the mistake one time and tried to say something about coaching, but he put her back in line and she did very well from then on.

Most of the coaches chose to show how well their wives stayed away from trying to coach by describing how they supported them in whatever they wanted to do. For instance, when it came to moving often, Knox (1988) explains that Shirley said, "Whatever you want to do" (p.81). By emphasizing his wife's compliance with the demands of his job, he relegates her to minor status in the family; in other words, the football coach expects his wife to exist in a world of paradoxes. She is to do most of the work for the family, yet she has no voice in major decisions about the family. She is to lead the family and be independent when the husband is not around, but she is to follow him wherever he wants to go. This would especially be true for football coaches' wives who are constantly asked to change from being independent to being dependent and then back again.

When Paterno became famous he could not go anywhere with his family without being recognized and attracting a crowd, leading his wife to taking the kids on summer vacations alone and attending the children's extracurricular activities alone. In the same vein, Mike Holovak (1967) dedicated his book to his wife Edith, "the football widow." Chuck Knox (1988) explained that he was so immersed in football that he almost didn't notice the birth of his third daughter.

The efforts of a coach's wife are for others: Her husband, her children, the players, other coaches, and their families. Nowhere is this more apparent than in the next section, which explores the theme of the "General Caregiver," where the wife becomes the constant entertainer, with the added pressure of the idea that her success at entertaining will keep her husband's career afloat.

## The Public Sphere: General Caregiver

The concept of caregiving in a general sense means to give care, basic needs, and/or emotional support to those both in one's immediate family and/or an "adopted" family. It is considered a form of hosting. Keywords used to conduct the cluster analysis in the this theme included anything having to do with "food" or "party," such as "cooking," "dinner," "restaurant," "catering," "social," "open house," "luncheon," and other similar terms, or "odd jobs" that coaches' wives were asked to perform.

For instance, Bo Schembechler's wife was asked to be the master of ceremonies at a football banquet, while others had to step in for their husbands as a surrogate at social functions and in other instances. Paul Deitzel (1971) called it "a must" for coaching staff and wives to get together. Chuck Knox (1988) claimed he and his wife often had dinner parties after games for the other coaches and their wives. Earl Blaik (1960) wrote that it was a "custom" for him and his wife to hold an open house after home games for their friends as well as newspaper reporters. And Joe Paterno (1989) joked that during recruiting season his wife is, "Almost in the tour guide and restaurant business" (p.180).

The "odd jobs" aspect of hostessing can entail a great deal of pressure. For a football coach, success as a "hostess" (and thus, as a wife) means she must have the ability to incorporate a lot of that "patient humor" into her daily life. She should have patience when dealing with recruits and their families, being able to humor and entertain them. She should have patience with fans and reporters who show up at her house, who might scrutinize her family and take souvenirs from her home. Finally, she should be able to display her humor tactfully and pleasantly, and constantly see her own life as humorous, not filled with obstacles and things to dread.

Issues of surrogacy are evident in the general caregiver category as well. For instance, the coach's wife, especially the wife of a high school or college football coach, is often a surrogate mother to the football players. Earl Blaik (1960) boasts, "[My wife] took as much interest in my players as if they were her own sons" (p.67). Ralph Sabock (1973) notes that the most rewarding part of being a coach's wife is probably the involvement with the "boys": "Getting involved in [the players'] lives and enjoying their lasting friendships" (p.129). Because she tutored his players, Coach Joe Paterno (1989) describes his wife as Penn State's "secret weapon" (p.20). Because the school had a policy against coaches asking professors for leniency, he involved his wife by making her a surrogate teacher (or a tutor) for players who were not making good grades. She did this for no pay and, according to Paterno, with no complaints.

Not only is the football coach's wife a surrogate mother for those outside her family, she also must often become a surrogate for her husband at social functions. Many coaches mention that their wives have to attend social functions alone. Ironically, some of these functions were often *in honor of* their husbands, other attendees reportedly believing he was not there because he was so busy (read: important). Often, on the day of the game, the football coach's wife is sought out to attend luncheons and other gatherings where important community leaders will be in attendance. It is here that the wife will find herself sought out by reporters for quotes from her husband or for her thoughts on her husband's state before leaving for the game. This is in lieu of asking the coach, because rarely is a coach available before a game. Even more often people find the wife alone at parties *after* a game in which her husband's team lost.

To be able to plan and carry out proper hostessing duties takes a great deal of skill and leadership abilities. Many coaches describe their wives as leaders, as women who stand out from their female peers because of such qualities. This factor puts the coach's wife into a life full of paradoxes: While she should be able to lead friends and family, the coach's wife is continuously following her husband.

The situational paradox of the football coach's wife is that a woman who marries a football coach must have leadership qualities, but must be willing to follow him at all times. Yet, sometimes when she follows too well, she is banished into "aloneness" and expected to accept this fate with "patient humor." Some coaches openly state that they looked for a "leader" or someone who was "independent" when they looked for a wife. Joe Paterno (1989) reveals when he realized that Sue would be the perfect wife: "She was very bubbly and would say whatever came into her head, which I liked. I could see her smarts, especially when I went out to her house and saw what kind of leader she was among her roommates" (p.78). Bo Schembechler (1989) talks similarly about his future wife: "It became pretty apparent this was the right woman for me. She was smart, independent . . ." (p.181). Such descriptions help support the process whereupon the coach piles burdens on his wife. Once again, if she has the characteristics of someone who can take the burden, then it is okay to burden her.

Paul Deitzel (1971) acknowledges that, "The wife of a football coach has a tough row to hoe. Indeed, it takes a remarkable girl to adjust herself to being the wife of a football coach" (p.13). This is certainly true when considering the constant moving football families go through. In all these coaching books or autobiographies, there is mention of frequent moves, decisions to move or stay, and the toll it takes on a coach's family. The decision and the move are always hardest for the family of a coach. Knox (1988) describes it best: "I've always been lucky. It's easier to leave when you leave right away. When it comes to my work, I've never had much use for a rear-view mirror, it only distracts from your forward vision" (p.228). In other words, when he gets an offer for a new job and his wife has acquiesced, he packs up and leaves immediately, while she stays behind and waits for the house to sell, for the kids to finish a school year, and so on.

Actually, the fact that the wife is mentioned at all in these autobiographies functions rhetorically as praise for the wife because, in her husband's eyes, she has succeeded as a football coach's wife. It also reifies her status and role to future readers who are often coaches with wives or coaches' wives themselves. Many of the coaches describe their wives' independence, assertiveness, and toughness, the irony being that she is only talked about as assertive when she is taking on the role of surrogate father or surrogate coach.

A coach's wife must be able to gage when to be stern, when to be consoling, when to politely laugh at a rude comment, and when to assert herself. The dangers of not knowing the proper timing for these reactions are clear: She could put her husband's job into peril. Or her family could even be in danger. It appears to be imperative that the coach divulges both his wife's independence and strength as well as her weaknesses and ability to follow him unquestionably. By describing her as someone with the greatest tact and strength, but also as someone who needs comforting from him, the coach helps to keep his wife on the pedestal as a role model for other wives, at the same time showing that he is needed as well.

## CONCLUSIONS

To summarize, according to football coaches, to be successful at her role, a football coach's wife must have leadership qualities. Specifically, she must be smart, patient, and have a bubbly personality. She should be loyal and dedicated to her family and her husband's career choices. Finally, she needs to be tough toward her husband's critics, and patient enough to follow him around, pick up his slack, and be his personal cheerleader at all times. She should not mind doing any of this, "Because it is something so special" (Sabock, 1973, p.121). In fact, "A coach soon learns that it is virtually impossible to keep his wife immune from the special life she leads by being married to a coach' " (ibid). So, in the mind of some coaches, the wife's life is pretty good because the benefits outweigh the costs.

However, we are never really given a good idea of what those benefits are beyond her husband's winning record or just the "privilege" of being married to him. Mostly, readers are left with images that lead them to believe the life of a football coach's wife is nerve-racking and hardly ever peaceful.

It is the language that football coaches use when talking about their wives that makes her role seem enjoyable. It works in a hierarchical manner, reinforcing the polarization of genders. At the same time, coaches' rhetoric stabilizes the football domain as distinctly "male." Most of the coaches refer to their wives as "cute," "little," or "beautiful," terms antithetical to how one might describe someone involved in football. In other instances, the coaches distance their lives from their wives, leaving readers to equate the football coach's wife with home, the coach with the field—thus extending the Victorian doctrine of separate spheres. Many of the coaches describe their wives as "perfect" football coaches' wives because they adhere to the stereotypical images for women. Wood (1992) explains that such language shapes our perceptions because the names we apply emphasize particular aspects of reality, neglecting others. By using such language in their autobiographies, these mostly famous and often revered coaches communicate to their readers—often other coaches—that, "This is how a 'good' football coach's wife conducts herself." Juxtaposed with descriptions of how elegantly many of the wives behave and how compassionate and sacrificing they are, readers are left believing that "paying the price" is supposed to be a benefit. While the wife does a lot of work at home and for her husband's team, she is usually left alone most of the time, sacrificing her own life for her husband's. This invokes the paradox: The football coach's wife just cannot win unless her husband wins, and even then she must be careful.

Many scholars have argued for continued study of sport because it is through sport that male domination is constructed and reiterated (Bryson, 1987; Trujillio, 1991). While many examine sport and its relation to violence toward women, few have studied the more subtle ways language and sport intersect, relegating men and women to "separate spheres." This study focuses on one sport and the women who are connected to that sport because of who they married. Such projects are important because they bring to light the fact that not only can sport demean women, certain sports, such as football, and the language surrounding it, can effectively take over and run women's lives.

### REFERENCES

Blaik, E.H. with Cohane, T. (1960). *You have to pay the price*. New York: Holt, Rinehart and Winston.

Bryson, L. (1987). Sport and the maintenance of masculine hegemony. *Women's Studies International Forum* 10: 349–360.

Burke, K. (1941, 1973). *Philosophy of literary form*. Berkeley, CA: California University Press.

Campbell, K.K. (1989). *Man cannot speak for her: A critical study of feminist speakers*. Westport, CT: Greenwood Press.

Dietzel, P.F. (1971). *Coaching Football*. New York: Ronald Press.

Glanville, J. with Miller, J.D. (1990). *Elvis don't like football: The life and raucous times of the NFL's most outspoken coach*. New York: Macmillan.

Holovak, M. with McSweeny, B. (1967). *Violence every Sunday: The story of a professional football coach*. New York: Coward McCann.

Knox, C. with Plaschke, B. (1988). *Hard Knox: The life of an NFL coach*. San Diego: Harcourt, Brace, Jovanovich.

Kraditor, A.S. (Ed) (1968). *Up from the pedestal*. Chicago: Quadrangle.

Matthews, G. (1987). *Just a housewife*. Oxford: Oxford University Press.

Paterno, J. with Asbell, B. (1989). *Paterno: By the book*. New York: Random House.

Picket, J.P. (Ed.) (2000). *The American heritage dictionary of the English language*, 4th ed. Boston: Houghton Mifflin.

Reid, B. (1994). *Big-time football at Harvard, 1905: The diary of coach Bill Reid*. Urbana, IL: Illinois University Press.

Rodgers, P. with Thomy, A. (1976). *Pepper! The autobiography of an unconventional coach*. Garden City, NY: Doubleday.

Sabock, R.J. (1973). *The coach*. Philadelphia: W. B. Saunders.

Schembechler, B. with Albom, M. (1989). *Bo*. New York: Warner.

Trujillio, N. (1991). "Hegemonic masculinity on the mound: Media representations of Nolan Ryan and American sports culture. *Critical Studies in Mass Communication* 8 (September): 290–308.

Welter, B. (1966). The cult of true womanhood: 1820–1860. *American Quarterly* 18: 151–174.

Wood, J. (1992). *Spinning the symbolic web: Human communication and symbolic interaction*. Norwood, NJ: Ablex.

# CHAPTER 21

# GirlSpeak: Adolescent Females Talk about their Athletic Identities

*Susan G. Zieff*

*Chuntal (age 13): "I'm good at playing basketball, that's why I play this sport."*
*Anna (age 14): "I would never quit a sport if it was too hard or too easy."*
*Grace (age 14): "(I joined this team) to show my talent."*
*Jennytte (age 15): "You are more disciplined and have strong feelings of accomplishment."*
*Jasmine (age 13): "I like to work hard so I can play in the WNBA and (I) can fulfill my dream."*
*Lisa (14): "The boys get mad if you mess up. I think I don't have the faith that I'll do good."*
*Alejandra (13): "People make fun of you if you don't play right or don't Know how to."*
*Erika (14): "I fear I won't be skilled enough."*

## GENDER AND ATHLETIC IDENTITY: THE FOCUS OF THIS STUDY

With these words, eight adolescent females speak to both positive and negative aspects of playing sport, learning physical skills, and demonstrating athletic competence. For some, perceived lack of physical ability can influence their decision to drop out of organized school sport; for others, the belief in their physical competence contributes to their identification as an athlete and the decision to stay involved in scholastic athletics.

This essay examines some factors contributing to the adoption or rejection of athletic identity as expressed by adolescent females. The notion of athletic identity has received some attention from sociologists and psychologists investigating the sport experience, especially Brewer, Van Raalte, and Linder (1993), who take as their starting point the extent to which an individual identifies with the athletic role. There is little information about how school-age girls develop and integrate an athletic identity. This study suggests that, for this population, it includes a sense of self-incorporating perceptions of sport-related competence and enjoyment, with aspirations of personal improvement and self-growth through physicality. In addition, important implications for lifelong physical activity involvement emerge.

Another factor at work here is the language these girls use to describe their sport experiences. Early scholars of gender and language such as Lakoff (1975) wrote about "women's language" notable for its lack of confidence, laden with passive and submissive vocabulary, suggesting it was reflective of women's broader social status. O'Barr and Atkins (1980) said that rather than gendered language, these characteristics describe "powerless language," reflecting women's powerless social position in many contexts. Sport scholars have conducted analyses of the reiteration of gendered language in the sport domain demonstrating how strength and power descriptors are used for male athletic performance while trivializing, minimizing, and overtly sexist language is used to describe female athletic performance (Halbert and Latimer, 1994; Messner, Duncan, and Jensen, 1993).

Among the athletes in this study, both the style and vocabulary selected serve to illustrate their feelings of confidence and satisfying physicality. They use powerful, skillful adjectives to describe their experiences and assert their abilities and interests without hesitation, atypical for adolescent females (Corson, 2001).

To address issues associated with adolescent female athletic identity and physicality, results of an open-ended questionnaire given to over 150 eighth grade students and over 50 high school female athletes asking about their sport experiences were examined. Of the 26 experiential and demographic questions included, we stressed their decision-making about expected future involvement in sport with the view that positive or negative responses are indicative of the extent to which an athlete might adopt an athletic identity. A brief discussion about the roles of sport history and involvement in competing extracurricular activities serve as backdrop for explanations about relationships between focused attention on a particular sport and identification as an athlete.

The sport sociology literature on the experience of girls in sport extensively documents adolescence as a time in which sport tends to be abandoned. Yet, sport scholars have also documented health-related and fitness benefits girls receive from sport, most noticeably a lower teen pregnancy rate (Sabo and Melnick, 1996). A secondary mission of sports scholarship has been documentation of sport *experience* for young female athletes to discover activities and types of programs that will attract the greatest number of participants and minimize the factors that diminish their enjoyment.

The surveys were delivered between spring 1998 and fall 2000 in an ethnically diverse city in the western part of the United States with a population of 750,000. The project was supported in part by a research grant from the Women's Sports Foundation. Due to its unique social and political climate, the conclusions drawn here reflect only the participants in this study; however, there are several messages about the factors that contribute to girls' accessing of school-based sport programs that are important for school sport administrators and community school boards who make such program decisions. These have to do with the emphasis on a "power and performance" model (Coakley, 2001), implying that athletes demonstrate a high level of skill as a prerequisite to participation and that the decision to play school sport must be made by junior high school or the student risks elimination from sport entirely.

The scholastic athletes in this study, particularly at the junior high level, articulate a clear sense of their physicality. Sport was described as a joyful arena, providing an opportunity for physical self-expression. Pride in personal accomplishment, the sharing of goals, hard work among peers, and the social and psychological benefits that come from dedication to the team were also widely reported. With equal conviction, the non-participants articulated a sense of physical inability and diminished physical self-confidence, sometimes to the extent that their decision to withdraw from school athletics had been made before reaching high school.

There are two assumptions that undergird this analysis: First, the idea that the decision to continue or abandon sport involvement is related to the extent to which an athletic identity is internalized; Second is the notion that an athletic identity is developed in part by participation in organized school sport.

Future sport team membership expected by the middle school girls was strongly connected to perceived ability to demonstrate physical skills, while continued play for senior high school athletes was linked to length of involvement and extent of participation in competing extracurricular activities. Both populations expressed concern about time commitment required for team membership as a factor to be considered in decisions to continue.

Among the high school athletes, 40 percent of the 11th and 12th graders were playing their *first* season of interscholastic sport. Roughly two-thirds of them were born primarily in China and other Asian countries, where cultural biases constrain female participation in sport. Many have little exposure to *typical* American school sports. Of these immigrant athletes, only 11 percent expected to continue playing sport after high school. Not surprisingly, after only one or two years in organized sport, they did not anticipate playing intercollegiate sport that typically requires extensive preparation, advanced skill, and devotion.

## The Gendered Physical Domain

Psychologists and sociologists (Orenstein, 1994; Pipher, 1995) have recently focused attention on the social and emotional worlds of preadolescent and adolescent females, suggesting that self-esteem and a sense of personal agency diminishes for girls reaching puberty, undermined in ways persisting into early adulthood (AAUW, 1992; Wolf, 1997). Gendered educational practices and the progressive influence of social expectations of traditional feminine behavior through junior and senior high school combine and continue to inhibit some girls' efforts to retain their autonomy and self-confidence (AAUW, 1992; Eder, Evans, and Parker *et al.*, 1995; Orenstein, 1992). Academic, social/emotional, and physical domains are all subject to gendering, resulting in disturbance of the path toward agency for some girls.

Historically, American society has viewed sport primarily as a masculine domain (Kimmel, 2000; Messner, 1988). Although sporting opportunities have increased for female participants on many levels, male athletes still outnumber females. Social perception that muscularity is linked to masculinity, and that sport is a dominant vehicle for the development of this aspect of masculinity persists, a perception contributing to a generalized social belief in the incompatibility of sport with femininity (Dworkin and Messner, 1999; Hall, 1996). For the athletes in this study, gender was not frequently or explicitly stated as a factor in their sport experiences, either concerning decisions to participate or the quality of their experiences; yet, expressions of connectedness to physical activity are coded in statements of perceived physical ability and confidence in their place as members of a sport team.

# Female Athletes' Perceptions of Physical Competence

The ways sport and other forms of organized physical activity contribute to or challenge the development of agency for young females remains unresolved by scholars. It is well documented in the sport sociology literature that parents, peers, teachers, and coaches influence children to become involved in sport (Coakley, 2001). Then, once girls enter sport, they may feel physically empowered (Chapman, 1997), or may be limited by efforts to conform to hegemonic views of femininity (Krane, 2001). McDermott (1996) and Chapman (1997) consider the role of perceived physical competence and empowerment as factors influencing the female experience in sport.

Perceptions of physicality also appear in the language used by the participants in this study describing their sport experiences. Among the girls who reported positive experiences with sport and physical self-confidence were terms such as "challenge," "strong," and "demonstrate skill." Conversely, girls who reported negative experiences used terms such as "low self-esteem," "stress," and "inadequate physical skill." Among these adolescent athletes, perception of personal, physical competence, and interest in skills required by a particular sport were also reported as important factors in their becoming involved in and continuing an active connection with team sport. In response to the question, "What do you like best about being on a team?" one athlete reported she wanted "To try to play my best," another stating she liked "pushing myself," a third noting, "The feeling that you have accepted a challenge everyday and tried your hardest" was personally fulfilling. One athlete simply stated that she enjoyed "Just playing the game." Satisfaction from winning was mentioned by many athletes, one track and fielder adding that, "Breaking personal records and achieving goals" was a personally fulfilling aspect of team membership. One junior high school athlete commented that she would "Never quit a sport if it was too hard or too easy." Sport demands "lots of grueling hard work" but "it eventually pays off."

Being good at a specific skill or sport was connected to enjoyment. Reasons given for participation by one athlete were typical: "Because I am good at both (sports) and they are fun to play." A high school softball player observed: "It feels good to know I can excel at something and have people appreciate me for one of my skills." Competition was another valued aspect of the sporting experience. While learning and developing skills contributed to a sense of personal accomplishment, testing one's skills against an opponent was a desired outcome for many of these athletes. One player noted, "I get to compete against other schools," another observing, "The competition keeps me on the edge."

Learning new skills was a benefit of team membership frequently expressed, pride in "perfecting a new skill" or working toward "better skills" being challenges seemingly approached without anxiety. The opportunity to try new physical movements by changing sports was a route taken by one junior high school athlete in search of a "new experience." And a high school soccer player reported that she changed sport teams because she was "Bored with individual sports and wanted to see what a team sport was like."

The desire to perform well was viewed as important for oneself, as well as gaining positive feedback from others. "Teachers and students respect me for being on the sports team," stated one athlete, while another appreciated the "recognition" gained from being an athlete, and having your name in the newspaper. Feelings of connection to school and team were reported to have an effect on players' self-concept. According to one soccer player, "I feel like I'm really active in school which makes me have higher self esteem." She also enjoyed the support gained "from these people"—her teammates. Skill improvement led to feelings of "confidence," noted one soccer player.

Athletes who expressed sentiments about their bodies tended to focus on fitness and health aspects of sport participation. Several junior high school athletes expected to continue their athletic involvement in high school because it is "healthier" to play and would help them "stay in shape." One middle school basketball player said continued participation "Will increase my chances of having a well-fit body," and anticipated observing the "differences from middle school" in her bodily development through further sport activity. One high school soccer player appreciated "The satisfaction of a good work out," while another noted how sport "Is a cool way to stay in shape," and that she liked "being a jock," observing that being an athlete led her to feel "Capable of doing things other than just studying and doing feminine required tasks."

## EXPECTATIONS TO CONTINUE PLAYING

### *Junior High School Participants*

An examination of the middle school girls' expectations to continue sport participation in high school and later reflects, in part, the extent to which athleticism is an integrated, rather than fleeting aspect of each girl's identity. This section is based upon a survey question that asked, "How long do you think you will continue playing this sport?"

Among these girls, those currently playing are much more likely to indicate positive expectations for the future than those who are not, with some notable exceptions.

Some junior high school players and non-players were uncertain, or hesitant, about involvement in high school sport. For those already playing, many respondents reported looking forward to "getting better" and "improving skills" by playing in high school, while one athlete stated that she would continue her athletic involvement because, "I know how to do it now." A softball player reported that she would continue playing in high school, "Because I want to get better" and high school sports "will be more challenging." Another, confident in her physical capability, reported she was certain to play sports in high school because, "I want to get my school the championships." Several middle school basketball players referenced potential professional sport futures, one athlete stating, "I need to work hard so I can play in the WNBA and fulfill my dream." One high school badminton player found that when she watches professional players, "It really encourage(s) me to play harder."

### High School Participants

When asked about post high school sport, over half the respondents reported being *uncertain*. Just over one-tenth indicated definitively that they would continue, while one-third noted that their sport days would finish with high school. Sophomore level athletes were the most ambivalent, accounting for over one-third of "maybe" responses. Tenth graders also reported the highest anticipated dropout rate for post-high school sport involvement. Typical reasons for ambivalent responses included the following:

- "Maybe, if it doesn't interfear (sic) with college." (9th grader)
- "Maybe because it's good excercise (sic)." (9th grader)
- "I hope that I have the time to play (in college) because I have to (have) time to study but hopefully I'll manage." (10th grader)
- "I also (sic) not sure whether I will play sports after high school since I don't know how many (sic) homework I will have in college." (11th grader)

## Assuming an Athletic Identity

Brewer, Van Raalte, and Linder (1993) concluded that strong athletic identity is more often found in individuals who interpret events in their lives from the perspective of its impact on their functioning as an athlete. Among the junior high school girls, evidence for this is seen in their comments about anticipating play in professional and elite arenas such as the Women's National Basketball Association and the Olympic Games.

Goals of improved performance and learning new skills were often framed as efforts to secure future achievements as higher-level athletes. The few negative reflections on their sport experience offered by the junior high school athletes tended to take the form of complaints about losing or practicing too often and for lengthy periods such that it interfered with school work and social life. As one multi-sport athlete stated simply, "It's a lot of hard work." An eighth grade soccer player noted, "You have to stay after school and practice a lot when I could do other stuff." One disappointed track athlete observed how school sport became less fun when "other players don't play fair."

## Perceived Lack of Physical Competence among Non-Participants

Eighth grade girls who chose not to play sports or who anticipated abandoning sport provide express complicity with the assumption held by "athletes" that only good players should play. Common reasons given for their withdrawal from sport included perceived lack of athletic ability and an associated diminished self-confidence. One former athlete "Decided not to play this year because of lack of self-esteem," while another eighth grader stated: "I don't really think of myself as athletic . . ." Yet another former player avoided trying out for the team because she "Didn't think I would make it."

The connection between performance and the decision to participate could be rigid; for example, several respondents noted that an individual should "Quit when not playing well." Typical comments by several former players:

- "I fear I won't be skilled enough."
- "You should quit when you're not playing well."
- "Sometimes people want to try something they're not good at."

Criticism from others confirms the negative self-assessment of those who ultimately decide to avoid school-based sport, although many of these girls participated in other extracurricular activities. For some, fear of humiliation from a public display of lack of physical ability was a deterrent to participation; as one girl complained, "When I make a mistake the next day everyone knows about it." More than one sport dropout noted that, "You get talked about." According to one non-athlete, "The boys get mad if you mess up. I think I don't have the faith that I'll do good." Public criticism sometimes focused on an athlete's ability; one girl's experienced that, "People make fun of you if you don't play right or don't know how to," contributing to her decision to abandon school sport.

## DISCUSSION

Although the results of this study are particular to this population and context, several important points regarding the general experience of girls in sport are to be noted. First, a significant population of adolescent females receives the message that being involved in sport requires a high skill level. The values of expressing oneself in movement and the enormous health and wellness benefits are not being heard, or are missing from their experiences.

Second, the extent to which these messages are delivered to immigrant girls must be carefully considered. At one high school in this study, a group of recent Chinese immigrants joined the badminton team under the supervision of a highly supportive coach who had introduced them to the nuances of the American scholastic sport system. Of these girls, most of whom were in their first year of scholastic sport involvement, two-thirds indicated lack of certainty about continuing sport involvement after high school, one-third reporting they would not play sport in the future.

Finally, there is the widely held belief that if one is not skilled by eighth grade, then the question of playing interscholastic sport should not even be considered. Within a system focused solely on skill and performance, the needs and interests of some girls is marginalized, even absent from the discourse about sport offerings and the system of competition. Lack of junior high school sport experience does not seem to completely deter girls from initiating sport team involvement during high school; such choices are dependent, in part, on the types of sports offered and the extent to which sport is available and accessed in venues outside of school.

Although sport has historically been viewed as a male domain, the results of this study suggest that for this population of teenage girls, sport is not only a place for the actual demonstration of physical prowess, it is also a place where power and physical competence can be articulated seemingly outside of typical gender dynamics. It has given this population of adolescent females the opportunity to voice their lived experiences in sport. Their views challenge us to rethink older, less complex views about the ways adolescent females experience sport and acknowledge the empowered language of the participants.

### References

American Association of University Women Educational Foundation. (1992). *How schools shortchange girls.* New York: Marlowe & Company.

Brewer, B., Van Raalte, J., and Linder, D. (1993). Athletic identity: Hercules' muscles or Achilles' heel? *International Journal of Sport Psychology* 24: 237–254.

Chapman, G. (1997). Making weight: Lightweight rowing, technologies of power, and technologies of the self. *Sociology of Sport Journal* 14: 205–223.

Coakley, J. (2001). *Sport in society: Issues and controversies,* 7th ed. Boston, MA: McGraw Hill.

Corson, D. (2001). *Language diversity and education.* Mahwah, NJ: Lawrence Erlbaum Associates, Inc., Publishers.

Dworkin, S.L. and Messner, M. (1999). Just do . . . what? Sport, bodies, gender. In *Revisioning gender: The gender lens,* vol. 5, ed. Ferree, M.M., Lorber, J., and Hess, B. Thousand Oaks, CA: Sage.

Eder, D., Evans, C.C., and Parker, S. (1995). *School talk: Gender and adolescent culture.* Rutgers, NJ: Rutgers University Press.

Halbert, C. and Latimer, M. (1994). "Battling" gendered language: An analysis of the language used by sports commentators in a televised coed tennis competition. *Sociology of Sport Journal* 11 (3): 298–308.

Hall, M.A. (1996). *Feminism and sporting bodies: Essays on theory and practice.* Champaign, IL: Human Kinetics.

Kimmel, M. (2000). *The gendered society.* New York: Oxford University Press.

Krane, V. (2001). We can be athletic and feminine, but do we want to? Challenging hegemonic femininity in women's sport. *Quest* 53: 115–133.

Lakoff, R. (1975). *Language and woman's place.* New York: Harper & Row.

McDermott, L. (1996). Toward a feminist understanding of physicality within the context of women's physically active and sporting lives. *Sociology of Sport Journal* 13: 12–30.

Messner, M. (1988). Sports and male domination: The female athlete as contested ideological terrain. *Sociology of Sport Journal* 5: 197–211.

Messner, M., Duncan, M.C., and Jensen, K. (1993). Separating the men from the girls: The gendered language of televised sports. *Gender and Society* 7 (1): 121–137.

O'Barr, W. and Atkins, B. (1980). Women's language or powerless language? In *Women and language in literature and society,* ed. McConnell-Ginet, S., Borker, R., and Furman, N. New York: Praeger.

Orenstein, P. (1994). *School girls: Young women, self-esteem, and the confidence gap.* New York: Anchor.

Pipher, M. (1995). *Reviving Ophelia: Saving the selves of adolescent girls.* New York: Ballantine Books.

Sabo, D. and Melnick, M. (1996). *Athletic participation and risk for adolescent pregnancy: Is there a connection?* Paper presented at the Population Council Family and Development Program Conference, New York City.

Wolf, N. (1997). *Promiscuities: The secret struggle for womanhood.* New York: Random House.

# About the Contributors

**Kimberly L. Bissell** (Ph.D., Syracuse University) is an associate professor in the Department of Journalism at the University of Alabama, where she teaches undergraduate courses in photojournalism and design and graduate courses in the social effects of mass communication. Her primary research interests include media and body image distortion in women and girls. Widely published, Bissell is an avid tennis, gymnastics and college football fan.

**Susan Burris** is an associate professor of Communications/Humanities at Owens Community College, Ohio, where she teaches popular culture. In her free time, she watches entirely too much ESPN and waits patiently for her Cleveland Browns to win a Superbowl.

**Melissa Camacho** (Ph.D., Michigan State University) teaches media criticism in the Department of Broadcast and Electronic Communication Arts at San Francisco State University, where her research focuses on the various relationships that exist between women and the media. A certified aerobics instructor, she teaches a variety of aerobic classes as part of an overall health and wellness program.

**Cheryl Cooky** is a Ph.D. candidate and Haynes Dissertation Fellow at the University of Southern California. Her research interests are in children and youth, focusing specifically on sports, gender, and popular culture. When not at her computer, Cheryl enjoys running with her dogs, Kalbi and Suki, cycling, or indulging in her secret pleasure: watching her favorite television show, *Sex and the City*.

**Scott A.G.M. Crawford** (Ph.D., University of Queensland) is a Scottish New Zealander who teaches in the College of Education and Professional Studies at Eastern Illinois University. A book review editor for the *International Journal of Sport History*, he is a passionate follower of rugby football and equestrian competition, and has contributed multiple entries to the *Encyclopedia of World Sport* and *The Encyclopedia of British Sport*.

**Julie E. Dodd** (Ed.D., Kentucky) is a professor in the College of Journalism and Communications at the University of Florida. A former health and fitness columnist for *The Oak Ridger* (Tennessee), Dodd has run road races in more than 20 states.

**Linda K. Fuller** (Ph.D., University of Massachusetts), a professor of Communications at Worcester State College, is the author/(co)editor of more than 20 books and 250+ professional publications and conference reports, including *Sportscasters/Sportscasting: Principles and Practices* (Haworth, forthcoming). Awarded Fulbrights to teach in Singapore in 1996 and do HIV/AIDS research in Senegal in 2002, she has been a Senior Fellow at Northeastern University for the 2004–2006 academic years.

**Kim Golombisky** (Ph.D., South Florida) is a former advertising executive who teaches in the School of Mass Communications at the University of South Florida. An award-winning teacher and researcher, she has written widely about sex/gender issues in popular culture and communication education. Currently, she is completing a critical discourse analysis of Title IX debates in school sports, sexual harassment law, and education reform movements since 1972.

**Joannie Halas** (Ph.D., University of Alberta, Canada) is an associate professor and research affiliate with the Health, Leisure and Human Performance Research Institute of the Faculty of Physical Education and Recreation Studies at the University of Manitoba. A former physical education teacher and avid cycle tourist, her research focuses on the development of culturally relevant physical education programs for marginalized youth.

**James R. Hallmark** (Ph.D., University of Oklahoma) is Dean of the Graduate School and Research and Professor of Communication at West Texas A&M University. His research interests primarily focus on subtle uses of influence in the media, in public interests groups, and in religious bodies.

**Marie Hardin** (Ph.D., Georgia) is an assistant professor of Journalism and associate director of the Center for Sports Journalism at Penn State University. Interested in diversity and sport media, she has been an avid runner and sports enthusiast since age 12.

**James G. King III** is a master's candidate in Liberal Studies at Skidmore College specializing in the sociology and psychology of sport. His undergraduate degree is from Williams College, where he majored in American Studies and Political Science. He is an instructor in Physical Education at Hamilton College, in Clinton, NY, where he coaches both the men's and women's squash and tennis teams.

**Jennifer Smith Maguire** (Ph.D., City University of New York) is a lecturer in the Department of Sociology and the Centre for Mass Communication Research at the University of Leicester, U.K. Her research on the contemporary commodification of body in the U.S. examines health clubs, exercise texts, and fitness as a consumer lifestyle. She has been published in the *Sociology of Sport Journal* and *International Review for the Sociology of Sport*.

**L. Marlene Mawson,** Professor Emerita at Illinois State University, spent 22 years at the University of Kansas teaching sport management, sport sociology, and research methods as Women's Athletic Director and head coach of women's basketball and volleyball. A competitor in AAU basketball and USVBA volleyball, she was a selected participant for two U.S. Olympic National Institutes for Girls and Women in Sport. Mawson has authored 50+ journal articles on sport, has served as President of the North American Society for Sport Management, and now, in retirement, enjoys playing golf and spectating at a variety of sporting events.

**Katherine L. McDowell** earned her undergraduate degree in Romance Languages from Skidmore College in 1965 and, in 1995, its first M.A. in Liberal Studies in 1995. Next came her J.D. from the State University of New York at Buffalo School of Law; she currently practices civil litigation in Scottsdale, Arizona.

**Sally Cole Mooney** is an ex-soccer mom whose three children played for a club team in New Orleans and whose life, for many years, was spent watching (and hearing) soccer. She teaches English at Delgado Community College in New Orleans and writes personal essays. Currently, she is working on an anthology of writings on illness.

**Treena Orchard** (M.A., Memorial University, Newfoundland, Canada) is a doctoral candidate in Medical Anthropology at the University of Manitoba. Her previous research projects with several Canadian Aboriginal communities focused on the topics of youth identity, women's cancer experiences, and male sex workers dealing with HIV. She is currently conducting her Ph.D. fieldwork on sexuality and coming of age with female sex workers in southern India, supported by a fellowship from the Canadian Institute of Health Research.

**Nancy G. Rosoff** (Ph.D., Temple) is an associate dean for Administration and Academic Program Development for the Faculty of Arts and Sciences at the Camden campus of Rutgers University, has conducted research on historical and contemporary images of athletic women. Her interest stems from experience, and moderate success, as an athlete, a coach, a sports journalist, and a fan, having played field hockey, lacrosse, and softball. As a graduate of Mount Holyoke College, she takes great pride in a Smith student's declaring that the Holyoke women played a "terrible hard" game of basketball in 1906.

**Catherine Sabiston** is a doctoral student in the School of Human Kinetics at the University of British Columbia. With research interests in body image and the physical self, as well as physical activity and sport participation during adolescence, Cathi has published work in *Medicine and Science in Sport and Exercise, Aviation, Space, and Environmental Medicine, the Canadian Journal of Public Health, and the Canadian Journal of Applied Physiology.*

**Jeffrey O. Segrave** is a professor and Director of Athletics in the Department of Exercise Science, Dance, and Athletics at Skidmore College. He specializes in the sociology of sport and has published widely in journals such as *Culture, Sport, Society, Journal of Sport and Social Issues, International Review for the Sociology of Sport, and Sociology of Sport Journal.* He writes extensively about the Olympic Games as well as feminist issues in sport, especially language.

**Mike Sowell** is an assistant professor at Oklahoma State University and the author of three nonfiction books (*The Pitch That Killed*, 1989; *July 2, 1903*, 1993; *One Pitch Away*, 1995—all Macmillan), as well as several articles on baseball history and the early days of sportswriting. An award-winning sportswriter and columnist for newspapers in Texas and Oklahoma for more than 20 years, he teaches courses on writing, editing and sports journalism.

**Jane M. Stangl** is visiting assistant professor in the Department of Exercise and Sport Studies at Smith College in Northampton, Massachusetts. Her academic interests include a critical re-examination of sports language/rhetoric and issues of the body as a socially constructed site of meaning, and she has published on the demise of women's coaches since Title IX.

**Jennifer Stark** (BPE, BE.d., University of Manitoba) is a third year physical education and language arts teacher in Winnipeg, Canada. A former international Ultimate player, she now competes provincially for the Manitoba Canadian Ultimate Team.

**Diana L. Tucker** (Ph.D., Southern Illinois University, Carbondale) is an assistant professor of Communication Arts at Ashland University, Ohio, where she teaches public relations and organizational communication. Growing up as the daughter of a football coach, she still roots for her father's team, The Ohio State University Buckeyes, and thinks her mother is one of the best-ever football coaches' wives, mothers, and kindergarten teachers.

**Faye Linda Wachs** is an assistant professor of sociology in the Behavioral Sciences Department at Cal Poly Pomona. She has published articles on gender relations of power and privilege in the world of coed softball, as well as work on media coverage of HIV+ athletes, and is currently coauthoring a book on gender relations of power and privilege manifest in health and fitness magazines. Having retired from softball, Faye stays active mountain biking, hiking, and running.

**Brian Wilson** is assistant professor in the School of Human Kinetics at the University of British Columbia, researches youth culture, media constructions of race and gender, audience studies, social movements, and the sociology of sport and leisure. His most recent work focuses on the production and consumption of alternative media by youth and subcultural groups. Brian has been published in the *Sociology of Sport Journal*, the *International Review for the Sociology of Sport*, the *Journal of Sport and Social Issues*, the *Canadian Journal of Communication*, and the *Canadian Journal of Sociology*.

**Susan G. Zieff** (Ph.D., University of California, Berkeley) teaches in the Department of Kinesiology at San Francisco State University, where she writes about the cultural and historical aspects of sport and exercise. A sports enthusiast, Susan is committed to experimenting with a new sport skill each year.

# Index